THE NEW REVELATIONS

A CONVERSATION WITH GOD

BOOKS BY NEALE DONALD WALSCH

Conversations with God, Book 1

Conversations with God, Book 2

Conversations with God, Book 3

Friendship with God

Communion with God

Conversations with God for Teens

Questions and Answers on Conversations with God

The Little Soul and the Sun: A Children's Parable Adapted from
Conversations with God (with Frank Riccio, illustrator)

Meditations from Conversations with God

Conversations with God: Guidebook

Moments of Grace

Bringers of the Light

Recreating Yourself

Neale Donald Walsch on Abundance and Right Livelihood

Neale Donald Walsch on Holistic Living

Neale Donald Walsch on Relationships

The Wedding Vows from Conversations with God

Honest to God: A Change of Heart That Can Change the World

Meditations from Conversations with God, Book 2: A Personal Journal

Conversations with God: Re-Minder Cards

THE NEW REVELATIONS

A CONVERSATION WITH GOD

Neale Donald Walsch

ATRIA BOOKS
New York London Toronto Sydney Singapore

"Lutheran Pastor Assailed" by Stephanie Simon originally appeared in the *Los Angeles Times* as "Heresy Charges Leveled at Pastor," and is reproduced by permission of the *Los Angeles Times*.

"A Holy War of Words" by Cathy Lynn Grossman appeared in *USA Today*, and is reproduced by permission of Cathy Lynn Grossman.

Extract from *Conversations with God: Book 1 (CWG 1)* by Neale Donald Walsch, copyright © 1995 by Neale Donald Walsch. Used by permission of G.P. Putnam's Sons, a division of Penguin Putnam Inc.

Extract from *Conversations with God: Book 3 (CWG 3)* by Neale Donald Walsch reproduced by permission of Hampton Roads Publishing Company, Inc.

Extract from *Holy Terror: Inside the World of Islamic Terrorism* by Amir Taheri (Adler & Adler Publishers), reproduced by permission of Amir Taheri.

ATRIA BOOKS
1230 Avenue of the Americas
New York, NY 10020

Copyright © 2002 by Millennium Legacies, Inc.

ISBN: 0-7434-5694-7

First Atria Books hardcover printing September 2002

10 9 8 7 6 5 4 3 2 1

ATRIA BOOKS is a trademark of Simon and Schuster, Inc.

For more information regarding special discounts for bulk purchases, please contact Simon & Schuster Special Sales at 1-800-456-6798 or business@simonandschuster.com

Printed in the U.S.A

The soul is the perceiver and revealer of truth.

We know truth when we see it, let skeptic and scoffer say what they choose. Foolish people ask you, when you have spoken what they do not wish to hear, "How do you know it is truth, and not an error of your own?" We know truth when we see it, from opinion, as we know when we are awake that we are awake. . . .

We distinguish the announcements of the soul, its manifestations of its own nature, by the term Revelation. These are always attended by the emotion of the sublime. For this communication is an influx of the Divine mind into our mind. It is an ebb of the individual rivulet before the flowing surges of the sea of life.

RALPH WALDO EMERSON
Emerson's Essays

AUTHOR'S NOTE

As in all conversations, there are things repeated here that have been said before. I want you to know that I am aware of that. No attempt was made by me to "edit out" material that makes the same point (sometimes in the same words) made in previous books I have produced. I assume these matters wouldn't have come up again if they weren't important within the context of what is being discussed here. I have thus forgiven all redundancies, and invite you to do the same.

The list of fallacies about God and Life in this book seems, in particular, to be very similar to the Ten Illusions of Humans given to us in *Communion with God*. They are plainly based on those illusions, and are recontextualizations of them. Yet not everyone who has come to this current dialogue has read that previous book, and the present material was clearly meant to stand alone.

INTRODUCTION

The world is in trouble. Bigger trouble than it has ever been in before.

This book provides an explanation of the crisis we are facing in a way that not only clarifies the crisis, but clarifies *how to resolve it.*

Here is an extraordinary insight into what's really happening to us right now on this planet, why we've gone astray, and how we can get back on the path that we say we wish to take.

We can look away from what's happening — the sudden and eruptive disintegration of life as we know it — for only so long before the fact that we really *are* in big trouble presents itself to us in ways that we cannot ignore.

That is what is occurring right now. We are being confronted by events and conditions that we cannot ignore.

This does not mean that now is a time for despair. Despair, in fact, is the last thing this is a time for. Despair is what has *created* the problem. More despair is certainly not going to solve it.

No, now is not the time for despair, but for repair.

As we seek to repair the damage that we are doing, we are invited to explore the matter of why we are doing it. What has led us into the depth of despair that would cause us to begin destroying ourselves? That is the key question addressed by this book. It is a question many people do not want to ask. The answers are too threatening to our very way of life — and many humans would apparently rather destroy their way of life than change it. They would rather see their lives end than see their lives altered.

This is a life-altering book. It contains New Revelations. It provides the tools with which to pull ourselves *out* of despair, lifting the whole human race to a new level of experience, to a new understanding of itself, to a new expression of its grandest vision.

This book was given to us, sent to us at just this moment, to help us. It presents its revelations in the form of a conversation with God. You do not have to believe that such a conversation took place to derive benefit from it. You have merely to be willing to follow the conversation, consider its contents, explore the possibility of applying them in your life, and observe the results.

The human race has reached a Time of Choosing. Our options are being placed before us by the tide of events — and by those who are creating them. We can either move forward, building together at last a new world of peace and harmony based on new beliefs about God and Life, or move backward, separately and continuously reconstructing the old world of conflict and discord based on old beliefs about God and Life.

How long we can keep ourselves going if we continue to choose the Old Ways is open to speculation. But ultimately our civilization—assuming no dramatic alteration in our present pattern—will simply cave in on itself. And everything I see tells me we are just years—not centuries, not decades, but years—away from that.

For those who are ready to embrace new beliefs (or at least to consider them), the issue becomes, what would they be? And what outcomes could they produce? I believe these new revelations have been given to us to offer some possible and powerful answers to these questions.

This conversation with God began as a simple plea from one humble human being to the God of his understanding, in the way that works best for him. I asked God to reveal to us what we now need to know if we want to help change the self-destructive direction in which humanity is moving.

Now the God of my understanding may not appear to be the God in which you believe, but It is, I am convinced, the same God nonetheless. And I believe that if any person goes to this same God in purity, sincerity, and with deep desire, God responds.

This book is God's response.

I believe it can save the world.

I

God, please be here. We need help.

I am here.

We need help.

I know.

Right now.

I understand.

The world is on the brink of disaster. And I'm not talking about natural disaster; I'm talking about man-made calamity.

I know. And you're right.

I mean, humans have had disagreements before, and serious ones, but now our divisions and disagreements can lead not simply to wars—which are bad enough—but to the end of civilization as we know it.

That is correct. You have assessed the situation correctly.

You understand the severity of the problem; you simply do not understand the nature of the problem. You do not know what is causing it. So you keep trying to solve it at every level except the level at which it exists.

Which is?

The level of belief.

The problem facing the world today is a spiritual problem.

Your ideas about spirituality are killing you.

You keep trying to solve the world's problem as if it were a political problem, or an economic problem, or even a military problem, *and it is none of these.* It is a spiritual problem. And that is the one problem human beings don't seem to know how to solve.

Then help us.

I am.

How?

In many ways.

Name one.

This book.

This book will help us?

It can.

What do we have to do?

Read it.

And then what?

Heed it.

That's what they all say. "It's all in The Book," they say. "Read it and heed it. That's all you have to do." The problem is, *they all hold up a different book.*

I know.

And every book says something else.

I know.

So now we should "read and heed" *this book?*

It's not a question of what you should do. It's a question of what you may do if you choose to. It is an invitation, not a requirement.

Why would I want to read this book when I've already been told by True Believers that all the answers are in the *other* books — the books that *they* are telling me to heed?

Because you have not heeded them.

Yes, we have. We believe that we have.

That's why you now need help. You believe that you have, but you have not.

You keep saying that your Holy Book (your cultures have many different ones) is what has given you the authority to treat each other the way you are treating each other, to do what you are doing.

You are able to say that only because you have not really listened to the deeper message of these books. You have read them, but you have not really *listened* to them.

But we *have.* We are doing what they *say* we should be doing!

No. You are doing what YOU say that they say you should be doing.

What does that mean?

It means that the basic message of all the sacred scriptures is the same. What is different is how human beings have been interpreting them.

There is nothing "wrong" with having different interpretations. What may not benefit you, however, is separating yourself over these differences, making each other wrong because of these differences, and killing each other as a result of these differences.

This is what you are now doing.

It is what you have been doing for quite some time.

You cannot agree even within a particular group of you, much less between groups, about what a particular book says and what it means, and you use these disagreements as justifications for slaughter.

You argue among yourselves about what the Qur'an says, and about what its words mean. You argue among yourselves about what the Bible says, and about what its words mean. You argue among yourselves about what the Veda says, what the Bhagavad-Gita says, what the Lun-yü says, what the Pali Canon says, what the Tao-te Ching says, what the Talmud says, what the Hadith says, what the Book of Mormon says...

And what of the Upanishad, the I Ching, the Adi Granth, the Mahabharata, the Yoga-sutras, the Mathnawi, the Kojiki?

Okay, we get the point.

No, actually, you don't. And *that's* the point. The point is, there are *many* holy writings and sacred scriptures, and you act as if there is only *one.*

It is *your* sacred scripture that is *really* sacred. All the rest are poor substitutes at best, and blasphemies at worst.

Not only is there only one Sacred Scripture, there is also only one way to *interpret* that Scripture: your way.

This spiritual arrogance is what has caused you your greatest sorrow as a species. You have suffered more—and caused *other* people to suffer more—over your ideas about God than over your ideas about anything else in the human experience.

You have turned the source of the greatest joy into the source of your greatest pain.

That's *crazy.* Why is that? *Why have we done that?*

Because there is one thing for which human beings seem willing to give up everything.

They will give up love, they will give up peace, they will give up health, harmony, and happiness, they will give up safety, security, and even their sanity, for this one thing.

What?

Being right.

You are willing to give up everything you've ever worked for, everything you've ever wanted, everything you've ever created, in order to be "right."

Indeed, for this you are willing to give up Life itself.

But isn't that how it should be? I mean, you have to stand up for *something* in life. And the Word of God IS what's right!

Which God?

Which God?

Yes, which God?

Adonai? Allah? Elohim? God? Hari? Jehovah? Krishna? Lord? Rama? Vishnu? Yahwey?

The God whose words were brought to us clearly by the Master and the Prophets.

Which Master and which Prophets?

Which Master? Which Prophets?

Yes.

Adam? Noah? Abraham? Moses? Confucius? Siddhartha Gautama? Jesus? Patanjali? Muhammad? Baha'u'l-
lah? Jalal al-Din Rumi? Martin Luther? Joseph Smith?
Paramahansa Yogananda?

You're not equating all of those with each other, are you?

Why not? Is one greater than the other?

Certainly!

Which one?

The one in whom I believe!

Exactly. *Now* you get the point.

So what do you want me to do, give up my beliefs?

I don't "want" you to do anything. The question is,
what do you want to do?

I want to find a way to get past all of these mixed-up beliefs
that humans have.

There is a way.

Which is?

Transcend them.

What does that mean?

Transcending means to go beyond, to move past. It
does not mean to completely reject or totally destroy.

You do not have to destroy a thing in order to move past it.

You would not want to destroy your old belief system in any event, because there is too much of it that you will wish to retain.

"Transcending" does not mean always being "other than," it means always being "larger than." Your new, larger belief system will no doubt retain some of the old—that part of the old belief system that you experience as still serving you—and so it will be a combination of the new and the old, not a rejection of the old from top to bottom.

Can you see the difference?

I think so.

Good. Then you can stop your resistance.

The reason humans have hung so tenaciously to their old beliefs is that they do not want to dishonor those beliefs by rejecting them completely, out of hand. They think that this is the choice they have: Reject the old or accept the old, totally. Yet that is not the only choice you have. You can review the old and see what parts of the old no longer work. You can expand the old to make some parts of the old work better. You can add to the old to make some parts of your belief system new.

Rejecting completely your present beliefs would be to discredit so much of what has been taught, so much of what has been understood, so much of what has been done—and so much of what has been *good*.

It would make too much of the world feel "wrong." It would make ancestors "wrong," it would make entire scriptures "wrong," it would make present-day *lives* "wrong." People would have to admit that all of the spiritual aspects of the human experience have been a mistake, a misunderstanding.

This is more than most people can acknowledge. It is more than they *should* acknowledge, because it is not true.

In fact, you don't have to declare that you were "wrong" about anything, because you weren't. *You simply didn't have a complete understanding. You needed more information.*

Transcending current beliefs is not an outright rejection of them; it is an "adding to" them.

Now that you have more information that you can add to what you presently believe, you can enlarge your beliefs—not *completely reject* them, *enlarge* them—and move on with your lives in a new way.

A way that works.

But I don't have more information.

Yes, you do.

I do?

You have this book.

2

Let me see if I understand. You're saying that this book is on a par with the Torah, the whole Bible, the Bhagavad-Gita?

I did not say that. But, for the sake of discussion, were not those books written by mortals, guided by Divine revelation?

Well, yes, but surely you're not equating the words here with the words of Confucius, the teachings of The Buddha, the revelations of Muhammad . . .

Again I say . . . these were mere human beings, were they not?

I wouldn't call them "mere" human beings. They were very *special* human beings. Human beings who understood enormous truths. Human beings who were deeply inspired.

You, too, can understand enormous truths. You, too,

can be deeply inspired. Do you think these experiences are reserved for the very few?

I tell you, they are meant for the very many.

Divine inspiration is the birthright of every human being.

You are *all* very special. You simply do not know that. You do not believe it.

Why not?

Because your religions have told you that you are not. They have told you that you are sinners, that you are unworthy, that only a very few among you have achieved a level of worthiness to be inspired directly by God—and that all of those people are dead.

They have convinced you that no one living today could possibly achieve that level of worthiness, and, hence, no book written today could possibly contain sacred truths or the Word of God.

Why have they done so? Why have they told us this?

Because to tell you otherwise would be to leave open the possibility that another master, another prophet, another messenger of God could come along, bringing new revelations and opening you to new understandings—and that is something that already established organized religions could not abide.

And so, while your world's religions may not be able to agree on which book contains the highest truth and the deepest wisdom and the True Word of God, there is one thing on which they *are* able to agree.

What's that?

> Whatever book it is, it's an old one.
> Definitely.
> It's an old book.
> It could not be a new book. It could not be a book written today.
> God's direct revelations ended long ago, your religions agree. Only old sacred books can contain divine revelation.
> Most people can accept that God's great truths have come *to* humans *through* humans. They simply cannot accept that this could be true of humans living today.
> This is how you think. This is how you have it constructed.
> If it's old, it's worthy; if it's new, it's unworthy.
> If it's old, it's true; if it's new, it's false.
> If it's old, it's right; if it's new, it's wrong.
> If it's old, it's good; if it's new, it's bad.
> This peculiar mindset is what makes progress on your planet so difficult, and evolution so time-consuming.
> What complicates all this is that, as you have constructed it, this mindset applies only to things—that is, inanimate objects—and to ideas. Ironically, when it comes to *people* you have it constructed the other way around.
> If it's new, it's worthy; if it's old, it's unworthy.
> Thus, your society dismisses out of hand some of the brightest new ideas and some of the wisest older people.
> Ask Hermann Kümmell.

Hermann Kümmell?

> A medical doctor in Hamburg in the late 1800s who had a terrible time convincing other physicians that it was a good idea to wash their hands before surgery.
>
> The idea of "scrubbing up" was summarily dismissed by "those who knew better," with Kümmell turned into a laughing-stock and practically driven out of his beloved medical profession for even suggesting that such a practice could save lives.
>
> This stubborn tendency of human beings to cling to their past, to refuse innovation or new thinking until they are forced to do so by an ultimately embarrassing weight of evidence, has been slowing your evolutionary process for millennia.

Yet now it does not seem as if we can afford to have that process drag on. It feels as though, now, time is of the essence. We have reached a crossroad here.

> Yes. You are facing now a new and startling danger— a danger posed to your entire species. A threat to your very survival posed by the combination of a *split in ideology* and an *advance in technology,* which makes it possible for you to seek to resolve your differences with tools of human destruction unlike anything you may have heretofore dreamed of in your worst nightmare.

My God, what can we do?

There are five things you can choose now if changing your world, and the self-destructive direction in which it is moving, is what you wish to achieve.

1. You can choose to acknowledge that some of your old beliefs about God and about Life are no longer working.
2. You can choose to acknowledge that there is something you do not understand about God and about Life, the understanding of which will change everything.
3. You can choose to be willing for a new understanding of God and Life to now be brought forth, an understanding that could produce a new way of life on your planet.
4. You can choose to be courageous enough to explore and examine this new understanding, and, if it aligns with your inner truth and knowing, to enlarge your belief system to include it.
5. You can choose to live your lives as demonstrations of your highest and grandest beliefs, rather than as denials of them.

These are the Five Steps to Peace, and if you take them, you can shift everything on your planet.

Why all this emphasis on God and our beliefs? Why are you not telling us to change our worldwide political or economic systems? Why are you not telling us to change our laws and stop our violence and share our resources and discontinue our discrimi-

nation and halt our oppression and redistribute our abundance
and end our wars and live in peace?

Because those are all changes in behavior.

Aren't our behaviors exactly what we need to change right now?

Yes. If what you decide you now desire is a world
living in peace and harmony, the answer is yes.

Okay, you've got me. I don't understand. Why are you talking
about beliefs when what we need to do is change behaviors?

Because beliefs *create* behaviors.

3

All behaviors are created by beliefs?

All behaviors.

Aren't there such things as "automatic reactions"?

Even those reactions are based on what you *believe* is occurring, is about to occur, or could occur.

All behaviors are sponsored by beliefs.

You cannot make a long-term change in behaviors without addressing the beliefs that underlie them.

I'm going to repeat that, because the brevity of the statement belies its importance.

I said:

You cannot make a long-term change in behaviors without addressing the beliefs that underlie them.

So it is on our beliefs that society needs to focus.

Exactly. And this is precisely where most of your societies have *not* been focusing—except those societies that are now causing, and have historically caused, the most upheaval.

But if we —

—Listen to me. I am telling you something very important here.

What I just said was . . . those societies that are now causing, and that have historically caused, the most upheaval in your world are those societies that have focused on *beliefs*.

Most humans try to change things by focusing on *behaviors*. They keep thinking they can make things better by *doing something*. So, everyone is running around trying to figure out what they can *do*. The focus is on doing something, rather than on *believing something*.

But radical forces within your societies have always sought to change things by using the power of *thought*, not action, for they know that thought *produces* action. Get a person *thinking* a certain way and you can get a person to *act* a certain way. *It is not easily done the other way around.*

Take killing, for example. You can rarely get a person to go out and kill another person simply by telling him to do so. You have to give him a *reason*. And "reason" exists only in *thought*. And thought is always based in Belief. So, if you want to get one person to kill another,

the fastest way to do that is to give him a *belief* that
supports the action, and can sponsor it.

Such as?

One such belief might be that killing is what God
wants, that it is doing the Will of God, and that one will
be rewarded in heaven for doing it.

That could be a very powerful belief, a very powerful incentive.

And so, while most of the world is seeking to bring
about change by telling people what to DO, those who
truly *know* how to motivate people are bringing about
change by telling people what to BELIEVE.

Do you get it?

Wow. Yes.

Your world is facing enormous problems right now,
and you must *solve the problems at the level of belief.* You
cannot solve the problems at the level of behavior.

Seek to change beliefs, not behaviors.

After you change a belief, the behavior will change by
itself.

But we are a very action-oriented society. The Western world,
in particular, has always found its solutions in action, not in quiet
contemplation or philosophy.

You can take whatever action you want to take to
alter someone else's behavior or to stop it, but unless
you alter the beliefs that produced such behavior, you

will alter nothing and stop nothing. You can alter a belief in two ways. Either by enlarging upon it, or by changing it completely. But you must do one or the other or you will not alter behavior.

You will merely interrupt it.

In other words, the behavior will return.

Is there any question about that? Do you not see your history repeating itself?

I see that, yes. And it's frustrating.

Your species does the same thing over and over again because your species has not changed its basic beliefs—about God and about Life—*in millennia.*

Beliefs are taught in virtually every school on your planet, in nearly every culture, in one form or another. Often you present beliefs as "facts," but they are beliefs nonetheless.

This would not be so bad, and would not produce such terrible results, if what you believe, if what you taught, was what is so. But it is *not* what is so. You teach your children what is *not* so, and *tell them* "this is what's so."

For the most part you are not doing this intentionally. You do not know that these are falsehoods. They are, after all, the things that *you* were taught. You thus assume them to be true. It is in this way that the "sins of the father are visited upon the son, even unto the seventh generation."

In some schools—particularly some religious schools where children in their earliest years are encouraged to view life through the prism of particular religious doctrines and cultural prejudices—the result of this is the inbreeding of incredibly negative behaviors reflecting extraordinarily mistaken beliefs.

You teach your children to believe in an intolerant God, and thus condone for them their own behaviors of intolerance.

You teach your children to believe in an angry God, and thus condone for them their own behaviors of anger.

You teach your children to believe in a vengeful God, and thus condone for them their own behaviors of vengeance.

Then you send these, your children, to do battle with the demons of your own creation. It is not an accident that by far the highest numbers of "warriors" in any radical movement are the young.

When you move the youngest among you from religious schools or military academies directly into your fighting forces, promising them that they are struggling for "a higher cause" or "a grander purpose" or that *God is on their side,* what are they to think?

Are they to contradict their elders, their teachers, their priests, their *ulama?*

Yet if you are not careful, *your own children will undo you.*

So we must change the beliefs of the young.

> Yes. Yet that cannot happen unless you change the
> beliefs of those who are *teaching* the young. And that
> means all of you. For you are teaching your young not
> merely in schools, but in every moment of their lives,
> as they observe you, their role models, living *your* lives.
>
> This is something you must understand: *Your whole*
> *life is a teaching.* Everything that you think, say, and do
> instructs another.
>
> Do you imagine that others do not know what you
> are thinking? Is it your idea that they are not listening
> to what you are saying? Are you hoping that they are
> not watching what you are doing?
>
> Young people, especially, are eager to learn about
> life, and they learn the most about life from *life itself*.
> And they intuitively know this. That is why they observe
> so closely. Young people miss nothing. You think you
> are kidding them? Think again.
>
> They see the fear. They see the anger. They see the
> hypocrisy. They see the saying of one thing and the doing
> of another. And yes, they even know pretty much of
> what you are thinking. More than you think they know.

So we must change *our* beliefs before we can expect the beliefs
of our offspring to change.

> Yes. And if you do not, you will stand by and watch
> your young do unimaginably terrible things—and *won-*
> *der where they could have ever gotten such ideas.*

Like the young people who took a gay college student named Matthew Shepard to a lonely stretch of country road outside of Laramie, Wyoming, a few years ago, tied him to a cow fence, brutally beat him, and left him there to die?

Like those young men, yes.

They felt he deserved what they did to him.

Yes.

They didn't even feel that what they were doing was inappropriate.

No one does anything inappropriate, given their model of the world.

Now there is an enormously important statement.

It is. So let's repeat it.
I said . . .
No one does anything inappropriate, given their model of the world.

So what we have to do is *change our model of the world.*

Exactly. That is what I have been saying here.

And we have to change people's beliefs, because that is what their model of the world is based on.

Exactly.

Our offspring are simply mimicking us. *All* people are just imitating each other. We are all just doing what we see each other doing.

Do you know what one mirror said to the other mirror?

No.

"It's all done with people."

4

Okay, so humanity's beliefs about God and Life are *incomplete,* and it is these incomplete understandings that we have been passing on to our children from generation to generation, creating the political, economic, social, and spiritual crisis the world is facing today.

Correct.

And if we can just change these beliefs, we can change all this.

Yes.

We can end the killing and the suffering.

You can.

We can end the poverty and the desperation.

You can.

We can put a stop to oppression and aggression and repression.

Indeed, you can.

That sounds so hopeful. That makes me feel as if we've got a chance.

Oh, you have more than a chance, my son. You, and all the children of God, have a happy destiny to fulfill. And using the power and the wonder and the glory of all the gifts I have given you, you will fulfill it. Only if you do not use that power, only if you set aside the wonder of who you are and throw away my gifts, can you not fulfill it.

It is going to be very difficult for you to do that. I have made it very hard for you to not reach your goal. For my gifts to you are so extraordinary as to render that virtually impossible.

Just look at what you have done so far! Against all odds, you brought yourselves into being, and moved your species into consciousness.

Against all odds, you acquired sufficient understanding of the world around you to produce truly extraordinary physical achievements.

Against all odds, you grew in self-awareness to the point where you recognized that there was something greater than the limited experience of you, developing arts and culture, science, philosophy, and spirituality to express your expanded view of existence.

When you look around your Universe (which you will soon have the technology to do much more effectively), you will see that these are not small accomplishments.

Of all the life forms in existence, only a tiny minority has done it.

And look at your personal lives. Many of you have grown to become dynamic, productive, loving, caring, compassionate beings, deeply concerned with the feelings of others, deeply committed to the betterment of all, and deeply determined to courageously explore the edges of your knowledge, that you might create an even brighter tomorrow.

Do you see the magnificence of that? This is Who You Are, and it is only the beginning.

Is this true? Do you mean this?

I tell you, you are capable of achievements and experiences beyond your wildest dreams. You are standing even now at the edge of a Golden Age, the beginning of a Thousand Years of Peace, which could lead to a grander glory for the human species than your heart can now hold the knowing of.

This can be your gift to the future. This can be your destiny. You need but choose it.

You're talking about changing our entire experience of life on this planet. For with all of our accomplishments, with all of our understandings, we have not been able to achieve peace. When you talk about a thousand years of it, you are talking about changing our entire way of life.

That is what we are talking about, yes. That is what you asked me to help you with, is it not?

It is, but I just don't get that there is a panacea, a "magic pill" that can do all that it takes to have that.

> There is.

Our beliefs.

> Your beliefs.

Specifically, our beliefs about God?

> About God and about Life.

What about people who don't believe in God?

> It doesn't matter whether people believe in God or not. All people have beliefs about Life. And what you will find is that people's collective beliefs about Life pretty much reflect humanity's collective beliefs about God. This is understandable, given what I'm now going to tell you—which is something that some people may not accept.

What's that?

> *God and Life are the same thing.*
> You may call these things by two different names, but they are the same thing. God is what Life is, and Life is what God is. God is the energy that you call Life, and Life is the energy that you call God. It is all the same thing.
> Life is God, *physicalized.*

So, if we believe in Life, we believe in God, is that what you're saying?

Yes.

You cannot separate God from Life, and you cannot separate Life from God. You can say you believe in Life but not in God, but that is like saying you believe in the brain but not the mind.

You can see and touch the brain, so you know it is there. You cannot see or touch the mind, so you're not so sure what that is, or whether it is there or not. The brain is the mind, *physicalized*. Yet it is your mind that allows you to even contemplate your brain. Without your mind, you would not even know that the brain exists.

It is exactly the same way with God and Life.

So we don't have to "believe in God" in order to change the world.

Not at all.

But those people who do believe in God have a head start.

Not necessarily.

What?

I said, not necessarily.

You mean a belief in God is not a benefit here? It's not an advantage?

It could actually be a disadvantage.

How can you say that a belief in God can be a *dis*advantage in changing the world?

Everything depends not on whether you believe IN God, but on what you believe ABOUT God.

I've already told you that you don't have to believe in God at all in order to use beliefs to change the world. All you have to believe in is Life. And you *do* believe in Life, because you are experiencing it.

Yet if you are one of those who does believe in God, *what* you believe *about* God can have an extraordinary impact on what you believe about Life—as well as how you *live* your life, and how you *experience it.*

So your belief *about* God becomes crucial.

And, to repeat, the world is in the place it finds itself in today—a place of crisis, of violence, of killing, and war—because of what we currently believe about God?

That is true.

Okay, then, let's start there. What are the beliefs that we have about God that create crisis, violence, killing, and war?

First, you believe that God *needs* something.

Second, you believe that God *can fail to get* what He needs.

Third, you believe that God *has separated* you from Him because you have not given Him what He needs.

Fourth, you believe that God still needs what He needs so badly that God now *requires* you, *from your separated position,* to give it to Him.

Fifth, you believe that God *will destroy you* if you do not meet His requirements.

These Five Fallacies About God have brought more
pain and destruction to your day-to-day existence than
all of your other beliefs combined.

Well, okay…we could discuss those beliefs in detail, I
suppose. . . .

It could benefit you to do so.

And I would like to do that, later. But right now, I don't see how
these beliefs about *God* create crisis, violence, killing, and war
between *people*.

That's easy. *You think it is appropriate to act with each
other in the same way that you believe God acts with you.*
You also think that when you create crisis, violence,
killing, and war, you are doing so *in order to meet God's
requirements*. You think that you are *helping God meet
His needs*.
Many of you believe that God *wants* crisis, violence,
killing, and war, if that is what it takes for you to fulfill
His requirements. In this context, you believe wanton
killing to be God's Will.

Human beings believe that? I don't know of any human beings
who believe that.

You may not know them personally, but I can assure
you they exist, and have existed on your planet for a
very long time.
From the very earliest days you have described the
worst human experiences and disasters—even man-
made acts of terror—as "the Will of God."

In fact, your effort to understand the bad things that happen to you is how you came to believe in the existence of a God in the first place—and to believe in a God who does bad things.

Please explain that.

In your most primitive times, what you would call the caveman era and before, humans did not comprehend the simplest aspects of life around them. All they knew was that there *was* life around them. That is, there was something *other than them.*

This *other thing* that existed demonstrated itself all around them. It showed up as wind and rain, sun and moon and clouds, plants and trees and tiny living things that you now call insects and large living things that you now call animals, and as spectacular effects such as fires that started spontaneously in the forest, thunder and lightning from the sky, huge waves on the ocean, and, sometimes, a frightening shaking of the very ground itself.

Now, *Homo sapiens* did not know what to make of all these things. They did not know why people died, why hurricanes or tornadoes or droughts came along and destroyed everything, or why anything happened at all.

In order to make some sense of these things, early humans concluded that there must be some power greater than theirs that made these things occur. They imagined "spirits" that caused good and evil to manifest itself in their lives in many ways.

As they watched day turn into night and night into day, grass grow and flowers bloom, and trees lose their leaves and get them back again, they began to deify nature. They imagined "rain gods" and "the sun god" and many other gods that did things according to mood and whim. What had to be done, they reasoned, was to somehow *affect* this mood and to *please* the gods, and then the gods would do as they asked.

All manner of rites and rituals were created to "call forth" the spirit of whatever gods might be needed or desired at the moment, to placate them and to honor them and to get them to do what humans earnestly requested. There were rites of fertility and rites of passage and rituals of every kind and intention. These developed through the centuries into what became what some of you now call pagan customs.

Myths grew up around how sacred powers directly influenced life on earth, and about how life on earth can directly influence sacred powers. These myths became oft-told stories, which turned into beliefs. That is, *they became true* for people.

When myth turns into truth, it becomes organized religion.

From so-called pagan religions to the mainstream religions of your time was not a very big leap. Most humans today continue to believe in a power greater than themselves, and most humans continue to believe that there is something they must do to placate the Source of that power.

Today on your planet there are thousands of religions, some honoring a plurality of gods, and some
worshiping a single god.

Yes, but there's only one true religion.

Here we go again. This is the answer to your question. This is how beliefs about *God* create crisis, violence, killing, and war between *people*.

But it's *true!* There's only one religion that has it *right.* The rest
of them may *mean* well, but they just don't have it right. And we
have to be careful not to be *lured* into false beliefs that may *sound*
good, but have nothing to do with God's Law. Because if we deny
the one true God, and God's Law, we will not be saved, but go
straight to hell.

When?

When?

Yes. When will this happen?

When you die, of course.

And, if true believers feel that you *deserve* to go to hell because
you do not believe in the One True God, nor follow God's Law,
they are allowed to *send* you there immediately, by killing you.
Indeed, in some cases they are obliged to. When leaders of a religion issue a mandate, all true believers are required to follow it,
and kill whomever the leaders tell them to kill.

Who told you that?

You did.

I did?

Yes. You said that we can destroy any person, government, or nation whose actions amount to apostasy. That's what we use as our authority. Your Word.

You use my word as your authority in these matters?

Of course. Knowing that we are doing God's Will is what guides us, directs us, gives us courage, and provides us comfort when we slaughter people.

But I would never will that.

What do you mean? You *did* do it.

I did?

Did you not part the Red Sea to let your people escape? And did you not then close the sea, burying under tons of water some 600 of those who followed? Did you not destroy nearly every person living in Sodom and Gomorrah? And have you not killed many others, or required or approved of the killing of others, throughout the ages?

From these and other recountings of the instructions and demands of Deity found in the Bible, in the Qur'an, in the Bhagavad-Gita, in the Book of Mormon, and in other Scriptures, every schoolchild of every culture knows about the Wrath of God.

Yes, that's the problem.

Why is teaching our children the truth a problem?

Because it is *not* the truth.

There is no such thing as the Wrath of God.
It is one of your false beliefs about God. But I am
clear that you think it is true, and that you think it is
appropriate to act with each other in the same way that
you believe God acts with you. Your religious leaders
have actually done this. They have called upon "all True
believers" to "kill the apostates."

Well, sometimes we say "Kill the infidels!" but it means the
same thing. "Infidel," "apostate," it doesn't matter. They're just
words. The point is, if others don't believe what we believe, God
says we get to kill them.

Christians have done it. Muslims have done it. Many groups
of believers have done it.

You know the history of some of this?

Oh, yes. Pope Urban II issued a call to a "crusade" at Clermont,
France, in 1095 that resulted in a series of military expeditions
organized by Western Christians against Muslims and other "infidels." These crusades went on for *two hundred years,* resulting in the
death of hundreds of thousands.

Muslim leaders, likewise, have sponsored through the centuries
aggression after aggression, assassination after assassination, slaughter after slaughter, in the name of eradicating apostasy.

And these behaviors have not been limited to medieval times.
In 1989 Ayatollah Ruhollah Khomeini, then the spiritual leader
of revolutionary Iran, publicly condemned a book called *The Satanic
Verses* and issued a *fatwa* against its author, Salman Rushdie.

It was said that Muslims around the world had a duty to exe-
cute Rushdie on sight, and that any Muslim doing so would go

straight to heaven. The man had to go into hiding for ten years, until the Iranian government finally revoked the *fatwa.*

Most recently, in the late 1990s, radical Muslims, many of them living in Afghanistan, declared war on Western civilization, telling Muslims throughout the world that it was their duty to bring "death to America" and "death to Israel"—among other specified enemies.

In other words, your history is repeating itself.

Over and over again. And we can't seem to find a way to stop it. Now we are dealing with horrible terrorist acts and the killing of many innocent people.

Meanwhile, the *Encyclopedia Britannica* 2001, in an article on the 200 years of Christian attacks, contained an ironic comment describing those crusades. It said that such random acts of terrorism "with their combination of idealism, ambition, heroism, cruelty, and folly, are a medieval phenomenon and, as such, outside modern man's experience."

I expect that line will have to be rewritten for the next edition. . . .

5

So the Five Fallacies About God create crisis, violence, killing, and war.

Yes. That is observable.

You also said there were beliefs about Life that were leading us astray.

Yes.

What are those?

The Five Fallacies About Life that create crisis, violence, killing, and war are:

1. **Human beings are separate from each other.**
2. **There is not enough of what human beings need to be happy.**
3. **To get the stuff of which there is not enough, human beings must compete with each other.**

4. Some human beings are better than other human beings.

5. It is appropriate for human beings to resolve severe differences created by all the other fallacies by killing each other.

These Five Fallacies About Life, combined with the Five Fallacies About God, make for a deadly litany of error that has created, and continues to create to this very moment, a world of deep anger, brutal violence, terrible loss, unrelenting sorrow, and unremitting terror.

You think you are being terrorized by other people, but in truth you are being terrorized by your beliefs.

These are what you must change if you are ever to realize your dream of a world living in peace, harmony, and happiness.

I say again, and again and again, you cannot change the conditions of anger, violence, loss, sorrow, and terror by political or economic means. You can *affect* these conditions—that is, you can alter them somewhat for a short period of time, or you can interrupt them—but you cannot eliminate them without a change in your beliefs.

Because "belief creates behaviors."

That is correct.

Well, as I said earlier, I want to discuss these false beliefs, all of them, later.

Good, because that is the point of this dialogue.

But first, in the early part of this conversation, you said that there were five things we can do now if changing our world, and the self-destructive direction in which it is moving, is what we wish to achieve. You called these the "Five Steps to Peace," yet none of them sounded like much of an action plan to me. They seemed like mostly philosophical meanderings. Forgive me, I don't mean that pejoratively. I just wonder if this is the kind of information that will help people and that will serve the world right now.

The purpose of this dialogue is to *awaken* people and to *heal* the world. That will both help *and* serve.

Now what I said was, there are five things you can choose. I said nothing about five things you can do.

I am making the repeated point here that peace on your planet will only be achieved when you change beliefs because unless you "get" this point, you will be able to achieve nothing in the way of healing your planet.

What you seek to heal are the wounds created by your beliefs. Your deepest beliefs have created the behaviors that have produced the wounds.

The overriding desire of humankind is peace, and I am showing you that your current beliefs do not render you very peaceful.

"Peaceful" is not something you do. "Peaceful" is something you are.

One does not say, "I am doing peaceful." One says,

"I am *being* peaceful." And *beingness* is an expression of the soul and the mind.

Again, please?

"Beingness" is an expression of the soul and the mind. "Doingness" is an expression of the body. All experiences of the body arise out of experiences of the soul or the mind. You get to choose which. If you choose the mind, as your mind feels, so the body does. If you choose your soul, as the soul feels, the body does.

The soul always feels joy, because the soul *is* joy. The soul always feels love, because the soul *is* love. The soul always feels connected with the wonder of life, because the soul *is* the wonder of life, expressed.

In order to feel this always, you have to be out of your mind. You have to get "out of your head" and into your heart.

I thought you were going to say, into your soul.

The heart is the bridge between the mind and the soul. First get out of your mind and into your heart space. From there it is a quick jump into your soul.

When you are in your heart space with another, that is when you can have a real soul talk. When you are in your heart space with yourself, that is when you can experience connecting with your soul at a very deep level. That is when you can experience communion with God.

If you stay in your mind, you will be affected by the constructions of the mind. If the mind is dampened or weakened, the body will function in ways that reflect that. If the mind is uplifted, strengthened, or renewed, the body will function in ways that reflect that.

If the mind is discouraged, diminished, restricted, frustrated, angry, wounded, or agitated, the body will demonstrate that. If the mind is excited, enlarged, unlimited, exuberant, joyful, healed, and peaceful, the body will behave in an entirely different way.

But isn't that just the way "old time religion" makes people feel? Doesn't it talk about "the renewing of your mind"? Doesn't it make people feel excited, enlarged, unlimited, exuberant, joyful, healed, and victorious? Isn't that *precisely its appeal?* Isn't that *explicitly its promise?*

Indeed. Yet it is a promise your old religions have not been able to keep for humanity as a whole.

Why is that? If religion can make individuals ecstatic, why can't it heal the world?

Because organized religion as you currently create it is largely an exclusive experience. It is exclusive to the individual or the group experiencing it. You have not found a way to include everyone in the same experience—that is, society as a whole—because you have not found a way for everyone to agree on *how the experience should be experienced.*

Indeed, you *disagree* on this question so dramatically

that it has caused you to interrupt your own ecstasy to express your disapproval of another for not experiencing their ecstasy in the same way.

You have argued with each other, battled with each other, and killed each other in your anger over this ecstasy.

Why? Why have we done this? And why can't religions heal this?

Organized religions *by their nature* exclude as many as they include. This would be non-problematic if religions were tolerant of those they exclude, yet far too often this is not the case.

Religions, which you count on to teach tolerance, have not learned how to practice it, and so, teach just the opposite.

I am so sad about that. And I wouldn't have believed how serious the problem was—and *is,* to this *very day*—if I hadn't come across evidence with my own eyes. The most recent, and to me a shocking, evidence of exactly what is being discussed here was contained in a newspaper article in the *Arizona Republic,* written by Stephanie Simon and originally appearing in the *Los Angeles Times,* on December 1, 2001. I want to reprint that story here, in full, because I want all the world to know just how insidious—and how serious—this problem is. Most people to whom I've shown this story are aghast. Their mouths drop.

Here's the article . . .

LUTHERAN PASTOR ASSAILED
Joining Interfaith Event Called Heresy

St. Louis—To the Rev. David Benke the ceremony at Yankee Stadium was a blessing, an opportunity to join other religious and civic leaders in offering comfort to a nation raw from the terrorist attacks on the World Trade Center and the Pentagon. He joined the celebrities and politicians on stage to sing patriotic songs and to pray.

It was, he thought, his duty as a pastor.

But some fellow clergymen took quite a different view. They saw his participation in an interfaith event as heresy.

Six pastors from the Lutheran Church–Missouri Synod filed formal charges last week calling for Benke's expulsion from the church.

Others have petitioned to oust church president Gerald Kieschnick for condoning Benke's participation in the event and himself for praying with chaplains from other Lutheran denominations after a tour of the World Trade Center wreckage in October.

Benke "participated in idolatry by participating with non-Christians" at the Sept. 23 service, one of the dissidents, the Rev. David Oberdieck, told the *St. Louis Post-Dispatch.* Oberdieck would not comment further Friday, saying the dispute was a "family matter" that should not be aired in the "secular media." But he stood by his interpretation of Benke as an idol worshiper.

He and other clergy also accused Benke of

"syncretism," which means promoting the view that all religions are equal. The 10-page petition against Benke called his participation in the New York ceremony "an egregious offense against the love of Christ" that gave "the impression that the Christian faith is just one among many by which people may pray to God."

According to these critics, by standing alongside "heretics" such as Muslims, Jews, Hindus and Christians of other denominations, Benke implicitly endorsed their faiths, giving the impression that all offer an equal path to salvation.

Church leaders hold that they must not pray in public with anyone from another faith, even Lutherans of other denominations. They believe in worshiping only with those who interpret the Scriptures and understand God in precisely the same way they do.

"We can't go to the communion rail with someone who thinks of communion in a completely different way," explained the Rev. David Strand, a spokesman for the church, which is based in suburban St. Louis.

The nation's largest Protestant denomination, the 16-million-member Southern Baptist Convention, hews to a similar tradition. "I do not have an ecumenical bone in my body," the Rev. Paige Patterson, a former president of the church, has often said. And indeed, many Southern Baptist clergy made a point of staying away from interfaith services after the Sept. 11 attacks.

Yet Benke and Kieschnick insist that the Yankee Stadium ceremony was not a formal worship service and thus was not off-limits to Missouri Synod members.

They viewed it as a secular event, organized by Mayor Rudolph Giuliani and hosted by actor James Earl Jones, that included some prayer.

When it was Benke's turn at the microphone, he recited a brief prayer that opened and closed with references to Christ. Although he stood in respectful silence while other religious leaders spoke, his supporters insist he was not worshiping with them. Nor was he assenting to their views.

"To suggest that when the imam was praying to Allah, Dr. Benke was praying right alongside ... it's an insult to even imply that was what he was doing," Strand said.

As for Kieschnick's impromptu prayer session with chaplains from other denominations, Strand said the same justification applied.

Now I read that story and I think to myself, I guess I must just be naïve. I mean, I thought I was a pretty savvy guy who knew what was going on in the world, but I'm seeing here that I have no *idea* of what's happening around me.

That story shocked me. I was shocked and saddened and sick at heart when I first read it. I just had no idea... I thought that I had to look elsewhere in the world to find that level of hysterical, radical *religious* intolerance.

It is time you acknowledged a human truth at which no one wants to look.

One of the biggest problems in the world today is organized religion.

Organized religions are a problem.

They are not a solution, they are *a problem.*

Not all religions, but most. And certainly, most of the largest.

What you have in the case of most of your largest and most influential organized religions is the blind leading the blind.

Really. I mean, here is a nation in the midst of incredible grief, searching for spiritual support in a moment of need, seeking to experience its unity and oneness at a time of turmoil, only to have *its own religions letting it down.*

Here are a people wanting only to link arms and walk in-step, each person appealing to the God of his or her understanding, each person knowing that healing begins with the expression of tolerance for every other person's understanding, only to find that organized religion forbids it.

Religions forbid tolerance. Can you imagine? Baptists refusing to pray with Jews or Catholics. Lutherans refusing to pray with *other Lutherans.* As if there was a wrong time, or a wrong place, or a wrong person with whom to pray.

Is it any wonder that human beings around the world are asking, "What's wrong with this picture?" Is it any wonder that bumper stickers and billboards have begun to appear, saying, GOD, SAVE ME FROM YOUR PEOPLE? Who in the world wants to believe in a God who is less charitable and less tolerant than they are?

How can we ask the world to heal itself when organized religion—the very institution that was meant to provide that healing—does nothing but inflict more and more damage, open wider and wider the wound, spread further and further its righteous indignation, its non-acceptance, its utter distain, its total intolerance?

> Yet how can you blame religion if religions believe in a God who does exactly the same thing?
> *It is your understanding of God that is the main problem.*
> I will say again, so that you cannot miss it...the problem confronting humanity today *is spiritual.*
> You do not understand who you are. You do not understand who God is. You do not understand how the world works. You do not understand that love is the basis of all of life, nor can you comprehend *a love that is unconditional.*
> You imagine that God is a small, petty, jealous deity who says to people bowed in prayer, "Sorry, it's my way or the highway. Your prayer I hear. Your prayer I don't, because you didn't do it right. You did not please me." In this you turn me into a replica of the worst of humanity.
> You claim that you are striving to be God-like in your lives...and if this is the God you are striving to be like, you have succeeded brilliantly.
> You may thank organized religion for teaching you how.

Not all organized religions are in this category. Some of them teach tolerance and actually practice it. Some of them teach of a God who is inclusive, and actually live that teaching. The Unity

Church is one that comes to mind. The United Church of Religious Science is another. And there are more, such as the Metropolitan Community Church, and still others. So not all organized religions fall into this category.

> Your assessment is correct. Yet the majority of them do. When I say "organized religion," or "religion" in general, within the context of the dialogue that we are now having, I want it to be known that I am speaking of those religions that teach a doctrine of *exclusivity*. In other words, "our religion is the only true religion."
> *This kind of religion is the problem.*
> Not all religion. *This kind of religion.* The kind of religion that teaches separatist philosophy and exclusivist theology.

And as you said, most of the world's major religions, unfortunately, fall into that category.

> It could be more unfortunate than you know, because these religions base their understanding on spiritual beliefs that simply are not true, but that have a huge impact on society at large—believers in God and non-believers alike—as we shall show as this dialogue continues.
> Yes, there are other problems facing humanity. There are problems of hunger, of poverty, of crime and corruption, of political turmoil and governmental abuse and corporate greed, and many other social problems as well. But all of these—*all of these*—are spiritual problems at their base.

That is the point. That is the focus of this discussion. For if your spiritual understandings were complete, none of these problems would exist.

You would not allow them to.

Yet it is many of your largest and most powerful and influential organized religions that will not *allow* your spiritual understandings to be complete, for they do not provide a space for it. They do not permit your contemplations to seriously venture beyond the boundaries of their own doctrines.

And so, even as your planet faces a spiritual problem of gigantic proportion, you are trying to solve the problem by temporal means. You are rushing around treating the symptoms, rather than the cause, of your worldwide disease.

You are seeking to bring about, for humanity as a whole, excitement, enlargement, unlimitedness, exuberance, joy, healing, and peace. But you are attempting to do this with politics, with economics, with education, with social programs, even with bombs.

It cannot be done that way.

You are trying to fix everything except what needs to be fixed. You are trying to change everything except what needs to be changed.

You are addressing everything but your most basic beliefs. *Yet it is your most basic beliefs that are creating the problem.*

That is why the Five Steps to Peace have to do with God and the spirit, not with the body.

6

Okay, I've got it. I'm convinced. So let's get back to that. We never got to really discuss those Five Steps to Peace. Could we review them?

Yes. You can choose to take these steps now if changing your world, and the self-destructive direction in which it is moving, is what you wish to achieve. Make this declaration:

1. I acknowledge that some of my old beliefs about God and about Life are no longer working.
2. I acknowledge that there is something I do not understand about God and about Life, the understanding of which could change everything.
3. I am willing for new understandings of God and Life to now be brought forth, understandings that could produce a new way of life on this planet.
4. I am willing to explore and examine these new under-

standings, and, if they align with my inner truth and
knowing, to enlarge my belief system to include them.
5. I am willing to live my life as a demonstration of my
   beliefs.

Okay, let's take the first one. There are many people who are
nowhere near ready to admit that their beliefs are not working.
Particularly their religious beliefs. In fact, they say that a little bit
of Old Time Religion is exactly what this world needs right now,
that everything would work out fine if we would all just start listening to it, obeying it, doing what it says.

> Yes. One group of religious believers who have been
> saying this has come to be known as "fundamentalists."
> These are what some have termed religious purists,
> who believe that the way forward is the way back-
> ward, to the original and exact words of Holy Scrip-
> ture—whatever Scripture it is they happen to believe
> in—to be read verbatim, and applied literally.
> There are fundamentalists in every faith movement.

Are they right? Would the world be better off if we just listened to those exact words, and obeyed them?

> The first difficulty is that just listening to them is not
> enough. You have to *interpret* them—and the moment
> you do that, you become the decider of what they
> mean. In that moment they are no longer the Word of
> God. They are your words *about* the Word of God.
> And everyone has to assume that you know what you're
> talking about. Of course, there's simply no way to

know this, so other people have to *take your word for it.*

Several religions seek to bestow infallibility on scriptures or supreme authority on individuals in positions of spiritual leadership in order to get around this problem.

Haven't Roman Catholics done this with the Pope?

Yes. In Roman Catholic theology it is proclaimed that the Pope, acting as supreme teacher and under certain conditions—when he is speaking *ex cathedra,* or "from his chair"—cannot err when he teaches in matters of faith or morals.

And in the Bhagavad-Gita, isn't there some statement about the words attributed to Lord Krishna being infallible?

It is true that in the Bhagavad-Gita, Arjuna tells Lord Sri Krishna that he accepts whatever He says to be completely perfect.

"Sarvam etad rtam manye," are the exact words, or, *"I accept everything You say to be true."*

And have not Islamists proclaimed the Qur'an to be infallible, and also bestowed infallibility on the *ulama*—religious teachers and "learned ones" within the *umma,* or community?

Indeed. In Islam, *ulama* are given pervasive authority in matters of both moral and temporal dimension in the life of Muslims from birth until death.

Isn't there also a thought, in certain interpretations of Islam, that Muslims must always follow the way of the majority of the community, which had been charged by the Qur'an with a mis-

sion and commanded to accept a challenge, and which is said to
be always protected by the hand of God — and thus endowed with
infallibility?

> I see that you have taken a look at comparative
> theology.

Yes.

> And what have you concluded?

That no human being is infallible, and that the assigning of
infallibility to any person or group can be very dangerous. I see that
the doctrine of infallibility — the idea that "we are always right" —
invariably leads to making someone else *wrong.* It produces disagreement and conflict. It can also produce a certain *hubris,* which
is the opposite of the humility said to be the bedrock of all religions.

> It has, in fact, done so.

But I am curious. What would *you* say to people who assert that
following the words of their Holy Scripture verbatim, and interpreting them literally, is the only way?

> I would ask them to notice that these words were
> written at a different time and in a very different kind
> of place and circumstance. I would observe that, while
> these teachings were based on a firm set of principles,
> to now interpret their words literally, rather than seek
> to understand the underlying principle that they reveal,
> could lead, at the very least, to misunderstanding, and,
> in the worst case, to a loss of the original wisdom in
> which they were grounded.

> I would invite humans to explore whether they might derive more benefit from the original teachings of all faith traditions if those teachings were contextualized within the framework of a continually evolving society.

In other words, remain open to the possibility of new inter-pretations that might allow us to better apply ancient wisdom to contemporary life.

> Exactly.
> Yet in the end I would say to people everywhere: Believe as you wish, follow your heart and your soul where it leads you, but do not seek to impose your views on others—and certainly do not seek to do so by force.

Yet what if they still insisted that their way is the only "right way" to live? And what if they believe that *they are required to make others live in the same way?*

> I would ask, "Who *is* doing the requiring?"

And if they answered, "God"—?

> I would say, "You've got me all wrong. I am not ask-ing you to do that. I am not requiring you to do that. I would never give Free Will to people just so you could take it away from them."

That is a very powerful statement. It is very impactful, because *even radical fundamentalists believe in the doctrine of Free Will.* Yet now I want to understand something, and I have to get "case specific" in order to do it.

Go ahead.

How could religious fundamentalists such as the Taliban of Afghanistan demand that all women cover themselves head to toe in a *burqah,* and say that all men must wear beards of a certain length, and tell women that they may not come out of their houses without a male blood relative, and may not hold jobs, and that girls may not go to school until they redesign the curriculum to teach them only what they are supposed to hear? I don't understand this. I'm trying to understand this, and I don't understand this.

There are writings in the Qur'an and in the Hadith that could be interpreted as supporting all of those injunctions.

But those are such repressive requirements. Why would such things be required?

Repressive societies have existed from the beginning of recorded history. The demands and restrictions of the rulers in such societies are not based on the will of God, but on what religious leaders claim are the "Laws of God," based on their own fears that full freedom would allow people to stray from the path that those leaders wish them to take. And the fact is that many people probably *would* take another path, for the simple reason that *they prefer it.* Yet in a repressive society there is no room for personal preference. And in a repressive society based on the principles of an organized religion, there is room only for the preferences of God.

But who can claim to really know those?

The leaders and teachers in every repressed society. Just ask them!

Yet what kind of a leader leads by force? And what kind of a teacher must use fear to convince his students of the wisdom of his teachings?

And what kind of a society will not allow its own members to be educated, or exposed to any thoughts other than those with which that society agrees?

Is this not a society living in desperate fear? Anxious that, once heard, those other thoughts may sound more attractive? And with what tool can a fearful society fashion itself, other than fear itself?

It is, however, not surprising that human societies such as these would arise, for *this is how you imagine God's kingdom to be.*

You imagine God to require you to love Him, or else. To require you to accept His teachings, or else. To require you to behave in a certain way, or else.

Only a God in fear would do this. A God in love would never do this. A God in love would never have to. For love begets its own allegiance, but fear rejects it.

Yet if God behaves in a fearful way, using fear to get what He wants and needs, should you not do this also? Indeed, should you not do it *in His Name?*

This is the circle of logic you have created, and you have trapped yourself within it. It is a vicious circle, and you are experiencing its viciousness right now on your planet.

I know! That's why I'm asking you for help. Tell us what to do here. We all want peace. We all want an end to the sadness and the suffering, and to all the killing of each other that we are doing and don't seem to be able to stop. We seek a newer world. Tell us what will work.

Please.

> I have told you. First, you must acknowledge that what you are now doing *is not working*.
>
> And it is not only your religion that isn't working. Your political structures are not working. Your economic systems are not working. Your educational programs are not working.
>
> None of the constructions that you have put into place in your society are holding up your society. Indeed, they are bringing it down.
>
> All of these structures are soundly based on beliefs that do not reflect reality. They no longer serve you. *Get rid of them.*

Get rid of them? Dump everything we've done to create civilization?

> What you have created is not civilization. It is anything *but* "civilized."
>
> Yet I am not talking about "dumping everything." I was not saying destroy the structures of your society. When I said "get rid of them," I was referring to some of the *beliefs* that have created the structures of your society in their present form.

Change those.

Do not destroy the structures of politics, economics, and education; add to them, alter them, improve them.

Even our religions?

Especially your religions.

You are invited to create a new way to experience your religions by looking deeply into the wisdom within them, then using that wisdom to form a new expression of your spiritual nature.

You are invited to open yourself to new ideas, new thoughts, and new revelations as you explore this new spiritual expression.

So we require a complete overhaul, is that it?

If what you choose is what you *say* you choose—a world living in peace, in harmony, and in happiness—the answer is, yes.

You must remodel your world and its society at every level.

The universe now invites you to re-create yourselves anew, in the next grandest version of the greatest vision you ever held about Who You Are.

7

That all sounds completely impossible. I'm sorry. I hate to throw cold water on all this, but I don't see how we can achieve this.

> **Are you willing to?**

Yes, but it just all sounds so overwhelming.

> **You are being overwhelmed *now*.**
> **It's just a question of what you choose to be over-whelmed by: present conditions, which could destroy your lives, or magnificent ideas that could re-create them.**

Well, when you put it that way. . .

> **That is the only way to put it, because that is the way it is.**
> **Here is the question before all of humanity right now.**

BY WHAT DO YOU CHOOSE TO BE OVER-WHELMED?

Do you wish to be overwhelmed by something coming *at you,* or by something coming *from you?*

You are right, this does all "sound overwhelming." It is *supposed* to be overwhelming. With this force—the force of your ideas, the power of new beliefs—you can *overwhelm all the negativity in the world.*

Well, I hate to bring this up again, but that's what *organized religion* says that it can do. I don't want to belabor this point, but there are those who believe that the reason we are failing in our efforts to create the life that we want on this planet is not that religion has failed us, but that *we have failed religion.*

Well, let's look at that.

Organized religion has been around for thousands of years. It has touched many individual lives, but in your collective society it has changed little. As a group you are still dealing with the same problems that confronted you at the beginning. The problems of greed, envy, anger, righteousness, inequity, violence, and war.

Most organized religions have not led you away from these behaviors, but more fully into them. In some cases they have actually justified them, even by their own example.

Religion, it was hoped, would bring your world closer to God, creating a sense of communion with the divine. Yet many organized religions have not done that. They have touched some individual lives in this way, but your collective society experiences not communion, but estrangement; not unity with God, but separation. In some cases, it is organized religion that actually *teaches* separation from God.

Religion, it was hoped, would bring people closer to each other, producing a sense of community and integration. Yet many organized religions have not done that. They have touched some lives in this way, but your collective society has experienced exactly the opposite. In fact, in some cases it is organized religion itself that preaches *against* community and integration, claiming that God never intended people of varying races, cultures, and nationalities to commingle, much less intermarry and co-create.

It was hoped that religion would bring your world a greater sense of joy and freedom, but in too many cases it has not done so. In fact, few institutions have done more to bind and shackle and restrict the human spirit, presenting long lists of what one must and must not do, must and must not wear, must and must not eat, must and must not think, must and must not enjoy.

Indeed, some organized religions have encumbered many human joys with guilt by proclaiming that much of what you love is bad. Money is bad, power is bad, sex is bad, music and dancing is bad, in some places even being *seen* is bad. Cover yourself! Hide yourself! Protect yourself! *Be ashamed of yourself!*

These have been the lessons of so many of your religions. These have been their teachings. Yet the real message of God is not shame, intolerance, exclusivity, separation, and subjugation. The real message of God is joy, acceptance, unity, freedom, and unconditional love.

Most of the killing and most of the domination and most of the suppression and most of the terror on your planet has been carried out under the banner of organized religion and in the name of God. The two hundred years of the Christian Crusades are a prime example, during which people were slaughtered in the name of Christ.

Yes. Former U.S. President Bill Clinton said in a speech to students at Georgetown University in November of 2001 that the international terrorism of today, which had only just then reached the United States, dates back thousands of years.

"In the first Crusade," Mr. Clinton said, "when the Christian soldiers took Jerusalem, they first burned a synagogue with 300 Jews in it, then proceeded to kill every woman and child who was a Muslim on the Temple Mount. I can tell you that story is still being told today in the Middle East, and we are still paying for it."

This kind of religious insanity continues to this very day, on which you murder with the invocation, "Allah is great!" The enormous irony and the immense sadness is that some humans do not even see the contradiction.

This is the effect that your organized religions of exclusivity and righteousness and retribution have had on you. They have solved nothing. They have, in fact, *enlarged* the very problems they were intended to solve.

But religion has done a lot of good in the world. Look at its charity work. Look at the millions whose lives it has touched in positive ways.

Religion has indeed done good in the world. As a helping hand and as a change agent in the lives of individuals, it has produced many blessings. As a force for societal evolution, however, it has not fared well.

Why have your organized religions been so singularly ineffective in bringing about a general uplifting of human morals, motivations, and *modi operandi?* Why have they been totally unsuccessful in producing any significant shift in wholesale worldwide consciousness?

This is the issue humankind might do well to address. Yet this is the question you are afraid to ask.

And if we asked it?

You would find that it is not for lack of effort. Most organized religions have been sincere in their attempts to bring about social change and a new way of life.

It is for lack of understanding. And it is because of stubbornness.

Most of organized religion has not changed its basic point of view for centuries and, in some cases, for millennia.

Let me restate that, so that you can appreciate its full impact.

I said, there *has not been a significant new idea* brought into most major organized religions *in hundreds and thousands of years.*

Indeed, the very *idea* of "new ideas" is anathema.

This conversation, the conversation you are now having, will dare to present some new ideas. Do you dare to look at them? Do you have the courage to expose yourself to some new thoughts on the subject of God, even if you think that you may not agree with them?

Your largest religions and their leaders resolutely refuse to. They cannot acknowledge that there may be something they do not know, the knowing of which could change everything.

Yet it is true that when they insist that they have all the answers, religions provide none.

And so now you are faced with an important question. This is another stating of the question asked before, the question facing all of humankind in this moment.

Will you move forward into new and unchartered seas? Or will you allow the tide of events to sweep you back to the rocky shoals upon which you have already crashed your hopes a thousand times?

Will you go back to the exact words and phrases and to-the-letter interpretations and literal applications of your old religions, as fundamentalists of every religion would have you do, or will you dare to explore, suggest, recommend, and create a *new* spirituality— one that does not reject everything about the old, but improves upon it, carrying humanity to grander heights?

Do you have the courage to take the Five Steps to Peace?

What if I say that I'm ready? What if I say I can admit that many of our beliefs — not just our religious beliefs, but also many of our ideas about economics, politics, education, philosophy, and much of our culture — are no longer working? What then?

Then you are ready to explore what *could* work.

Then you are ready for new revelations.

Then you are ready to build a new tomorrow.

8

Okay, Step 1 of the Five Steps to Peace is admitting what I just admitted. Step 2 is acknowledging that there is something I do not understand about God and about Life, the understanding of which could change everything. All right, I stipulate that. I don't know everything about Life. I don't understand everything about God.

> You may not, but some people believe that they do, and many of your religions say that they do.
> Are you willing to look at that? Are you willing to be *a force and a source*, in your own way, in your own corner of the world, which brings about a change in these beliefs?

I think I could be that. A Force and a Source. I like that. But how? *How* to be that? That is the question.

First, you must *choose* to be. You must select yourself. It is a matter of self-selection. You must decide
that this is who you are.

Then, you must decide to demonstrate your decision about yourself, every hour of every day. You must
understand that every act is an act of self-definition.
Everything you think, say, and do defines you, announces
your choice about yourself.

Life is a decision conveyor. It conveys to the world
the decisions that you've made about yourself. It tells
people what you've decided about who you are, and
who *they* are, and why you are here, and why you think
they are here, and what life itself is about.

Those decisions have greater impact than you could
ever guess. They touch people in ways that go far beyond
what you might have imagined.

Yet it does not begin by trying to change the world.
It begins by seeking to change the self. Change the self
and your inner world changes. And when your inner
world changes, the outer world that you *touch* changes,
little by little. And when the outer world that you touch
changes, the world that *it touches* changes, and the world
that *it* touches. Outward and outward and outward this
spreads, like a ripple in a pond.

Yes, I have heard that analogy before. And perhaps now it is
time to make waves, to rock the boat.

If not now, when? If not you, who?

Indeed. I see this now. I see that I must get involved. Me, *personally.* I can't sit around waiting for others to solve the problem. None of us can. We can't afford to anymore. *Time is of the essence.*

You are correct.

I could begin by seeking to change the part of my self that does not believe I have any role to play in helping to create the outer collective world we all inhabit. I could change my inner beliefs *about* that world, about Life, and about God. Then I could talk to my community's religious leaders. We could all do that. We could go to our local spiritual leaders and ask them to sit down with us—heck, to sit down with *each other*—and talk about these things.

I know of a situation in my own community of Ashland, Oregon, where a local Muslim spiritual leader was hearing that terrible and inaccurate things were being said about his faith by a Christian minister in the community in sermons to his congregation. The Muslim called the minister's office to ask if a meeting might take place, but he could not even get a return phone call. Still, he refused to give up. He called every day, then every hour, gently asking if the minister would just sit down and talk with him. Finally, a layperson from the church did talk with the Muslim in a personal meeting for a few moments. But the minister never did. He refused. He has refused to this day.

**What would you tell your local religious leaders if
you could get them to sit down together with you?**

I would tell them about a conversation that I had not long ago with Sir John Templeton—he's the man who created the Templeton Prize in Religion—in which I asked him what he felt the world needed most right now. Sir John said, "humility theology." When I asked him what that was, what he meant, he replied, "It's a theology that acknowledges it does not have all the answers. We need a theology that is willing to continue asking questions."

Sir John is very wise.

But I wonder whether a way can be found to convince any of the world's major religions that they don't have every last answer. These religions are *based* on their *conviction* that the answers are theirs. They say that all we have to do is *just listen to them*. What could we say to our local ministers, to our local rabbis, to members of the clergy from all the faiths in our community, if they say this?

Ask them if they observe that people who listen to the teachings of the major organized religions are people at peace. Or is it the people who have been listening who find themselves angry, intolerant, rigid, abusive, and fighting in so many wars?

Ask them who has been at war in Ireland? Who has been at war in the Middle East? Who has been in constant conflict in the Balkans, on the Indian-Pakistani border, in Afghanistan? Who has sown the seeds of intolerance of gays, of women's inequality, of discrimination against minorities in the United States?

Yet know that the banner of organized religion is not the only banner that is waved in humanity's many struggles. There is also the flag of nationalism. So you must talk with your local political leaders as well.

You have said that the problem is not political, and it is not economical, it is spiritual.

> That is correct. It is your current spiritual under-
> standings that create and support your present politi-
> cal and economical constructions. So sitting down with
> religious leaders makes sense. But so, too, does sitting
> down with political and business leaders, because their
> spiritual understandings drive the engine of their poli-
> tics and their economics.
>
> Politics is your spirituality, *demonstrated.*
>
> So, too, economics.
>
> So engage the entire community, not only your reli-
> gious community, in explorations of a new spirituality
> that could change everything.

That's an idea! Maybe ordinary, common citizens in cities and towns around the world could create an informal movement, sitting down together to see what might be done within their own communities to sow the seeds of peace, then inviting their own local religious and political and business leaders to come in and begin to dialogue with them — and, more important, with each other — about all this.

Maybe we *can* change some beliefs — or at least get people to start thinking, to at least start looking at some *new ideas.*

Ah, but what would the new ideas be? That's the question. We've been searching for ways out of our dilemma for centuries. What *is it* that we don't understand about God and about Life, the understanding of which would change everything?

I, myself, have been trying to think, what would I say if I were asked this question? What could I offer as a new idea for people to think about, a new thought for humans to consider?

We need some guidance here. We need some insight. We need a new angle from which to approach all this.

What is it that we don't understand about God and about Life?

> Are you really ready for some insight? Are you truly prepared to look at things from a new angle? Do you really want to know what you don't understand?

Yes.

> All right, here goes. And remember, this is not going to be easy for some people to accept.

I understand. Go ahead. At the very least we'll have something new to discuss. Talking and talking and talking about the old theologies in the same old ways has gotten us nowhere. We're going around in circles here. And in the meantime we're killing each other, because the old theologies haven't worked in stopping us.

> Fair enough. So here's the truth that you don't understand:
>
> Your entire civilization—your religion, your politics, your economics, your social structures, everything—is based on fallacies.

Well, that could open up a conversation. I assume that these are the fallacies we've been speaking of here?

Yes. These are the five about God and the five about Life that have become firm beliefs held by human beings.

The Five Fallacies About God have produced organized religion, and the Five Fallacies About Life have produced nationalism.

These are the two causes of your world being in a constant state of turmoil for centuries.

Oh, good, so I can tell people that we shouldn't have religions and we shouldn't have nations! Have I left anything out?

That's not what I've said.

Sure sounds that way.

Then you have not been listening.

I have not said anything about abolishing religions, and I am not saying anything about abolishing nations. While organized religions and nationalism have been the two main causes of turmoil on the Earth, it is also true that religions and nationalism and cultures and traditions all provide humans with a sense of identity and of community.

In other words, there are some things that work and some things that do not work about religion and nationalism. I would never suggest simply abolishing those things.

These are not things that you "shouldn't have." What is clear, however, is that you must now improve—not eliminate, but improve—the way you experience and express your religious and national identities if you truly wish to create a world in which humans live in peace and harmony and happiness.

And how can we make those improvements?

One way would be by looking at the fallacies upon which your present beliefs about God and Life are based. This can only happen if you, and the other people with whom you discuss this, take the Five Steps to Peace.

So that could be our first assignment—to see if we can get everyone in our sphere of influence, all of our local religious and political and business leaders, to agree to take the Five Steps to Peace.

Do you think you can do that?

It may not be easy.

It's a start. It's a place to start. You can't even begin to try to improve things if you can't agree that there's something that needs improving. You can't make anything work that isn't working if you can't agree that it isn't working right now.

Right now life on your planet—and the belief upon which it is based—is not working. Not if what you want to experience is what you say you want to experience. Yet if you cannot agree that these things are not working, you are lost, and there is nothing further you can do.

Well, I'm going to try. I'm going to promote the Five Steps to Peace. Publish them. Ask for comments from the public about them. Generate support for discussing them in our communities.

I may even announce a Five Steps to Peace dialogue or conference, and invite local leaders. I'll make it a public invitation. I'll try to make it irresistible.

This is *spiritual activism,* and I think this is what we need more of today. We need to begin with open, honest dialogue about our respective points of view. We need to make it all right to dissent, all right to criticize, all right to ask questions—and to *question the answers* we get when we ask them.

Many of our religions themselves stifle such discussion and debate. While in most Christian circles it is now conceded that not every single word in the Bible should be taken literally, many fundamentalist Christians continue to believe the Bible to be the unadulterated and absolute Word of God, down to the last crossed *t* and dotted *i*.

In the Islamic tradition, there is not even any such thing as a "fundamentalist." *All* of the Muslim faithful profess to believe that the Qur'an as revealed through Muhammad is the unadulterated and absolute Word of God, down to the last crossed *t* and dotted *i*. There can be no deviation from this. Anyone who does not adhere to this belief is deemed an apostate. In some places such apostasy is punishable by death.

Some may think I am exaggerating when I say these things, but the fact of the matter is that some religious followers have now gotten down to *arguing over pronouns.* So trivial have our clashes over God become, so petty do we imagine our God to be, that a publishing firm in America has created a firestorm by simply printing a Bible that seeks to be gender neutral.

Writer Cathy Lynn Grossman reported on this event in March 2002 in *USA Today* under the headline, A HOLY WAR OF WORDS. Grossman informs us that "a new 'gender accurate' translation of the New Testament"—called *Today's New International Version* and published by a company named Zondervan—"is creating a furor among believers who see every sacred word as a cobblestone on the path to Jesus and salvation."

Grossman's story goes on to say that the new Bible "is threaded with revisions that swap *they* for *he* and *children* for *sons* from Matthew to Revelation. Zondervan president Scott Bolinder claims it 'honors biblical principles' yet shows today's readers that 'the Bible isn't only for boys.'

"But critics such as James Dobson, founder of the conservative Focus on the Family ministry, say muting 'the masculinity intended by the authors of Scripture' violates the Gospel by 'obscuring the fatherhood of God'...'and the true identity of Jesus Christ.'"

Reporter Grossman sums up the point of view of many of these critics: "mess with the Bible and you're messing with God."

The gender-neutral Bible, these critics say, could "throw innocent believers and new converts off the track to eternal life...," Grossman writes.

The problem, the article quotes critics as saying, is that "changing pronouns in biblical text implies that something was wrong with the original"—and "among evangelicals 'you just don't say that the Bible is wrong,'" Nancy Ammerman of Hartford Seminary's Institute for Religion Research was quoted as saying.

The story also quotes R. Albert Mohler Jr., president of the Southern Baptist Theological Seminary, as saying that "capitulating to the treacherous winds of popular culture would be 'an insult to the very character of the Bible as the eternal, inerrant and authoritative word of God.'"

Now, just what kind of insult are we talking about here? Reporter Grossman's story offered an example. In *Today's New International Version* the wording of John 11:25 . . .

"He who believes in me will live, even though he dies, and whoever lives and believes in me will never die."

. . . has been changed to . . .

"Anyone who believes in me will live, even though they die, and whoever lives and believes in me will never die."

Grossman came up with other examples as well, including a change in Titus 2:12, where, elaborating on Paul's teaching, older Bibles say that the grace of God that brings salvation has "appeared to all men," whereas the controversial newest translation says that this grace "offers salvation to all people."

Now, I'm not sure that such changes constitute an "insult to the very character of the Bible," but I am sure that it is just this sort of petulant bickering over the "inerrant" word of God that produces so many of the *errant behaviors of humans*.

"Accuracy and fidelity to the word of God is always the high moral ground," says Susan Harding, an anthropologist at the University of California-Santa Cruz, identified in Grossman's *USA Today* article as a writer on fundamentalist language and politics. The story quotes Ms. Harding as saying that the kinds of gender changes in the Bible cited earlier create "the slippery slope to perdition."

So that's it, then. We're on our way to Hell if we change the pronouns in the Bible from "he" to "they."

The Harding quote concludes, "You can't have a community of believers who literally don't agree on what the Bible says."

I respectfully disagree. I observe that it's when we have a community of believers who do *not* disagree on *anything* that we are all in very big trouble.

What we need is *open dialogue* about the revelations of God, about the truths of life, about who we are and who we choose to be and how we can all best get to where we want to go as a human society.

> The conversation that we are having right here is a good example of an open and candid dialogue. Share it with others, so that they can know the kinds of things being talked about.
>
> Now, through our discussion here, you, yourself, have already taken the first two steps to peace. You've admitted that your old beliefs are no longer working and you've acknowledged that there is something you do not understand about God and about Life, the understanding of which will change everything. Are you ready to take the third step?

Let's see ... Step 3 is choosing to be willing for a new understanding of God and Life to now be brought forth. Okay, I'm willing for that to happen.

> Are you? Are you really?

> This idea is very threatening to some people. That anyone living today could bring forth a new understanding of God and of Life that would be even worth considering shakes the very foundation of orthodoxy.

I'm willing to step away from that for a moment. I'm willing to have someone try.

> No, no, this is not about having someone "try." This is about your being willing for a new understanding to be brought forth, not your being willing for someone to *try* to bring it forth.

What's the difference?

> The difference has to do with how wide you are opening the Space of Possibility.
>
> The believers in Muhammad and Jesus and Baha'u'llah and the others do not say that those men "tried" to bring forth great truth. They say that they *did*.
>
> Now, are you willing to announce and declare that it is possible for someone to *try* to bring forth a new understanding of God and Life, or that it is possible for someone to actually *bring forth* a new understanding of God and Life?
>
> There is a huge difference.
>
> You see, in your world it is very difficult to experience anything that you do not believe is possible. Even if it happens, you will deny it.

That doesn't feel true. Many things have happened in my life that I didn't think were possible.

Yes, but other people around you verified it for you. They swore that it was happening. They said that it was true. So it became true for you.

On the other hand, if the majority of people in your culture—virtually everyone in your society—says that something is not possible, it would be very difficult for you to experience it. Indeed, it may not be possible for you to experience it at all.

Even if you are looking right at it you may not see it. Or you will look right at it and see it as something else, because you simply do not understand it.

Yes, I remember my elderly grandmother watching man's first walk on the moon. She stared at the television and said, "Isn't this a good movie?" When my father and my aunt told her, "No, Ma, this is real. They're really on the moon," Granny said, "It's a wonderful movie. So imaginative." She simply could not hold the reality of it. She simply did not understand how such a thing could be possible.

And what you do not understand—?

You will deny!

Exactly.

And so, if you do not think that it is *possible* for someone living today to bring forth a new understanding of God and Life, to bring to the world a new revelation, you will find it incomprehensible. You will not understand it. Which means?

We will deny it.

Even as your heart beats with the excitement of its message. Even as your body trembles with growing awareness. Even as your soul dances with joy and ignites your mind.

Yet now I invite you to open wider the Space of Possibility. Not to acknowledge that it is possible for someone to *try*, but that it is possible for someone to *do*, the thing called "bring forth a new understanding of God and Life."

The Space of Possibility must allow room for a New Truth—a *huge* New Truth.

Okay, I'm open to that. I'm going to be open-minded enough to consider that there could be something new here for me to look at.

Good.

Can you state it directly?

Yes. Let's call this the **FIRST NEW REVELATION:**

God has never stopped communicating directly with human beings. God has been communicating with, and through, human beings from the beginning of time. God does so today.

This is what you can tell others when they ask you, "What are these new ideas you would like us to consider? What is it that we may not know, the knowing of which could change everything?"

What I am inviting you to do is to *change your belief about this. Let go of your idea that God ever stopped com-*

municating directly with human beings. Be willing to con-
sider a new thought about it—the thought that God is talking
to everyone all the time.

Can you do that? Can you hold the space of that
possibility?

I'm trying. I've been trying very hard since the beginning of
this dialogue.

You can't "try." If you wish to have the experience
that you *say* you wish to have, if you truly wish to be
one of those who assists in changing the self-destructive direction in which your world is heading, you must
do more than "try." You must do it.

You asked me if I would do something. You asked
me if I would help you. You asked me if I could give you
some tools with which you could join in changing the
world.

Yes.

Well, I'm going to invite *you* to do something.

Yes?

Use the tools that I give you.

Do not say that you are "trying" to use them. Do not
do as some others have done and dismiss them as not
being the "right" tools, or lay them aside, saying they
are "too difficult" to use.

I would not give you these tools if I did not know
you could use them. It is not my function to frustrate

you or to test you. (Nor to *punish* you if you do not *meet* the test.)

It is my function to glorify you, and so, to glorify Me. For only in the glory of you will the glory of Me be found. Only through the wonder of you will the wonder of Me be made known. Only through Life Itself, expressed in its next grandest way, can Life Itself be *experienced* in such a way.

9

I am ready! I am inspired and I am ready! *I will do it.* I will shed any last remaining doubt. I will move into full faith and knowing. I am willing for a new understanding of God and Life to now be brought forth, and I am completely open to the possibility that this can happen.

> **Good. Because now I'm going to ask you to open the Space of Possibility even wider.**

Okay.

> **I'm going to ask you to be open to the possibility that new understandings and new revelations can be brought forth, and are being brought forth, through *you.***

Yes, I understand that is what you are asking me. Yet that could feel so . . . self-serving, so self-aggrandizing, and so . . . heavy a burden.

It will only feel that way if you think that you are the only one given such abilities.

Such an idea would require you to think of yourself, and even to declare yourself, as someone special. Someone more special than anyone else.

You *are* someone special, but you are *not* more special than anyone else.

So know that you do not have to feel burdened, or somehow totally responsible for bringing to the world the New Message it awaits. For all people everywhere are capable of bringing forth this new message, sharing this new understanding, and revealing this new truth.

If that is true, everybody everywhere could claim to be the New Messenger of God. How do we sort it all out? To whom shall we listen?

Listen to no human who declares himself or herself to be more special than anyone else.

If a man or a woman seeks to set himself or herself separate and apart from the rest of humanity, or claims to be higher or better or holier than the rest of humanity, by declaring themself to be "more than" or "greater than" others, or to be the messiah, or the savior, or the only true parents of humanity, or the only true prophet, or any other such exalted thing, run from them as fast as you can.

Yet if men or women declare themselves to be messengers of God even as you *all* are messengers of God, and saviors even as you *all* are saviors, and holy even as you *all* are holy, then listen to them carefully, for they will not tell you to follow *them,* but to follow the God who lives within you.

For it is within your heart and within your soul and in the deepest reaches of your own mind that Divinity resides, and it is there in which it will be found, and only there in which it can be fully experienced, and only there from which it can emerge in purity and in truth, and through no other person, place, or thing.

Divinity realized through any other person, place, or thing is Divinity by Projection. You are witnessing all around you in the outer world the expression of Divinity, but that is not the same as the *experience* of Divinity.

Never confuse expression with experience.

A beautiful flower is an expression of Divinity, yet only when you see, feel, smell, and touch the beautiful flower *that is You* can you know the *experience* of Divinity.

Outer expression can *lead* to inner experience, but it can never substitute for it. Yet when inner experience leads to outer expression, the circle is complete—and this is the purpose of Life, and the function of the World, and of the entire Universe as well.

Oh, wow, I've never had things explained to me that simply before. Will you elaborate on this just a little for me?

The purpose of the World, the reason for its having been created, is to provide a contextual field within which you may achieve an awareness of your own Divinity. Part of the way that this may be accomplished is through observing the Outer Expression of Divinity that Life presents, provides, and produces.

Yet do not confuse the two. For the Expression of Divinity is not *your* Experience, but the Experience of something or someone *other* than you. And when you make *that* experience *your* experience, you substitute the Outer for the Inner. In so doing you move further from the power of Divinity within you, and give your power away. This, no true avatar or master will ever request or require you to do—nor will they even allow you to do it of your own accord. *Beware, therefore, of those who prepare a place and a way for you to pay them homage.*

Ah! *That* is what is meant by the saying, "If you see The Buddha walking down the street, run away from him."

Yes. If it is so obvious from the way that people are treating him—and from the way that he is *allowing* people to treat him—that he is The Buddha, then he is *not* The Buddha, for The Buddha would never allow others to think of him or to treat him as if he were more special than they.

Those who govern you in the outer world sit in the highest seats, so you must obey them and do everything they tell you. But do not do what they do, for they do not practice what they preach.

They create heavy burdens and place them on the shoulders of people, but they themselves are not willing to lift a finger to move them.

And those who claim to be teachers of the highest spiritual law, but do not live it, can likewise be easily identified. Everything they do is done for men to see: They make their robes wide and the tassels on their garments long; they love the place of honor at banquets, and the most important seats in the synagogues and churches and gathering places of all kinds; they adore being greeted in the marketplace, and they encourage others to call them Father and True Parent and Highest Teacher and Master and Rabbi and Prophet.

Yet you are not to be called 'rabbi,' for there is only one rabbi, and that rabbi is in your heart.

And you are not to be called master, for you have only one master, and that master is in your soul.

And do not call anyone on Earth your spiritual "father," or "true parent," for you have only one Spiritual Father/Mother God, the Source of All Creation, and you are all children of that One God, brothers and sisters and equal offspring—One with The One That Is.

Nor is anyone to be called your highest teacher, for you have one highest teacher, the Divinity within you— which means the wisdom and the knowledge and the truth that *is* you.

There will be others who may instruct you about how to find this Highest Teacher within you, and that person may be called "a" teacher, one of many who will come to you during your lifetime to remind you of Who You Really Are. Yea, even you, yourself, may call yourself a teacher, or may be called a teacher by many others.

> Yet should you choose this form of service to human-
> kind, do it with humility, for whoever exalts himself shall
> be humbled, and whoever humbles himself shall be
> exalted.
>
> I tell you this: The greatest among you will be rec-
> ognizable, for they will be servants.

You mean, there is no such thing as a Highest Teacher or a
Divine Being to whom we should pay homage? You mean that
Moses and Jesus and Muhammad were no more special than any-
one else?

> Let's put that in the reverse. *Everyone else is as spe-
> cial as Moses, Jesus, and Muhammad.*

That's a very daring thing to say. Saying something like that
could create trouble. I could be killed for saying something like
that. That could be called *apostasy*. I could have a *fatwa* put out against
me, calling for my death.

> Yes, you could.

I don't mean to dishonor Muhammad by making a statement
like that.

> Yet how could that be construed as dishonoring
> Muhammad? *It is what Muhammad's followers say that peo-
> ple should do.*

What?

> Muhammad's followers say that all people should
> strive to be as special as he. They *call people to that*

journey. That is what the *Hadith* is all about. Through it, the followers of Muhammad use his life as their template.

People may say that they are *modeling* their lives after Muhammad, but they don't say that they have *duplicated* his life. It is *blasphemy* to say that we are as holy as Muhammad. It is *heresy* to claim that we are as special as Jesus. It is *the height of spiritual arrogance* to imagine that we are as wise as Moses.

Is it? Did Jesus not say, "I and the Father are one," and "Those who hear the word of God, and do it, are my brothers and sisters"?

Maybe, but being brothers and sisters does not mean that one brother cannot be more special than the rest.

Ask a mother which of her children is more special. And did Jesus not say of his own miracles, "The works that I do shall you do also; and greater works than these shall you do"?

Yes, but he said that about those who believe in *him.* "He that believeth in *me,*" he said, shall do these things, and greater still.

Meaning, "If you believe that I am the Son of God and can do these things, *you can do these things too,*" yes?

I suppose it could be interpreted that way.

Jesus was setting an example. So was Muhammad. Masters have always set such examples, encouraging others to follow their lead, to live as they have lived, to be as they have been.

All Muslims seek to emulate the life of Muhammad. All Christians seek to emulate the life of Christ. All Buddhists seek to emulate the life of Siddhartha Gautama.

Do you not believe that you would do well to emulate the lives of your greatest spiritual masters?

Yes, I suppose I do.

Well, to "emulate" means "to strive to equal or excel." Now, look at the last two words in that last sentence. *Look at them.*

Do you understand their implication?

Now would it not be the cruelest hoax of all to encourage you, in one breath, to do that, and in the next breath declare that it is impossible?

I never thought about it that way.

Well, think about it that way. For I tell you this:

A true master is not the one with the most students, but one who creates the most masters.

A true leader is not the one with the most followers, but one who creates the most leaders.

A true king is not the one with the most subjects, but one who leads the most to royalty.

A true teacher is not the one with the most knowledge, but one who causes the most others to have knowledge.

And a true God is not one with the most servants, but One who serves the most, thereby making Gods of all others.

For this is both the goal and the glory of God: that His subjects shall be no more, and that all shall know God not as the unattainable, but as the unavoidable. (From *CWG 1.*)

Oh, I *love* that! "God is not the unattainable, but the *unavoidable.*" That is an extraordinary statement.

You consider it extraordinary only because you have been told that the opposite is true. You have been told that you *cannot* attain godliness, and that you certainly should never claim to.

Yet is it not true that the Masters whose teachings many of you follow have done exactly that?

Yes.

And have they not encouraged you to follow their example?

They have, yes.

Then why would you declare it apostasy or blasphemy to do so?

I don't know.

It is an example of the contradictions found in your understanding of what the messengers honored by your religions have said.

But now, here is a **SECOND NEW REVELATION:**

Every human being is as special as every other human being who has ever lived, lives now, or

ever will live. You are all messengers. Every one of you. You are carrying a message to life *about* life every day. Every hour. Every moment.

Everything you think, say, and do is a message. Your whole life is your teaching. If you thought that others, tomorrow, would walk in the path that you have taken today, would you take the same path?

You may think that people do not look to you, but they do. More people than you know. Everyone, in fact, whose life you touch is touched by your example. You are giving them data about life. You are telling them how it is, how things operate, how things are, and they will emulate you, they will copy you, they will take your data into their world and make it part of their own lives.

Your children will do this. All young people, children or not, who see you and know of you and are touched by you, will do this.

Your family will do this. All people, family or not, who see you and know of you and are touched by you, will do this.

Your neighbors will do this. Your nation will do this. You *are* the nation. The nation is made up of *you*. You *are* your religion. Your religion is made up of *you*.

Everything starts with you.

You are the first domino. All the rest of the dominoes fall when you do. What you "fall for" is what they'll fall for! Therefore, don't fall *for* anything... but, rather, fall *in*.

Fall in step with your highest self, for your highest

self steps on The Path. Fall in line with your grandest thoughts, for your grandest thoughts lead you to that Path. Fall in love, for love *is* that Path. Then, watch things *fall into place,* all because of *you.*

You are such a messenger. This is God work we're up to, you and I. So keep on!

I never thought of myself as a messenger.

You are. And this is important for you to know. Otherwise, you will be looking all your life for The One Who Brings The Message, even as the whole human race has searched throughout its history for that One.

Your species has announced, occasionally, that The One has been found. And, having made that announcement, humans then decided that there could be no other messenger, then or ever.

This was not something that I told you. *This was something that you made up.* This was something that you decided on your own.

The fact is that you know, you *all* know inherently, intuitively, what works and what does not work in getting you where you say you choose to go, and in creating what you choose to create.

You have already said that what you choose to create is a world of peace and harmony and happiness. There is a compass inside of you pointing you in that direction. There is a yardstick against which you can measure every option, a scale on which you can weigh every decision.

You have within you an Internal Guidance System, and you can call this whatever you wish—intuition, hunch, confidence, or a "feeling in your bones"—but you cannot deny that it is there.

It is a greater awareness. It is a *felt sense of sureness.* And the more you rely on it, the more you will know that you can rely on it.

IO

Okay, I'm still working on Step 3. I'm willing for a new understanding of God and Life to be brought forth. But let me see if I've got this straight. Are you saying that we should pay as much attention to the words of a cab driver in Phoenix as we do to the words of Moses, Jesus, or Muhammad?

> Why pose your question this way? Why not ask this question about Confucius? Or Siddhartha Gautama? Or Patanjali?
> Why not single out for comparison, Baha'u'llah? Or Jalal al-Din Rumi? Or Joseph Smith?
> And what's wrong with Paramahansa Yogananda?

That's the second time you've brought up this question. Are you saying that people like Siddhartha Gautama were as holy as Jesus?

> He was called The Buddha, wasn't he?

Okay, I picked the wrong one. What about Joseph Smith? Surely you're not putting him in the same category with The Buddha, Moses, Jesus, and Muhammad!

Why not?

Because . . . it just isn't *right,* that's all.

Now let *me* see if *I've* got this straight. Muhammad inspired the Qur'an, correct?

Yes. That's my understanding.

And Joseph Smith produced the Book of Mormon.

Yes.

So you're saying that the Qur'an is more sacred than the Book of Mormon, because Muhammad is "more holy" than Joseph Smith?

Well, I'm not saying that — but I suspect that most Muslims would say that.

And Christians would say the same thing about the New Testament and Jesus as compared to Joseph Smith, and Jews would say the same thing about the Torah and Moses as compared to Joseph Smith, is that what you're telling me?

I don't want to speak for anybody else. I can only speak about my observation through the years. It is my observation that the majority of Christians would not say that the Book of Mormon is as authoritatively the Word of God as the New Testament, in spite of the fact that members of the Church of Jesus Christ of Latter-day Saints — Mormons — very definitely consider themselves Christians . . . and I don't know what Jews would say about whether the Book of Mormon is as clearly the Word of God as the Torah. They might say, "Who can know?" They would probably have a good debate about it. Like I said, I'm confused.

Okay, let's move to some other comparisons. Who is more "holy," Jesus, Moses, or Muhammad?

I don't know. You're asking me something that I don't know.

Well, Moses brought down the Ten Commandments, didn't he? And Jesus brought forth the teachings in the New Testament, yes? And Muhammad's words are what the Qur'an is all about, no? So who is more "holy"?

Are you trying to start an argument here?

No, *but human beings are.* In fact, they started one a long time ago, and they've never finished it. In their effort to finish it, they're threatening to finish *you.*
That's the point.
That's part of what's going on in the world.

You keep saying this.

Yes, because I am preparing you for the **THIRD NEW REVELATION.**

Which is?

No path to God is more direct than any other path. No religion is the "one true religion," no

**people are "the chosen people," and no prophet
is the "greatest prophet."**

If this is true, then we have to set aside every assumption we
have made in the creation of our beliefs. We have to rip out every
building block we've put down.

> Those building blocks no longer support a structure
> housing a world of peace, harmony, and happiness.
>
> I have said to you here that the problem now con-
> fronting the world is a spiritual problem. It cannot be
> solved by political means. It cannot be solved by eco-
> nomic means. It cannot be solved by military means. It
> can only be solved by a change in beliefs.
>
> The beliefs that you are now invited to explore, and
> may wish to adopt, are all expressed in the New Reve-
> lations, given to you here.
>
> Examine these New Revelations carefully. Consider
> them seriously. They have not been given to you with-
> out reason.
>
> You have asked for help. You've asked, what are the
> new ideas the human race can consider? What is our
> opening point for discussion? What are the new thoughts
> with which we can be inspired, and with which we can
> hope to inspire others?
>
> These New Revelations are given to you in answer
> to your call for help.

But you're asking us to take all of our present beliefs and turn
them upside-down!

> Your present beliefs are turning your *world* upside-

down. And inside-out. You are tearing yourselves apart, blowing yourselves up, ripping yourselves to pieces, pulling yourselves in every direction, poisoning yourselves with your beliefs. Your present beliefs are not supporting you, they are killing you.

You can stop all this by taking the Five Steps to Peace.

Okay, I'm taking Step 3 right now. I declare that I am willing for a new understanding of God and of Life to be brought forth.

Good. Now, do you remember Step 4?

Step 4 is choosing to be courageous enough to explore and examine new understandings, and, if they align with our inner truth and knowing, to enlarge our belief system to include them.

That is exactly right. And that is exactly what this dialogue is intended to give you a chance to do. Are you ready to take an exploration?

Okay, but I'm nervous. It still feels a bit scary. It feels as though you're going to shake the foundation of everything that the people of the world hold true.

Yet this is exactly what your planet needs right now. Very few people are exploring these ideas. Very few are even willing to look at them. You have to have courage to do that, because new ideas can be challenging. Do you have the courage?

Well, if I don't have to agree with you . . . if we're just going to talk . . .

In some societies that's a very big thing. People are not encouraged to do that. In fact, in some places they are not even *allowed* to. There is no doubt that in some circles this very book will be banned.

Well, I guess I'm among the courageous ones, then.

Not just you, but everyone reading this book. If they haven't put it down by now, they're courageous, too.

Well, here we all are, so let's get to exploring. We're going to be examining beliefs, right?

Yes. These are the underpinnings of all human experience. Although some of them seem to pertain only to God, and, hence, might seem as though they affect only those people who believe in God, you will see presently how these ideas about God have deeply impacted secular life.

Yes, you were talking about that before.

One does not have to believe in God to be impacted by the social conventions created by those who do. These social conventions produce cultural imperatives— ways that all people feel they have to live their lives, because that's just "how things are."

So religion often affects the non-religious.

That's the point, exactly. Organized religion in the end is nothing more than a system of beliefs. All human behaviors are based on human beliefs, and one set of beliefs feeds another, creating what you might call Super Beliefs that transcend particular religious or secular philosophies.

With beliefs, as with all things, the whole is greater than the sum of the parts. So, it is pertinent to explore basic religious beliefs whether one is religious or not.

I got us into this briefly out of respect for sincere atheists and the agnostics. I wanted to give them a reason to stay with the discussion.

All that anyone who cares about life has to do is take a look at the world around them. That should be reason enough.

We are in a very precarious place, that's for sure.

And it is your beliefs that have put you there.

There are, of course, many beliefs about God promulgated by the hundreds of religions now established on the Earth, yet five of these are foundational. They are shared by the majority of organized religions, and it is upon these that they have based their fundamental, if varying, dogmas.

The foremost of human beliefs about God is that God needs something.

This idea is very foundational in most people's construction of God. According to this formulation, God is a Being in the universe who needs and wants something in order to be happy.

Although God is described as the Supreme Being, it

is nevertheless true, according to this formulation, that under certain experiences and conditions God becomes displeased. This displeasure ultimately turns into anger, and this anger finally produces retribution.

In short, God has things He wants you to be, do, and have, and things He does not want you to be, do, and have. These are God's expectations and requirements, and if they are not met, woe be unto you.

That's exactly what the nuns used to say to me in Catholic elementary school! "If you do not obey God's Laws, then *woe be unto you.*" So said the Sisters of Mercy.

These requirements of God have been articulated and summarized in different ways in the canons of your various religions, but they all say pretty much the same thing. Perhaps the most familiar précis is known as the Decalogue, or the "Ten Commandments."

The belief that God needs something in order to be happy is a fallacy. It is fallacy #1 of the Five Fallacies About God.

God is all there is, all there ever was, and all there ever will be. There is nothing that is not God, and God is therefore wanting and needing nothing at all.

Here, then, is a **FOURTH NEW REVELATION.**

God needs nothing. God requires nothing in order to be happy. God *is* happiness *itself.* Therefore, God requires nothing of anyone or anything in the universe.

That can't be true.

It is.

It *can't* be. Practically every Holy Scripture of all the religions of the world has a long list of requirements that God has placed on the human race. These involve behaviors, rituals, observances, and even such things as diet and clothing.

His Divine Grace A.C. Bhaktivedanta Swami, founder of the International Society for Krishna Consciousness, who produced the book *Bhagavad-Gita As It Is,* said in its introduction that one has to understand that the central point of the Bhagavad-Gita is this:

Instead of satisfying his own personal material senses, man has to satisfy the senses of the Lord. That is the highest perfection of life. The Lord wants this, and He demands it.

That is not true.

His Divine Grace was wrong?

His Divine Grace was inaccurate in that writing. That is an inaccurate statement.

Okaaaay... then let's take the Torah. It has a long list of dos and don'ts handed down as the Law of God. So does the Qur'an, to name just two more of humanity's holy scriptures.

Yes, they do. That is correct. So let's look at some of what these scriptures say. Let's see if these are the kinds of statements you'd attribute to God.

In the Book of Deuteronomy it says that if a man marries a woman and finds that she is not a virgin, and if her family cannot prove that she was a virgin before her marriage, "she shall be brought to the door of her father's house and there the men of her town shall stone her to death."

Wait a minute. This is God's Law?

As Moses is said to have handed it down, yes. The *Torah* also says that, if found to be in an adulterous relationship, both the man and the woman are to be taken to the city gates and also stoned to death.

Uh, can we hold it here just a second?

And God is concerned about other real life matters as well. Apparel, for instance. A woman "must not wear men's clothing...for the Lord your God detests anyone who does this," the Torah says.

Well, there go slacks and tailored suits.

Also, "Do not wear clothes of wool and linen woven together."

Now, wait a minute ...

Then, too, only certain people are welcome in God's house of worship. If you happen to be a child born out of wedlock, you cannot go there.

You can't?

No. No illegitimate child, "nor any of his descendants may enter the assembly of the Lord, even down to the tenth generation."

Also, if a certain part of your body happens to be

injured in an accident or as a result of war, you cannot join with other worshipers of God, either.

I beg your pardon?

The Bible says: "If a man's testicles are crushed or his penis is cut off, he may not be included in the assembly of the Lord."

Okay, okay, let's hold it right there.

But these are words right out of the Bible. Do they upset or embarrass you?

Those words are in the Bible?

Turn to Deuteronomy 23:1–2, New Living Translation.

Oh, one of those *modern* Bibles.

Yes. The King James Version has it this way: "He that is wounded in the stones, or hath his privy member cut off, shall not enter into the congregation of the Lord," but it means the same thing.

Well, I'll be doggone . . .

And I have some startling news for women who take some of those self-defense classes that are offered these days.

Really?

Yes. They can find themselves in a lot of trouble with some of what they learn in those classes.

What do you mean?

> The Bible says, "If two men are fighting and the wife
> of one of them comes to rescue her husband from his
> assailant, and she reaches out and seizes him by his pri-
> vate parts, you shall cut off her hand. Show her no pity."

Boy, the writers of the Bible had a real thing going on about
male genitals, didn't they?

> Who do you suppose was doing the writing?

I *get* it.

> Oh, and they also had some thoughts about children
> who don't obey their parents. These are probably not
> thoughts that many mothers would have.

Okay... what does this particular Holy Scripture have to say
about children who don't obey?

> Kill them.

What?

> According to the Torah, God says to kill them.

I don't believe that.

> Well, it's right there, plain as day:
> "If a man has a stubborn and rebellious son who does
> not obey his father and mother and will not listen to
> them when they discipline him, his father and mother
> shall take hold of him and bring him to the elders at
> the gate of his town.

"They shall say to the elders, 'This son of ours is stubborn and rebellious. He will not obey us. He is a profligate and a drunkard.' Then all the men of his town shall stone him to death.

"You must purge the evil from among you."

I guess that would do it, all right. . . .

But God does not always rely on His subjects to do His punishing. Very often—according to your various "holy scriptures"—God does the punishing directly.

Wait a minute. You mean you don't wait for Judgment Day? You punish people while they are on earth?

Certainly I do! Especially if they don't believe in Me, and in my goodness! Wouldn't you? If you were all-powerful, all-wise, all-good and kind and all-loving, wouldn't you punish those who didn't believe in you? I mean, wouldn't that make you really mad?

You're kidding me here, right? You're pulling my leg, yes?

Are you calling your "holy scriptures" wrong? Be careful! That could get *you* punished.

Oh, come on.

The Qur'an clearly states, "As for those who disbelieve, their deeds are like a mirage in the desert which the thirsty takes for water, until he reaches it to find that there was nothing, and finds God with him who settles his account, for God is swift at the reckoning." (Sūrah 24:39)

> Muslims know what action by God awaits those who believe in my goodness and those who do not.
>
> Sūrah 9:26—"But Allah did pour His calm on the Messenger and on the Believers, and sent down forces which ye saw not: He punished the Unbelievers. Thus doth He reward those without faith."

So we're *forced* to have faith, or else.

> That's right.

I don't know about all this. It just doesn't seem reasonable that the Source of All Goodness and Kindness and Wisdom would punish people who, for one reason or another, simply do not believe in Him.

> But I always give people a chance! Isn't that reasonable? I never punish anyone without first sending them a warning that they had better straighten up and believe in Me. If then they still don't believe in Me, I destroy them utterly, true, but never, ever, without warning.

I don't know this God that you are talking about! I think you're making this all up!

> Am I? Or...are *you*?

What do you mean?

> Read your own holy scriptures, the writings of humans.
>
> Let's read once again from the Qur'an, at Sūrah 17: 15–16:

"...nor would We visit with Our Wrath until We have sent a messenger (to give warning).

"When We decide to destroy a population, We first send a definite order to those among them who are given the good things of this life and yet transgress; so that the word is proved true against them: then we destroy them utterly."

The fact of the matter is, the world is full of sinners everywhere—people who do not believe that I am God and that I am good, and who do things that I don't want them to do. In fact, human beings are so bad that I will have to destroy most of humanity, and punish all of it, before the final day.

What? What are you telling me here?

I'm telling you how angry I am! I said so in many of your holy scriptures, as in the Qur'an at Sūrah 17:58:

"There is not a habitation We shall not destroy before the Day of Resurrection, or not inflict severe punishment upon it. This is in accordance with the law (of God)."

But I thought that you were a loving, forgiving God.

I am, if you don't make me angry.

You're making fun of us, right? You've quoted a slew of out-dated entries in those scriptures in order to make a mockery of humans.

Quoting what you've said about *Me* is making a mockery of *you*?

> My good and wonderful friend, God is not making
> a mockery of humans; *it is humans who are making a*
> *mockery of God.*
>
> You are saying that God *wills* these kinds of things, and
> you are using writings that you call *holy* to prove it.
>
> Holding up these Holy Scriptures, you've justified and
> rationalized the most barbaric behaviors.

No fair. The passages you quoted are *outdated.* They are not meant
to be applied literally today.

> I thought that your sacred scriptures were *never* "out-
> dated." Isn't that what makes them sacred? Are you sure
> these words were not meant to be applied literally
> today?

Of course, I am sure. They couldn't be.

> You may want to tell that to some of your world's
> fundamentalists. They say something quite different.
>
> There are those among you who are literalists. They
> assert that their holy scripture—the Bible, the
> Qur'an, whatever it might be—must be read verba-
> tim, and applied literally.

Well, yes, I know that. But such fundamentalists are in the
minority. They are not having any real impact on everyday life.

> Oh, really?

Okay, I'll admit that there have been some places in the world
where governments actually made laws out of statements first
appearing in their scriptures. And authorities in those countries

did cut off the hands of thieves, stone adulterers, murder apostates, and often administer those punishments in sports stadiums as public events. . . .

Yes, primitive things happen in primitive times.

Well, I was not even talking about primitive times. I was talking about the the 21st Century. I was talking about these days and time.

So was I.

Oh. Well, most humans do not think of these as primitive times.

Then they aren't looking very closely at the world around them.

Still, the point I was making is that such radical fundamentalists are not having much impact on the everyday lives of most people.

Maybe not most people in the culture *you* live in, or in the circles in which you move, but there are other cultures and other circles within your own culture where strict fundamentalist views have a tremendous impact on everyday life.

I guess I have to agree with you when I hear stories about, for instance, Afghanistan, where for five years the ruling authorities followed what they said was a true and proper interpretation of Islam's holy writings as they chopped off the hands of thieves and killed unbelievers.

It is not just one country that has exhibited primitive behaviors.

No, but in this particular country things had gotten very strange — almost surreal. The government did not allow music other than sacred hymns and chants to be played anywhere. It prohibited television. It made it a punishable offense to display a picture or a photograph of any human being or animal, saying that it was a violation of sacred law to create or show "graven images." And I've already talked about its prohibitions against women.

The laws of some other countries are nearly as strict.

The world was horrified in April of 2002 when it was reported that over a dozen teenage girls died in a fire at their school in Saudi Arabia because they were apparently not allowed to run out of the burning building without proper Islamic attire. There are actually "religious police" in Saudi Arabia who have the authority to cite people for infractions of religious law as they interpret it. Women may be punished on the spot if they are judged to be dressed inappropriately in public. A woman may not have lunch with her fiancé in a restaurant. Couples going out together may not sit in such a way that a woman is seated next to a man other than her husband.

And when practices such as these are questioned, the questioner is said to be "insensitive" to the cultural norms and religious customs and long-standing traditions of the local populace. Yet, are we to abandon basic human values in order to honor religious or cultural diversity? Is it insensitive to be sensitive about laws that are insensitive?

I suppose a case might be made that it *is* insensitive if one is criticizing what the local people themselves say they want, but in most of these cases the people have no choice in the matter. These are "sacred" laws, having nothing to do with civil protections and everything to do with particular religious beliefs and prejudices, and they are *imposed* on people.

When the Taliban left the Afghanistan capital city of Kabul, it took all of half a day for women to start coming out of their houses without wearing head-to-toe coverings, men to shave off their unwanted beards, and merchants to begin playing music again.

**Now shall we examine the primitive cultural beliefs
and the surreal behaviors of some other countries?**

Oh, you mean such as the belief that people of a certain skin color should be bought and sold and used as slaves? Such as the idea that these same people should be treated with prejudice to this present day, provided with less respect, less education, less opportunity, and, in general, a lesser share of everything?

Or the thought that women, as well as people of differing sexual preferences, should fall into the same category?

Do you mean countries that believe that might is right? Nations that adjust their morals to fit their purposes? Governments that twist the truth to suit their own agendas? People who conquer and destroy and bomb and murder and plunder and economically overpower and systematically deny others one-tenth of what they have *in order that they may have more?*

You are making this list, not me.

But help me understand. Many people and nations around the world do what they do, say what they say, and believe what they believe based on what they know that God has proclaimed.

I do not make proclamations.

You mean it was not you — not God — who said that people must behave in these ways? Was it *not* you who selected one race to be your "chosen people," *not* you who placed one nation "under

God," *not* you who said, as the New Testament makes clear, that races must never intermarry, that gays are an abomination, or that, as the Torah declares, "If a man's testicles are crushed or his penis is cut off, he may not be included in the assembly of the Lord?"

What do you think?

I don't know what to think.

Yes, you do. You know exactly what to think. You know the truth about that. You know, thanks to that internal guidance system I talked about.

You have a *felt sense of sureness* that God could not possibly have said those things—or half of the other things attributed to me. You know it and I know it and everybody else knows it.

The question is not whether you know it, but whether you're able to admit it, to say it out loud, to contradict the prevailing notion, which has it that trampling on sacred beliefs and ancient traditions is very wrong.

Trampling on *each other* is permitted, but not trampling on beliefs.

In fact, it has become a tradition to trample on each other *because* of your beliefs. And so, absurdity has come full circle.

II

I have to admit that I always did find it hard to believe God would tell people they may not intermarry, or that women must not allow any portion of their body to be seen in public, or that couples may not use contraceptives, or that men must wear beards.

I never did understand why God felt he had to give human beings so many *orders*.

> I don't. I don't have to give orders to anyone, and I've never done so.

Never?

> No. And I never will.

You never will? You mean that we will never know what God really wants?

> No.

Why? *Why would you do this to us?*

Do what to you?

Why would you tell us to follow God's Law, to obey your wishes, and then not tell us what you really want?

Because there is nothing that I *do* want. And this is what you cannot understand or refuse to accept.

There is nothing that God wants or needs.

God demands nothing, commands nothing, requires nothing, compels nothing. Teach *this* in your seminaries and your madrasas.

God neither orders nor requests, insists nor expects, anything. Tell *this* to your young.

I am the Author of Everything. I am the Creator and the Created. There is nothing that is that I am not. I have no need to give orders to anyone.

To whom would I give orders? There is no one to command but Me. I am the All In All. I am the Alpha and the Omega, the beginning and the end. And whom would I punish were my orders not kept? Would I use my right hand to slap my left? Would I bite my nose to spite my face?

Your teachers and your doctors of law, your priests and your *ulamas,* tell you that God is to be feared, for He is a vengeful God. You are to live in fear of God's wrath, they say. You are to tremble in His presence. Your whole life you are to fear the terrible judgment of the Lord. For God is "just," you are told. And God knows, you will be in trouble when you confront the terrible justice of the Lord. You are, therefore, to be obedient to God's commands. Or else.

Most of you, therefore, spend much of your adult lives searching for the "right way" to worship God, to obey God, to serve God. *The irony of all this is that I do not want your worship, I do not need your obedience, and it is not necessary to serve me.*

These behaviors are the behaviors historically demanded of their subjects by monarchs—egomaniacal, insecure, tyrannical monarchs at that. They are not Godly demands in any sense, and it seems remarkable that the world hasn't by now concluded that the demands are counterfeit, having nothing to do with the needs of Deity.

Deity has no needs. All That Is is exactly that: all that is. *It therefore wants, or lacks, nothing*—by definition.

If you choose to believe in a God who somehow needs something—and has such hurt feelings if He doesn't get it that He punishes those from whom He expected to receive it—then you choose to believe in a God much smaller than I. You truly *are* Children of a Lesser God.

No, my children, please let me assure you again, through this present conversation, as I have done in conversations past, that I am without needs. I require nothing. (From CWG 1.)

Then you haven't given us "orders"?

No. It was human beings who felt they had to give human beings orders, in order to *keep* order. And the best way they knew how to get people to *follow* orders was to say that they came directly from God.

There were also those who sincerely believed that they were receiving directives from God about how life should be lived, and what they said that they received was passed on by others in good faith. Yet this does not mean that what was passed on was always accurate, nor does it mean that the person who claims to have been the original recipient of these revelations was infallible.

Any more than this book is infallible.

That is correct. That is exactly right. Any claim of infallibility for this book would be inaccurate.

It would be inaccurate to say that this book is accurate.

Yes.

So this book is accurate when it says that it is inaccurate.

That's clever, and that's another yes.

So if it's inaccurate, why should I believe it?

You should not believe it. You should apply it and see what works.

Incidentally, put every other writing that claims to be a communication from God to the same test.

We've already done that. We've been testing out the words of those other books for centuries, and life on our planet is our evidence of whether their teachings work or not.

So it's no longer a question of whether you *have* evidence, it's a question of how much evidence you *need*.

Apparently. Still, what you are saying here, in *this* book, is impossible to believe. It can't be true. It violates everything I have ever been taught. God *must* want *something*.

Why?

I don't know, but He *must*. If He doesn't, what reason would there be for us to do, or not do, anything?

You mean you need *God* to require you to do the things that are best for you, and to prohibit you from doing things that are clearly not good for you?

No, no, we need God to *determine* what is "best" or "not good." Once we know what *that* is, we can pretty much depend on ourselves to do or not do it. It's deciding what *is* "best" that's difficult.

But that should be easy. Simply decide what it is you are trying to do. Just look at what it is you want to experience.

Who? Us as individuals or all of us as a collective? And when? Now or in the future? Because, you see, the problem is that most of us decide what it is we, ourselves, want to experience, and what we want to experience now — *right* here, *right* now — and don't give a *thought* to the future. Not even to tomorrow, much less next month or next year.

Why are you so shortsighted?

Because we are selfish.

Why are you so selfish?

Because it is our habit to think first, and sometimes only, of the self.

You know this about yourself?

Yes. We can admit that.

Then the problem is easy to solve. The answer is obvious.

Really? What is it?

Simply expand your definition of "Self."

The problem is not that you are self-centered, the problem is that you have misdefined the Self around which you *are* centered.

When you center around a "self" that is much smaller than the Self really is, when you define the "self" as something less than the Self is in truth, *that* is when you get into difficulty.

As it turns out, your definition of "self" is too small. When you first became "self-conscious"—that is, when *Homo sapiens* first became *aware* of themselves—you experienced that "you" were over "here" and that everything else was "over there." And so, you defined the "self" in a way that was far too limited.

Later in this dialogue, when we explore the Eighth New Revelation, you will see in very dramatic terms just how limited your definition of "self" has been. Yet do not blame yourself. You couldn't have known any better. You didn't understand. *And this is where most organized religions have failed you. They have taught you to believe in a limited, tiny Self.*

I thought that Christianity teaches that I am my brother's keeper.

Yes, but you are over "here," and your brother is over "there." You see yourselves as separate from each other.

I thought that Islam teaches that the most important element in life is the *umma,* the community. The community is everything. The honor of the community, the sanctity of the community, the safety of the community, the character and piety of the community—all these things are what's important, and determine whether God lives as an experience in people's lives.

Yes, but the community still consists only of "your people." "Those other people" are not part of it. You see yourselves as separate from each other.

This drives to the nature of your most basic beliefs. You define the individual Self as the part of you that ends at your fingertips and your toes. And yes, some of you do have a sense of a "collective self" that extends to your family or your community—and in some cases that community can be quite large, but it is still not all-inclusive. It includes everyone who thinks like you, looks like you, acts like you, agrees with you, but it does not include others. In fact, it may systematically *exclude* others.

So many of your organized religions have taught you

exclusiveness. In this way they have created just the opposite of what they were intended to create. Instead of creating unity, they have produced division.

But we *are* different from each other. There's no denying that.

I've said nothing about differences. I'm talking about divisions. Differences are not divisions.

But we *are* divided from each other.

No, you are not. You only think that you are. You only act as if you are. In reality, you are not.

This is what most of your religions tell you. They tell you that you are separate from each other, and separate from God.

We are not separate from God?

You are not.

Of course we are. God is good. God is great. We are bad. We are sinners. We are but minuscule specks of dirt, unworthy of even being trod upon by the foot of the Lord. Ours is to humble ourselves before God, reminding ourselves of our relative nothingness before Him who created us.

According to some religions, we are to fall to our knees in humble supplication while saying our prayers. According to others, we are to prostrate ourselves, our face to the ground, five times daily while praising Allah. In still other traditions we are to bow deeply. We are to beat our chest. We are to whip ourselves with scourges. We are to —

—Wait! I understand. I get the picture.

Are you now telling us that we have this all wrong?

I am telling you there has been a misunderstanding.
I have brought my revelations to you by many means
and through many messengers, yet I have come to you
not to humble you, but to exalt you.

But we do not deserve to be exalted. We deserve only to grovel
before the Lord.

Why? Why do you think this?

Because we have failed you!

Ah, yes, the second fallacy about God.

12

You mean that we have *not* failed God?

> How can you fail God when there is nothing that God wants or needs?

Well, of course, I don't believe that.

> That's right. You believe in the First Fallacy.

And that's where I first went wrong?

> Correct. It is on that fallacy that all other beliefs are based. The first fallacy about God is that God needs something. The second fallacy is that God can fail to have His needs met.

But He can! He *did.*

> When?

At the beginning. In the Garden of Eden. He told humans not to eat of the fruit of the Tree of Knowledge of Good and Evil, but we did. So He threw us out of the Garden. He evicted us from Paradise.

This is all just a story, of course. It is a parable. It is meant to convey that we separated ourselves from God when we sinned.

> Ah, yes, the third fallacy about God.
>
> First, you believe that God *needs* something.
>
> Second, you believe that God *can fail to get* what He needs.
>
> Third, you believe that God has *separated* you from Him because it's your fault that He failed to get what He needs.

But it's *true*. You needed us not to sin and we have sinned. So our punishment has been that we are banned from Paradise. We are separated from God. Now we have to work our way back. We have to get back into God's good graces.

> My wonderful children, you are never *not* in my good graces. You have created in your imaginings a God whose feelings get hurt. My feelings do not get hurt. My sensitivities do not become offended. You cannot upset Me. You cannot make Me angry. Upset and anger are the very antithesis of Who and What I Am.
>
> You imagine that I am a Being like you, only bigger and more powerful, living somewhere in the universe—some kind of parent figure with ego needs and emotional agitations that match your own. Yet I tell you, that is not who and what I am.

Here is the FIFTH NEW REVELATION:

**God is not a singular Super Being, living some-
where in the Universe or outside of it, having the
same emotional needs and subject to the same
emotional turmoil as humans. That Which Is God
cannot be hurt or damaged in any way, and so, has
no need to seek revenge or impose punishment.**

Now I know and I understand that this upsets your
apple cart. This throws everything into disarray. For your
entire system of right and wrong, good and evil, justice
and injustice is based upon an opposite thought. It is
empowered through the thought that God *does* seek
revenge and impose punishment.

Most people don't want to "let go" of a punishing God because
they want to feel that there is *some* justice in the Universe. If the
"bad guys" don't get punished while on Earth, at least we can hold
the thought that "they'll get theirs" when they die—because "God
has promised us justice."

There is no such thing as reward and punishment in
my kingdom. Yet, saying that there is no such thing as
"punishment" is not the same as saying there are no
consequences.

When you do the thing called "die"—that is, after
you end your time with a physical body here on Earth—
you will be given the opportunity for a Life Review. In
fact, you will *ask for it.* You will *want it.* It will be a major
part of the process by which you come to know more
about yourself and about Life, by which you evolve.

During this Life Review process you will be allowed to experience every moment of your life, everything that you ever thought, said, or did. This experience will be comprehensive. You will not only experience this from your point of view, you will experience it from the point of view of *every person whose life you touched.*

You will be able to experience what *they* experienced as a result of what you were thinking, saying, or doing.

Let me see if I understand this. I will move through all of my life's interactions with others, one interaction at a time, *from the other's point of view?*

Exactly.

My God, that *would* be hell.

No. It would be remembering. You will remember Who You Really Are and who you can become by coming to know what others experienced at your hands. But even if it was painful for them, you will not suffer.

How can that be?

Suffering is a point of view. Remember that. Pain is an experience; suffering is a point of view *about* that experience. You will experience the pain—as a mother experiences the pain of childbirth—but you will not think of it as suffering. To complete the analogy, you will experience it as the joy of giving birth. In this case, to a New You. To a You who now understands more, comprehends more, realizes more, knows more—and is ready to experience the Self in a new way as a result.

This process is called evolution. And in this process of evolution the primitive concepts of "reward and punishment" have no place.

It can be difficult for many humans to understand that. Take away Reward and Punishment and everything seems to fall apart.

Unless it does not.

Unless humans empower themselves to create whatever understandings they wish to put into place about "right" and "wrong," "good" and "evil," "justice" and "injustice," *without using God to justify them.*

You're talking about a secular code. Many organized religions say that this is the Great Evil overtaking the world. They call it *secularism,* or *humanism,* or, worst of all, *secular humanism,* and they say it is the great enemy of God.

Of course they do, because it is a great threat to *them.*

God *has* no "enemies," because God cannot be hurt, damaged, or destroyed.

Yet our dictionaries define "secularism" as "rejection or exclusion of religion and religious considerations." And that's my point.

It says nothing about rejection or exclusion of *spirituality* and *spiritual* considerations.

What is the difference between religion and spirituality?

One is an institution and the other is an experience.

Religions are institutions built around a particular idea of how things are. When those ideas become hardened and set in stone, they are called dogmas and doctrines. They then become largely unchallengeable. Organized religions require you to believe in their teachings.

Spirituality does not require you to believe anything. Rather, it continually invites you to notice your experience. Your personal *experience* becomes your authority, rather than something that someone else has told you.

If you had to belong to a particular religion to find God, it would mean that God has a particular way or means by which you are required to come to Him. Yet why would I require that?

I don't know. Why *do* you require that?

The answer is, I don't. The idea that God has only one way of approaching Him, or one particular means of returning to Her, and that this way and only this way will work, is a fallout from the illusion of requirement.

The illusion of requirement?

This is another of the illusions of humans, another of those false beliefs we've discussed. It has nothing to do with ultimate reality.

I have no need to require anything of you, because I have no need to receive anything from you. And, contrary to your belief, I have absolutely no need at all to require you to come to me in a certain way.

Is saying a *rosary* better than saying the *savitu?* Is the practice called *bhakti* more sacred than the practice called *seder?*

Is a church more sacred than a mosque? Is a mosque

more sacred than a synogogue? Am I to be found in one
place and not in the other?

I want to say that the answer is no. But then, why do religions
insist that *their* way is the best way—no, no, the ONLY way—to
you?

It is helpful for organized religions to imagine this
because it gives them a tool with which to seek, acquire,
and retain members—and thus, to continue to exist.

It is the first function of all organizations to perpetuate themselves. The moment any organization serves
the purpose for which it was formed, that organization
becomes no longer necessary. This is why organizations
seldom complete the task that they are assigned.

Organizations are not, as a rule, interested in rendering themselves obsolete.

This is as true of religions as it is of any other organized undertaking. Perhaps, more so.

The fact that a particular organized religion has been
around for a very long time is not an indication of its
effectiveness, *but just the opposite.*

But if it weren't for religion, how would we know how to get
back to God?

In the first place, you cannot *not* "get back to God."
This is because you *never left* God, and God *never left you.*

The Third Fallacy About God is that you and I are
separated. Because you think we are separate from each
other, you keep trying to get back to Me.

Oh, wait! I've got a wonderful story to tell here! It's really great!

Okay! Let's hear it!

It's about this boy who keeps sneaking off into the woods for a moment or two every day. His father becomes concerned. What could the boy be doing out there every single day? One day the father asks the boy, "Why are you spending so much time in those woods?" And the boy replies, "To be closer to God."

"Well," says the father, relieved, "you don't have to go into the woods to do that. God is everywhere. God is no different in the forest than out here in the rest of the world."

"Yes, father," smiles the boy, "but in the woods, *I* am different."

Ah, that *is* a wonderful story.

Both the father and the son told a great truth. The son understood that God is everywhere, but that he was not able to slow down and perceive the presence of God everywhere as well as when he was in the woods.

This is very wise. The story tells you that if you will stop what you are doing for just a moment each day, you will be able to experience the presence of God.

The father, too, was wise. For he understood that going to the woods was not necessary. The story tells us here that it is when you take the woods with you wherever you are that you have begun to master life.

Here is the Fourth Fallacy About God: There is something that you are *required to do* in order to get back to me. There are certain stipulations you must meet in order to be reunited with God in what you call "heaven."

Now here is the Good News. *There is no other place to be.* The challenge is not to "get to" heaven, but to know that you are already there. For heaven is the Kingdom of God, and there is *no other kingdom that exists.*

Yet even if there were some place other than heaven and you were looking for "directions" to heaven, most organized religions would be very confusing places from which to get them.

There are a thousand different religions on the Earth, and each one has its own set of "directions," reflecting its idea of how "God wants it."

Of course, as has been said here now repeatedly, there is no particular way that God "wants" you to worship God. Nor, in fact, does God need to be worshiped at all.

God's ego is not so fragile that She must require you to bow down to Her in fearful reverence, or grovel before Him in earnest supplication, in order to find you worthy of receiving blessings.

What kind of Supreme Being would need to do this? What kind of a God would this be?

That is the question you must honestly ask yourself.

You have been told that God has made humans in His image and likeness, yet I ask you this: Is it possible that religions have fashioned God *in the image and likeness of humans?*

You have made that comment before.

Indeed. It is a question I invite you to deeply explore.

Because what *humans* do, when they don't get from others what they require from others, is become angry. Then, if they really think they *need* what they were requiring and they still can't get it, human beings *condemn and destroy* those who don't give it to them.

This is exactly what you say God does.

This is the Fifth Fallacy About God. You believe that God *will destroy you* if you do not meet His requirements.

Nothing could be further from the truth. Why would I destroy you? What purpose would be served by that?

Justice.

Justice?

God is just. If we disobey God's Law, we are punished.

And just what *is* "God's Law"?

It's all there, in The Book.

Which book?

Here we go again. You know which book.

Ah, yes, the book that *you* believe in.

Right.

Do you see the circle here? It is a vicious circle. It will go round and round, producing one human disaster after another, until you can all agree on one set of laws based on no religion in particular.

You mean, create a secular society.

I mean, create a spiritual community, as opposed to a religious community. A community based on spiritual principles, not a community based on the doctrines of the major organized religions, most of which are rooted in incomplete understandings and exclusivist theologies.

The community I am inviting you to create would have a deep foundation in all of the New Revelations, including the SIXTH NEW REVELATION, which puts to rest forever the Five Fallacies About God:

All things are One Thing. There is only One Thing, and all things are part of the One Thing That Is.

13

Does the statement "all things are one thing" mean that because everything is part of the same cosmos, we are all interconnected, or does it mean that we are all, quite literally, the *same thing?*

> It means that you are all the same thing.
>
> Everything in the universe is made of the same stuff. Now you can call that stuff anything you want. You can call it God, you can call it Life, you can call it Energy, or you can call it by other names, depending upon how it manifests Itself. That will not make it any less the same.
>
> You cannot, therefore, be in any way separate from Me.

Nor from any living thing.

> Nor from *anything at all.* All things are living. There is no such thing as a Dead Thing.

Rocks? Dirt? Other inert objects?

> How do you define an "inert object"?

Well, here we go with the dictionary again. It says that "inert" means "lacking the power to move."

> There is no such thing in the universe.

Rocks have the power to move?

> Rocks are movement itself, in a particular way, at a particular speed, with a particular vibration.
>
> *Everything* is in motion. Everything. Motion is the nature of the universe, and all things in it. There is nothing that is not moving. Nothing.
>
> Put a rock under a microscope and what will you see?

Molecules. Atoms.

> Yes. And what will they be doing?

Moving.

> Right. Now put it under a very *powerful* microscope and what will you find?

Subatomic particles. Protons, neutrons, electrons, hadrons, baryons, mesons, quarks, antiquarks.

> Good. And what will all those things be doing?

Uh . . . moving?

> Exactly. Will *any* of them be standing still?

No.

In other words, all things are made up of Things That Move. Is that right?

I guess so.

Now, here is the elementary question.

Okay...

What makes them move?

I'm not sure I know.

Take a guess.

Some invisible force. Gravity?

Actually, on the scale of atoms the effect of the force of gravity is practically nonexistent when compared to the other forces at work.

Other forces?

Your science has already discovered three other basic forces, all of them stronger than the force of gravity. Together with gravity, you call these the Four Basic Forces. In order of strength they are: the strong force, the electromagnetic force, the weak force, and gravity.

Wow, thanks for the physics lesson.

We haven't even begun, my son. We haven't even begun. We could talk here of leptons and neutrinos, of the muon and the tau—of many, many things. We could speak of the Unified Field of Everything, and still we would only touch the surface of what is True About Life.

There are more things in heaven and earth than are dreamt of in your philosophy.

So what *does* make things move? What does keep everything in motion?

In simple terms that you can understand?

Please.

I do.

You do?

I am First Cause. I am that which makes all the right moves. You could say, "God is cool. God has all the moves."

I am the Alpha and the Omega, the Beginning and the End, the Here and the There, the Before and the After, the Up and the Down, the Left and the Right, and The Space In Between.

I am the All—Not All, the Am—Not Am. I am That Which Is, and That Which Is Not. Which means, in effect, that there is nothing Which Is, because in the absence that That Which Is Not, that Which Is...is not. And that, in turn, means there is nothing Which Is Not.

Everything Is, and Is Not.

Do you understand?

Of course I do. Why, I was just sayin' that yesterday to a couple of fellas down at Murphy's. We were just kinda shootin' the breeze, see, and the subject of God came up, and I was just getting into all that when suddenly I realized how late it was and that I had to get goin'.

Uh-huh.

The point, therefore, of all this?

It is, as I said, that we are all the Same Stuff. We are all That Which Moves. There is nothing that does not move. *Everything* moves. Nothing stands still. Nothing at all. Everything is Stuff In Motion. That includes you, and rocks. You are all this Same Stuff. This "stuff" is called Life.

Everything IN Life IS Life.

Can you wrap yourself around *that* concept?

I don't think I've ever heard it put just that way before.

Can you embrace the concept? There is nothing in Life that is not a part of Life. Can you agree with that?

Well, yes, I think so. . . .

Good. Then you are only a step away from understanding a larger truth.

Which is?

That you and God are One.

I'm not sure I can make the leap. How can that be true?

It is true if "Life" is just another word for "God"—
and it is.

There is only One Thing, and that Thing can be called
God, or Life, or All That Is, or whatever it pleases you
to call it.

You are all manifestations of that One Thing, as is
everything else you observe with your five senses—and
everything you observe with your sixth sense as well.

In fact, your five senses are rather primitive recep-
tors. They pick up data relating to only about one-tenth
of the world around you. Your sixth sense picks up
much more.

My sixth sense?

Yes.

What is that? Intuition?

You have called it that. You have also called it your
extrasensory perception. It is at this level of perception that many of the mysteries of the universe may be
unraveled, and found not to be mysterious at all.

Well, this has all been very fascinating, but what does any of
this have to do with world peace, and the crisis the world is facing today?

Everything.

Everything?

Everything.

In what way?

Because you are using only your five senses to figure out the world around you. And you are using only
your five senses to build it. Yet to create the kind of
community I am talking about, to create the world of
your dreams, *you have to use your sixth sense.*

Why? How so?

Everything you believe about God and your world
has come to you through your five senses. This is
true for the largest number of people on your
planet. Learning about God through one's sixth
sense has always been forbidden. *Every human who
has done so and has proclaimed it publicly has been
humiliated and persecuted.*

And so, you have been asked to learn about God,
who lives *outside* of your five senses, by using *only* your
five senses.

In fact, you are using only *two* of them. What most
people know about God they know largely through
what they have heard or read. If they have a *feeling* about
what God must be like that differs from what they have
heard or read, they are told to dismiss it. Such feelings,
they are scolded, are "the work of the devil."

Your knowledge about God is *passed on knowledge.*
Somebody told somebody, who told somebody who
told somebody, who told somebody who told somebody, who told you.

Well, how else are we going to find out about God? Somebody has to tell us, because in and of itself, God is the Unknowable.

> Then how did those who told humans about God in the first place come to know about God?

They listened to the Masters and the Prophets.

> And how did the Masters and the Prophets, whom they quote, come to know about God?

Through direct revelation.

> *So direct revelation is a valid means of coming to know about God?*

Yes, but only if you were an old person, living in olden times. I know where you're leading me, and I'm not going there.

> You may want to consider the possibility that what would work for the world right now—given what the world says it wants to experience, which is peace and harmony—is a New Spirituality based upon New Revelations.

What kind of New Spirituality are we talking about?

> A spirituality that enlarges upon organized religion in its present form. For it is many of your old religions, with their inherent limitations, that stop you from experiencing God as God really is.
>
> They also stop you from experiencing peace, joy, and

freedom—which are *other* words for God as God really is.

Yes ... well, as I said before, this so-called "new spirituality" sounds an awful lot like *humanism,* having nothing to do with God at all.

And how does your dictionary define "humanism"?

"A way of life centered on human interests or values."

What's wrong with that? Why would anyone have a problem with that?

Because life should be centered on *God's* interests and values, not our own.

Do you imagine they are different?

Of course they are different. God wants one thing and we want another. That's the *whole problem.*

Your problems are not created by human beings doing things other than what they say "God wants them to do," your problems are created by people doing *exactly* what they say "God wants them to do."
Have you noticed that?

Uh, yes, in some cases, but ...

In *some* cases? In almost *every* case. More of your wars have been fought in the cause of organized religions than in any other cause. Millions of your people have been killed in the name of God.

Is this not the blasphemy?

Everything would change on your planet if you simply stopped telling yourself that you are doing the will of God when you harm each other.

Well, I don't think we put it that way. . . .

You put it *exactly* that way. And you insist that God puts it that way.

You even tell yourself that God wants you to go out and fight for him, to kill for him.

We do not. Nobody says that. And nobody says that God says that.

Really? Do I have to start quoting holy books again? In the *Qur'an* God not only says to go out and fight, He says that those who do not will go to hell.

No, no, no . . . a holy book urges peace, not fighting.

Well, God is not talking about fighting just anyone here. God is talking about fighting those who do not believe the way He has instructed you to believe.

God would not do that. God is the greatest peacemaker in the Universe. God is Peace Itself. God would not instruct His followers to fight others simply because they held a different religious belief.

But humans say that God does exactly that. In the Qur'an, Sūrah 9:123 declares:

"O ye who believe! Fight the unbelievers who gird

you about, and let them find firmness in you, and know that Allah is with those who fear Him."

And in the Bhagavad-Gita, Chapter 2, Text 31 says:

"...you should know that there is no better engagement for you than fighting on religious principles, and so there is no need for hesitation."

Okay, so maybe it suggests that true believers may want to go out and fight for their beliefs, but it does not say that they *have to,* and that if you don't, God will punish you. That's somebody's exaggeration. That's not God's word.

Really? Read Sūrah 9:38 and 9:39:

"O ye who believe! What is the matter with you, that when ye are asked to go forth in the cause of Allah, ye cling heavily to the earth?

"Unless ye go forth, He will punish you with a grievous penalty..."

Or read the Gita, at Chapter 2, Text 32–33. Happy are those, says the Gita..."to whom such fighting opportunities comes unsought, opening for them the doors of the heavenly planets.

"If, however, you do not perform your religious duty of fighting, then you will certainly incur sins for neglecting your duties..."

So, if you wonder where all of this "warrior mentality" is coming from, where these cultural tendencies to fight religious battles and to be suicide bombers originate, just look to your many holy scriptures and your

religious teachers. They have provided your species
guidance for generations. And almost all of them
promise that, whether you win or lose in battle, you'll
get your reward.

As the Bhagavad-Gita puts it, somewhat pithily:

"...either you will be killed on the battlefield and
attain heavenly planets, or you will conquer and enjoy
the earthly kingdom. Therefore, get up with determination and fight." (2:37)

There you have it. You can't lose! I've even heard that Muslim men are told that if they die as they kill others in an act of
jihad, as in suicide bombings, they will be rewarded in heaven by
being able to enjoy unlimited sex with 72 virgins.

Yes, that promise has been made. God also instructs,
in the Qur'an, Sūrah 8:67, to fight until all in the land
of your enemies are subdued, and until then, to take
no prisoners.

God says to take no prisoners?

That is exactly what God says in this passage. Not
until the people whom you fight have been completely
subdued. And when they are, God says it is then okay
to set up a system of bribery, whereby the remaining
unbelievers must pay you to not kill them. You could
call this God's Protection Racket.

That's ridiculous. No holy book would ever suggest such
a thing.

Really? Check out Sūrah 9:29.

It says, "Fight those who believe not in Allah nor the Last Day, nor hold that forbidden which hath been forbidden by Allah and His Messenger, nor acknowledge the Religion of Truth..."

And how long does it say to fight them?

Let's see, "...until they pay the *Jizya* with willing submission..." Oh, yes, I've heard of that. I've read that in order to stop the killing of all non-Muslims when a village or an area was over-run by Muslims, tribute had to be paid. This is usually in the form of a "jizya"—a fixed poll tax levied on non-Muslims for protection and other services—as well as a "kharaj," a land tax. But I thought that was just a barbaric custom; I didn't know that payment of a *jizya* for protection was a religious instruction actually given in the Qur'an.

Now you know.

Okay, but really, nobody in modern times actually believes or lives any of this. I mean, those words were written in ancient times. It was a different world back then. Nobody today believes that Islam instructs its followers to go out and subdue people or countries, or to kill nonbelievers. Nobody in places of importance, anyway. Maybe a few fundamentalist radicals say that, but nobody with any real credibility says that.

Would you consider the political or religious leader of an entire country a person with credibility?

Certainly. But national religious and political leaders do not say such things.

The Pope did at the time of the Crusades.

Okay, yes, but that was also a very long time ago. I'm talking about *today*. I'm talking about modern times. The human race has matured. It has evolved. Those attitudes would never be expressed by a religious or political leader in modern times.

Of course, there is the statement of Iran's Ayatollah Khomeini, quoted in the textbook *Holy Terror: Inside the World of Islamic Terrorism* by Amir Taheri, published in London in 1987.

Yes, there is that. Why don't you tell us all what it says?

Well, in that textbook the Ayatollah, the supreme religious leader of Iran and its *ipso facto* political leader as well, is quoted as saying:

"Islam makes it incumbent on all adult males, provided they are not disabled and incapacitated, to prepare themselves for the conquest of countries so that the writ of Islam is obeyed in every country of the world.

"But those who study Islamic Holy War will understand why Islam wants to conquer the whole world.... Those who know nothing of Islam pretend that Islam counsels against war. Those (who say this) are witless. Islam says: Kill all the unbelievers just as they would kill you all! Does this mean that Muslims should sit back until they are devoured? Islam says: Kill them, put them to the sword and scatter.... Islam says: Kill in the service of Allah those who may want to kill you! ... Islam says: Whatever good there is exists thanks to the sword and in the shadow of the sword!

People cannot be made obedient except with the sword! The sword is the key to Paradise, which can be opened only for Holy Warriors! There are hundreds of other psalms and Hadiths urging Muslims to value war and to fight. Does all this mean that Islam is a religion that prevents men from waging war? I spit upon those foolish souls who make such a claim."

> Now I tell you this: Humans have used the announcement that it is God's Will as an excuse to rationalize and justify the most barbaric behaviors you could ever have imagined, the most unfair behaviors you could ever have contrived, the most ungodly behaviors you could ever have foisted on unsuspecting and innocent people.
>
> You have used these behaviors to get *your* way, not God's way.
>
> I tell you, you must move away from your Old Ideas of "God's way" and move into a New Experience of Divinity if you ever want to see peace on Earth.
>
> You have said that your interests and God's interests are not the same, and that this is obvious. Yet now I have come to tell you that God's interests and human interests are not divergent, but are identical. The fact that you do not see them as one is what is causing problems.
>
> So long as you insist that you must serve *God's* interests rather than human interests, you give yourself permission to define God's interests as you wish. And you *do* so—according to *your own beliefs* about God and what God wants and expects.
>
> Humanity's interests cannot be so easily ill-defined, for *humanity's interests are self-apparent.*

The greatest interest of all humanity is Life. This is the greatest interest of God as well, *but you claim otherwise.*

You imagine that God has a *greater* interest than human life, and that is what allows you to *waste it with impunity.*

Pure humanism would never allow you to destroy life sanctimoniously. Only organized religion could justify such a travesty.

14

That is quite an indictment.

Indictment resides in your mind. It is part of your Guilty/Not Guilty, "right/wrong" mentality. What I have done is make an observation.

Observation is not judgment, and statement is not indictment. A statement of fact is just that, a recounting of what is so.

Observation is the "what's so" of any situation; judgment is the "so what?"

It is you who add the "so what?" to any set of facts. *Nothing has any meaning save the meaning you give it.*

It is you who decide whether "what's so" is "good" or "bad," "right" or "wrong," "okay" or "not okay," and you base this decision on your assessment of whether "what's so" works or does not work, depending upon what it is that you are choosing to be, do, or have.

The process of human witnessing, assessing, and choosing has always functioned this way, and it is circular.

You witness, assess, and choose, then witness the results of your choosing, assess that, and choose again, then witness again, assess again, and choose still one more time, in an ongoing cycle.

It is through this process that you decide Who You Really Are.

The constant making and remaking of this decision is what you call evolution.

The reason for the soul's having come to the body is to evolve. That is, to become a grander and grander version of itself.

This is the purpose of your life on Earth, and of life everywhere. Applying this process to that part of your life called religion has been hard for you because of the deep emotional attachment you have to your beliefs.

You have a deep emotional attachment to all of your beliefs, but your beliefs about religion have been particularly difficult to let go of. Therefore, the evolution of your religions has lagged far behind the evolution of your sciences, your technologies, your psychologies—indeed, your understanding of every other aspect of life.

You have done the things you have been doing to each other in the name of religion because many of your present organized religions—all well-meant, all well-intended, and most grounded in some sound spiritual principles—are simply incomplete in their understandings.

Religion has not been allowed to grow.

Indeed, you will not *let* it grow. You claim that any new insight that contradicts or modifies the old is blasphemous and heretical. You claim that New Revelations are not possible. Your position is that everything there is to say has already been said, everything there is to know is already known, everything there is to understand is already understood.

Your desperate struggle to keep your species alive—to stop its members from killing each other and from destroying all of life—will not end, and it may wind up ending *you*, if you are unable to make one simple statement:

There is something I do not understand about God and about Life, the understanding of which will change everything.

We must take Step 2 in the Five Steps to Peace.

Yes. This is an essential and irreplaceable step, for only with a new understanding of Life and of God can humans construct a more workable and uniform code of conduct.

As things now stand, creating such a workable and uniform code is very difficult, because so many of you believe that *your* code of conduct comes from God, and is, therefore, the only one that should be followed.

The fact that most of the exclusivist religions of the world say this, and that the world's sacred laws are all different, doesn't matter to you. All of you believe that *your* code of conduct is the *right* code of conduct.

It is this *righteousness* that is your undoing.

Your worldwide community cannot function this way. When your planet housed a group of smaller communities, most of them isolated and disconnected from each other, human beings could function that way. It wasn't a very smooth functioning, it often wasn't very happy, but the species at least survived.

Now you are a worldwide community, interconnected and interdependent. You are truly All One, whether you are ready to accept this belief or not.

Now, a disruption in one part of the community disrupts the whole. And so you are going to have to learn to *act as one* if you wish to survive.

This is something you have had very little practice doing. Many of you seem to think that "oneness" is, in fact, *threatening*. And so you continue your past behaviors, in which you allowed your differences to produce divisions, ignoring the fact that a house divided against itself cannot stand. *You do not see yourself as being in the same house.* So why bother to worry about divisions?

But does healing mean that we can no longer have different religions, or different ideas about how to experience God?

Of course not. It means only that you notice your Oneness.

Oneness does not mean sameness. Unity and individuality are not mutually exclusive. Differences do not have to mean divisions, and contrast does not have to lead to conflict.

> Your fingers are not at all the same. They look dif-
> ferent, and they all have different functions. Yet they are
> all part of one hand, and both hands are part of one
> body.
>
> Your nose looks not at all like your eyes, and your
> mouth bears no resemblance to your forehead. All of
> these have different functions. Yet they are part of one
> face—the face you show the world.
>
> Would you bite your nose to spite your face?
>
> Why do you allow your religions to do so to the
> face of humanity?

I keep thinking about that newspaper article about those pro-
testing Lutherans. They were not only upset that a Lutheran minister was praying with non-*Christians,* they were angry that he
prayed with other *Lutherans* who simply belonged to a different
Lutheran denomination! They said that this constituted "an egregious offense against the love of Christ."

> And what do you think?

I can't imagine that God would think that. I don't want to
have anything to do with a God who would think that. I want to
run out and buy one of those bumper stickers that says . . . GOD
SAVE ME FROM YOUR PEOPLE.

> And yet it's important to remember that these behav-
> iors are neither "right" nor "wrong," they simply no
> longer work. They do not *function* effectively, given that
> you say what you wish is to survive in peace and
> harmony.

> Functional behavior is what is now desperately needed
> if life as you know it on Earth is to continue.

Right now our behaviors are woefully dysfunctional. We have created a completely dysfunctional society.

> That is your witnessing, that is your assessment, and
> that is your choice.

No, it is not my choice. It is what I observe, but it is not what I choose.

> Of course it is. You are choosing it every day, by fail-
> ing to do anything about it.

That's not fair. What can I do? I can't be responsible for changing the entire planet this instant!

> I will ask you again. If not now, when? If not you, who?

15

How in the world can one person take on the task of changing the world?

If all it takes is one person to instigate self-destruction, can it not also be one person who inspires self-renewal?

The human race now yearns to renew itself. You can sense this everywhere. You can feel it in the air. All that people are waiting for is someone to stand up and show the way. Someone to get the ball rolling. One person to topple the first domino.

Yet let me make something clear. The era of the Single Savior is over. What is needed now is joint action, combined effort, collective co-creation. What is called for now is not one person *only*, but a large number of humans willing to be the "one person" in their family, in their community, in their circle of influence, who will take on the task of bringing about change right then, right there.

In this context one person can make a huge difference, for it is always one person within a group or cluster who calls forth the highest vision, who models the grandest truth, who inspires and cajoles and agitates and awakens and ultimately produces a contextual field within which collective action is rendered possible and becomes inevitable.

Are you that one person? Do you choose to be an inspiration for all those whose lives you touch?

That is the question your soul asks you now. That is why it has brought you to this book.

Perhaps one of us reading this book is that person. Perhaps several are. Maybe many. But however many of us may take up the call, we will still need your help. We need God's help.

I understand. That, too, is why you came to this book. It is, in fact, how you began this dialogue. You said that you wanted my help. That was a good beginning, but we cannot move forward if you believe that I am a confused God.

Who believes that?

Most of the human race does, judging by its actions. As I said, its codes of conduct are remarkably different from culture to culture, yet all are declared to be based on the Word and Law of God. If they all are, God must be terribly confused.

Of course, we would not say that it is God who is confused. We would say that it is humans who are confused.

> Yes, and if they would all just pay attention to *your* code of conduct, they would no longer *be* confused.

Exactly! That's right.

> Yet if God is the All-Powerful, why does He not simply make it clear which code of conduct is the correct code of conduct? Why does He not simply resolve the matter?

That is exactly what He is doing.

> He is?

Do you not know that the End Days are near? Do you not see that the Final Victory is at hand? Do you not observe the fruits of the struggle, the glorious outcome of the *jihad?*

> You mean the maiming and killing of thousands of people in God's name?

I mean the elimination of the traitorous *infidels.* I mean the cleansing of human society.

"You must purge the evil from among you," says the Bible. "Fight them until there is no more conflict and all faith goes to God," the Qur'an instructs. "To protect men of virtue, and destroy men who do evil, to set the standard of sacred duty, I appear in age after age," the Bhagavad-Gita informs us. So you see, this is the right and proper work of God's people.

> Do you really believe that?

No, I do not.

Then why are you saying it?

I want to be fair, and to give a voice to those who do believe it.

It is just such beliefs that have caused the havoc in the world that religious wars have produced. Do you see that?

I do, of course. Most people do — except those who are deeply enmeshed in them. The problem is, we don't know what to do about it. We don't know how to help those who are caught up in those beliefs to break the spell.

You can help them by telling them that you can understand how they could feel that way, that you recognize these are their beliefs, and that you would like to engage in a dialogue with them about those beliefs to see if there is more about them—and about other beliefs in the world—for you both to learn.

But what if what they are doing — the way they are acting — is causing you damage or harm? What if their beliefs are making them do things to you that are horrible?

Even people who do horrible things will stop doing them, if only for a moment, if you will ask them why they are doing them.

It is not the basic nature of human beings to be horrible. It is the basic nature of human beings to be loving. When humans are being horrible, it is because

of something they believe. Ask them, therefore—even in the midst of the horror—ask them:

What hurts you so much that you feel you have to hurt me to heal it?

Now *that* is a piercing inquiry.

It is a wonderful question to pose in the middle of any disagreement that is causing another to cast negative energy at you. It works in households as well as in international affairs.

But then, having asked the question, you must be willing to listen to the answer. You cannot write the answer off as so much propaganda, or dismiss it out of hand. You cannot ignore it or belittle it or devalue it because you disagree with it. And, of course, you *will* disagree with it, or no one would be fighting with you.

It is helpful to understand that when someone is fighting with you, they are usually *fighting for your attention.*

If they could get you to hear them, and to help them with what is hurting them, without going to battle with you, they would forgo the battle, if only to remove themselves from danger.

But then, why *do* they go to war, or start a battle? Don't they know that it is bound to place them in danger?

Because they perceive that dangerous things are *already* happening to them, or are about to happen to them—and that is what they are trying to *stop.*

Remember what I told you: When they attack, no

nations or groups or individuals think of themselves as
attackers. They all think of themselves as defenders.
*"What hurts you so much that you feel you have to hurt
me to heal it?"* can therefore be a very useful question.

Yet what if I can't do anything about what hurts them so much?
What if their point of view is skewered, and their demands are
unreasonable?

Everybody's point of view is skewered. Let's begin
with that. You should know that going in.
To be a healer you must understand that *nobody does
anything inappropriate, given their model of the world.*

Does that mean that I have to accept everybody's point of
view as valid?

It means you have to understand that it is *valid for
them.* You have to be ready to say Nine Words That
Could Heal the World:
"I can understand how you could feel that way."
This is a very powerful sentence. It does not indicate
that you share another person's feelings, or agree with
something they have done, but it does indicate that *you
can understand how they could have come to this feeling.*
That statement alone can put out huge fires.

Really? I mean, is it really that powerful?

Yes, because it says to the other, "You are not alone.
You are not going crazy, you are not the only one who—

given your beliefs, thoughts, and experiences—could come to your conclusions."

If you are to be a healer, you must understand that the biggest difficulty facing people with a problem is rarely the problem itself, *but the fear that nobody else understands it.* If nobody else understands it, the prospect of finding a solution can seem very dim.

That is why the feeling of not being understood leads to desperation. And, conversely, the feeling that *someone else understands* moves people back from the brink and opens the door to discussion.

That's still a mighty tall order. If someone is dropping bombs on you, or poisoning your water, or conducting biological warfare on your nation, or, for that matter, screaming in your face in the kitchen, it's pretty hard to say, "I can understand how you could feel this way."

If you *don't* say it, or at least *ask,* "What hurts you so bad that you feel you have to hurt me to heal it?" you will never end the violence. You may interrupt it, you may postpone it, but you will never end it.

This is because, I repeat: *All attack is seen by the attacker as a defense.*

Understanding this is the basis of all healing.

16

I found those last statements extremely provocative. Could we explore them further?

Certainly. We should.

What do you mean, "Nobody does anything inappropriate, given their model of the world?"

I mean, no one ever sees their actions as "wrong."

But some peoples' actions *are* wrong, whether they see them as that or not.

Perhaps this is a good time to bring up the SEVENTH NEW REVELATION.

There is no such thing as Right and Wrong. There is only What Works and What Does Not Work, depending upon what it is that you seek to be, do, or have.

How can you say that? How can you say, "There's no such thing as right and wrong"?

> Because it's true. "Right" and "wrong" are figments of your imagination. They are judgments you are making, labels that you are creating as you go along. They are values that you are *deciding upon,* depending on what it is that you want, individually and as a society. When what you want changes, what you decide to call "right" and "wrong" changes. Your own history proves this.

Nonsense. The basics don't change.

> They don't?

No.

> Give me an example of a "basic" value that doesn't change.

Okay, killing. "Thou shalt not kill" doesn't change. That's a basic human value.

> Unless what you want is to win a war.

No fair. That's self-defense. We have a right to defend ourselves.

> Well, not all wars are wars of self-defense. Your planet has known such things as wars of aggression.

Yes, but let's not talk about them. That only complicates things.

> I see.

Our country never aggresses upon anyone. The only wars that *we* ever fight are wars of *self-defense.*

Your country only fights wars of self-defense?

That's right.

Of course it's right.

And what does that mean?

It means that you've just proven what I said before. There is not a country and there is not a group of people on Earth that imagines itself to be an aggressor. Everyone who enters into war does so saying that *they are defending something.*

Do you see this now? I am making a repeated point of this because it is something you need to look at very closely.

On your planet there are no "attackers," only "defenders." You achieve this interesting paradox by simply calling all attack a defense. In this way you are able to change your basic values from moment to moment as it suits you, without seeming to change them at all.

You get to kill people with impunity to obtain what you want by simply saying that you had no choice. You had to *defend* yourself.

All attackers see their actions in this way. Indeed, you have seen your *own* attacks on others *exactly this way.* Not just in war, but in every situation of conflict in your life, from battlefields to bedrooms, command centers to boardrooms. Nobody attacks, everybody defends.

Seeing another's attack on *you* in this way can produce miracles. Yet you could never see another's attacks in this way so long as you imagine that there is such a thing as "right" and "wrong."

This is very hard to swallow, I hope you know that. The idea of a world in which there is no such thing as right and wrong is very difficult to accept. It seems to me that we really do have some basic values here on this planet. Values shared by all people . . . or certainly, by most of them.

Well, don't be shy. Give me another example.

Okay, the prohibition against suicide. Most people consider that the taking of one's own life is wrong. It is immoral.

Yes, on the question of ending one's life, it is the current imaging of the majority of people on your planet that it is "not okay" to do that.

Similarly, many of you still insist that it is not okay to assist another who wishes to end his or her life.

In both cases, you say this should be "against the law." You have come to this conclusion, presumably, because the ending of the life in question occurs relatively quickly. Actions that end a life over a somewhat longer period of time are not against the law, even though they achieve the same result.

Thus, if a person in your society kills himself with a gun, his family members lose insurance benefits. If he does so with cigarettes, they do not.

If your doctor assists you in your suicide, it is called manslaughter, while if a tobacco company does so, it is called commerce.

With you, it seems to be merely a question of time. The legality of self-destruction—the "rightness" or "wrongness" of it—seems to have much to do with *how quickly* the deed is done, as well as who is doing it. The faster the death, the more "wrong" it seems to be. The slower the death, the more it slips into "okayness."

Interestingly, this is the exact opposite of what a truly humane society would conclude. By any reasonable definition of what you would call "humane," the shorter the death, the better. Yet your society punishes those who would seek to do the humane thing, and rewards those who would do the insane.

It is insane to think that endless suffering is what God requires, and that a quick, humane ending to the suffering is "wrong."

"Punish the humane, reward the insane."

This is the motto that only a society of beings with limited understanding could embrace.

So you poison your system by inhaling carcinogens, you poison your system by eating food treated with chemicals that over the long run kill you, and you poison your system by breathing air that you have continually polluted. You poison your system in a hundred different ways over a thousand different moments, and you do this *knowing these substances are not good for you*. But because it takes a longer time for them to kill you, *you commit suicide with impunity*. (From *CWG 3*.)

What about stealing? It's a basic human value that we don't take from another that which is not ours.

> Unless you think that another has no right to it, and you do.

That's not fair. If someone else has no right to something and we do, then, precisely *because it is not theirs, but ours,* we have a right to take it away from them.

> Of course you do. According to your values, that is true. Particularly, your value called "ownership" (which we shall discuss later). Yet that is precisely my point. You are doing nothing here but proving my point.
>
> My point is that your values change as your perceptions change. They change as your desires change, as the things you *want* change.
>
> If you want something that another party thinks is theirs, and if you want it or imagine that you need it bad enough, you will justify yourself in taking it. Believe me. You have done this. You have done exactly this.
>
> Values are a moveable feast. You cannot think of a single "basic human value" that has not been temporarily set aside, altered, or completely abandoned at one time or another by human beings who have simply changed their minds about what it is they wanted to be, do, or have in a particular moment.
>
> If you think, therefore, that there is such a thing as absolute "right" and absolute "wrong," you are deluding yourself.

You mean, we are "wrong"?

That's very clever, and it points up a major problem with your word "wrong." It has for centuries been used in at least two different ways—to mean that which is "mistaken," and to mean that which is "immoral."

An action that is called "mistaken" is an action that does not produce a desired or predicted outcome.

An action that is called "immoral" is an action that violates some life code or larger law that a society has put into place—or that a society imagines its Deity to have put into place.

The difficulty with morals, as I have just pointed out, is that they change from time to time and place to place, depending upon what it is a society or its members are trying to accomplish. Morality is, therefore, extremely subjective.

The difficulty with "mistakes" is that in religious societies or contexts they are often equated with moral failure, rather than simply *operational* failure. This makes it not merely inconvenient or unfortunate to have made a mistake, but *sinful*. In certain religious or morality-based cultures, normal human error can be considered an *offense against God*—punishable by severe and disproportionate sanctions or suffering.

We have already looked at some examples of this. Here are more:

1. He that curseth his father or his mother shall be put to death.

2. A blasphemer shall be stoned to death.
3. A woman who fails to wear a covering over her entire body may be whipped and beaten.
4. A person who steals shall have his hand cut off.

Those who do not agree with such stringent, inflexible standards, to say nothing of the disproportionate responses required by them, are considered apostates— and can be killed.

This circumstance creates all the conditions for large-scale conflict and war, for now an attack may be justified as a *defense of the faith,* an act authorized by—and, indeed, *required by*—God.

That's *exactly what's been happening* on our planet. You've hit the nail right on the head. That's what's been going on in the world in these days and times.

It has been going on for centuries. Indeed, for millennia. That is why the Seventh New Revelation is so important, for it creates a context that separates "mistake" from "morality," removing God from the picture.

Do you really think I ever cared whether you ate meat on Fridays, or wore a head-to-toe body covering because you were female, or stood on the appropriate side of the Wailing Wall?

I heard that not long ago some women attempted to stand with the men on the "men's side" of the Wailing Wall, one of the most sacred sites in all of Judaism. They wanted to make a point: that it is time to end this infantile separation of women from the men because of a thought that women are unworthy or, because of their menses, somehow "unclean." The men — some of them rabbis — began shouting and cursing and spitting, and some even began scuffling with the women.

Is it truly your imagining that God is concerned with these things?

It does seem rather petty, even in the name of sacred tradition.

Perhaps especially so.

Yet do you not care at all about life on Earth, and what is going on here?

God cares about life on Earth enough to give humans all the help, all the support, and all the tools that they could ever need to make it a wondrous and joyful experience. And God loves human beings enough to give them the greatest gift of all: free will.

Now interestingly, a challenge that you have created for yourselves is that you believe God gives you this free will, but then takes it away from you by telling you exactly what it is that He requires you to do. Even what you are to think, and to say. In some cases, how you are to dress and to eat.

Some of you think that it is disrespectful even to write the name of God, and so you use dashes where the vowels would be in order not to complete the spelling (ignoring the fact that this writing custom simply grew out of the fact that the original language in which God's name was written *had* no vowels). Others

of you pass laws in your societies against possessing or displaying any pictures, or even *drawing* any, of God or of humans or animals, because you believe there to be a prohibition against these "graven images."

You have denied yourself many of your simplest pleasures—music and dancing, for example—claiming that your God says He doesn't want you to engage in such indulgences. These are, some of you say, sinful and immoral.

Indeed, in countries where civil law is based on religious law, you have made the smallest mistakes and the tiniest human errors matters of moral turpitude.

Yet true morality as an unchanging, objective criteria does not exist. It *cannot* in any evolving society, for the nature of evolution itself is change. And, of course, this is exactly what most governments that have their foundation in religion seek to stop. They seek to stop *change. Yet change is the nature of life.* And so, they seek to create a better life by denying Life Itself.

But Life will not be denied, nor will its process be corrupted. Great difficulty can thus arise when societies change and morals do not. A deep chasm is created between by-the-book rules and on-the-ground experiences. As this chasm widens, new and more practical standards of behavior spontaneously emerge within a culture. Yet as new standards emerge, old ones are defended by those who are afraid to make the adjustment.

And so, again, attack is justified in the name of defense.

> This is exactly the situation in many of your cul-
> tures today.
>
> It is an irony of life on your planet that freedom,
> which is *the very essence of what God is,* and free will,
> which is *God's greatest gift,* is nearly always severely
> restricted by those governments that are controlled by
> religions.

There are those who say that government should not *be* controlled by religions, that there should be a strict separation of Church
and State. Yet that is a very Western worldview. Other cultures
feel that only God should and can be the supreme governor of
human affairs, and that God's Law, as contained in holy writings
and interpreted by religious teachers and jurists, should be the
law of the land.

> > This is the clash of ideology that I spoke of early in
> > our conversation. It is essentially a clash between indi-
> > vidual freedom and personal restriction, between human
> > rights and what some people declare to be God's Law.
> >
> > In truth there is no clash, for freedom is the essence
> > of God, and human rights—personal liberty, equality
> > under the law, the fairness of trials—are expressions
> > of that essence.
> >
> > Yet there have been religions (there still are today)
> > that do not recognize basic freedoms and equalities as
> > every person's human right. According to some reli-
> > gions, as has been noted here already, women are not
> > equal to men. According to certain religions, atheists do
> > not have the right to live. A person who is not a mem-

ber of the faith cannot testify against one who is. And slavery is permitted.

No, no... there is no bona fide religious Scripture that fails to condemn slavery.

You had better read the Bible and the Qur'an more closely.

Now when such religious teachings become the law of the land or become the innermost beliefs and "morals" of a culture, a clash is certain to develop. Especially when those religions seek to make their beliefs the guiding principles of *other* people.

There have always been ideological differences on your planet, but the present widening of the *split in ideology* with a simultaneous *advance in technology* has created the conditions for rapid self-destruction.

Well, here we are again, at the same question. What can we do to stop this?

It will take an unprecedented act of courage, on a grand scale. You may have to do something virtually unknown in the annals of human history.

What?

You may have to give up some of your most sacred beliefs.

"I can't. *I can't.* I would rather die than do that."

That's what some people will say when they read this.

Then they are going to. Many people are going to die in order to be "right."

Only when enough human beings die over these ideologies will you decide that *maybe it was the ideologies themselves that were mistaken.*

Your life and your experience will cause you to change you mind, at last, about what is "right" and "wrong," and about "what works" and "what doesn't work."

Well, here we go! This is the very kind of *relativism* that fundamentalists claim is creating all of our problems in the first place. Isn't this what gives rise to even more radical fundamentalism?

Yes. Afraid of losing a way of life, unable to cope with rapid and endless change, having no new theological thoughts or ideas or spiritual models offered to them in centuries, some people know no other way to move forward than to go backward.

These people insist on returning to a narrow and literal interpretation of their particular sacred scripture, and upon adherence to the "fundamentals" of their religious traditions, even if some of those ancient fundamental teachings and requirements make no sense at all in present-day circumstances.

This creates a clash with those who see clearly that present-day situations cannot be addressed or resolved by such ancient interpretations. Yet people who wish to remain true to their innermost beliefs feel that it is these beliefs that are being attacked. And these they will defend to the death.

What, then, is the solution?

> The world must create a New Spirituality.
>
> Not something to completely replace the old, but something to refresh it.
>
> Not something to reduce the old, but something to expand it.
>
> Not something to subvert the old, but something to support the best of it.
>
> Human spirituality is in need of refreshment.
>
> It is now time to present the world with new theological thoughts and ideas, a new spiritual model.
>
> The world must have something new to hold on to if it is to release its grip on the old. If you were in the middle of a raging stream, would you let go of a log?

No.

> Build, therefore, a bridge.
>
> *Become* that bridge.
>
> Live the beliefs of a New Spirituality. Walk the path of a New Revelation. Do not merely speak of this revelation, but demonstrate the truth of it with your life, lived.
>
> Show the way.
>
> Be a bringer of the light.

I have to ask again, what can one person do?

> You are the light of the world. Do you not know this?
>
> *Everyone is,* when they choose to be.

A city on a hill cannot be hidden. Neither do people light a lamp and put it under a bushel. Instead, they put it on its stand, and it gives light to everyone in the house.

In the same way, let your light so shine before men that they may see your good works and praise the beliefs that have sponsored them.

By this means you can help others span the chasm between yesterday and tomorrow, and close the gap between the comfort of tradition and the necessity of innovation.

For the world must now invent itself anew. Yet honor the past as you envision the future. Do not completely reject old beliefs, nor require anyone else to. Enlarge upon them, alter them where alteration seems appropriate, and invite others to do the same.

Let your New Spirituality be not the rejection, but the *fulfillment,* of all that your old religious laws and your ancient prophets have promised you. And when others ask what you are doing, say: Do not think that I have come to abolish the Law or the Prophets; I have not come to abolish them, but to fulfill them.

17

You said something fascinating earlier. You said, "Nobody does anything inappropriate, given their model of the world." I can see how this applies. It is what made it possible for music of any kind other than Islamic religious songs to be outlawed by the Taliban in Afghanistan.

Exactly. That was their model of the world. To them this seemed perfectly reasonable.

So, if we find a person's behavior, or the behavior of a whole group of people, unacceptable to us, what we have to do to produce lasting change is to *affect the model of the world that is creating their behavior.*

You understand now. You understand the central point of this dialogue. That is what I am saying here. You can seek to alter behavior, but that will produce only short-term change, at best. Yet if you alter *beliefs*, you will impact behavior at its source.

That is why I have said that what would be benefi-
cial for human beings right now if they wish to live
together in peace and harmony is *a new spirituality,* a
new "model of the world" based on expanded and
changed beliefs.

How do we create that? I know you said before that in order
for others to feel "safe" with these new beliefs, we have to demonstrate that they work, using our own lives as the model. But how
do we come up with new beliefs to begin with?

You will not come up with any new beliefs unless and
until you decide that some of your old beliefs are not
working.

Beliefs are difficult things for humans to let go of.
Once you believe a thing, you believe it until it is proven
wrong. Even then many of you continue to believe it,
refusing to let go of old ideas long after they have been
proven inaccurate, ineffective, or unworkable. But at least
here, in this dialogue, you're willing to look at it. And
that's the first step to change. You can't change anything
that you're not even willing to look at. So, first you have
to decide which of your old beliefs are not working.

In this conversation we have explored Five Fallacies
About God. These are beliefs that no longer work for
the human community. There can be no serious argument about that. The fact that they do not work is
observable and demonstrable. The continuing condition
of conflict on your planet is the demonstration.

If your present beliefs about God were accurate,

conflict would have been eliminated on your planet long
ago. Instead, your beliefs about God actually create conflict. I have pointed this out now repeatedly. The intention is that you will not be able to miss this point—or
to ignore it.

You said earlier that there were ten fallacies that humans
believe. Ten in all.

> Yes. In addition to the Five Fallacies About God, there
> are also Five Fallacies About Life that make your expe-
> rience on Earth very, very difficult.

Are these fallacies about Life as important, do they produce
just as much impact, as the Five Fallacies About God?

> Every bit as much. They also create crisis, violence,
> killing, and war.

Then let's go over them now. We haven't discussed these yet.

> The Five Fallacies About Life are:
>
> 1. Human beings are separate from each other.
> 2. There is not enough of what human beings need to
>   be happy.
> 3. To get the stuff of which there is not enough, human
>   beings must compete with each other.
> 4. Some human beings are better than other human
>   beings.
> 5. It is appropriate for human beings to resolve severe
>   differences created by all the other fallacies by killing
>   each other.

Okay, let's go back to the top of the list and take a look at these.

> Good.
>
> The First Fallacy About Life is that human beings are separate from each other. This idea emerges from the Third Fallacy About *God,* and so we see how the Fallacies About God have a spillover effect.
>
> Your species' fallacies about God are very powerful. They impact every area of your collective experience, even for those who do not believe in God. Because they are connected so deeply with the root cause of all experience as you now understand it, your ideas about God affect and actually create your beliefs about Life— producing fallacies in the secular arena as well.
>
> You believe that God has separated you from Him because you have not given God what She needs. This idea, in turn, stems from your belief that there is something in particular that God *does* need, and that God can actually *fail to have His needs met.*
>
> Both of these ideas are almost ridiculous on the surface, but the absurdity of ideas has never stopped human beings from embracing them.

As you have pointed out, God is, *by our own definition,* the Almighty, the All-Powerful, and the Most High. You would think we would "get" that God needs and requires nothing to be happy. The idea that we must somehow placate God (in order to have His blessings, and not His curses, showered upon us, and to guarantee a place for us in Heaven) nevertheless persists.

And what humans have *done* to "placate God" is inhuman. You have persecuted others, causing them incredible suffering, and you have killed people by the millions, in order to please this God of yours.

In the earliest days of pagan worship, humans even sacrificed babies—tiny infants, the embodiment of utter innocence—placing them on pyres and burning them alive in hopes of causing the gods to smile.

This need to "make God happy" emerged from your errant thought that God is somehow *not* happy. This is a crazy idea, because God is Happiness Itself. Yet you have clung to your idea of a brooding, displeased Deity.

Your idea that God is not happy—*and that humans are the cause*—is what has created the insane basis for insane religions to inspire people to act insanely.

I have never heard it put so directly.

It is time that you did.

This really is a silly idea, isn't it?

It is more than silly. It is deadly.

It is also the epitome of arrogance for you to imagine that somehow something that human beings have done could make the Creator of the Universe give up Peace and Love—which is the Essence of Who and What the Creator IS.

In other words, you imagine that I am willing to *give up Myself* in reaction to something that you have done. The reason you imagine that I do this because *you do this.*

And we do not even see the connection.

No, you do not.

We say that we are made in the "image and likeness of God," yet you are correct in what you suggested before—what we have done is create God in the image and likeness of humans.

And so, you have imagined a God that separated humans from Him, because He was not happy with humans. This is what humans do to each other when *they* are not happy, and you have concluded that God would do the same.

This idea of The Great Separation created in you the experience of being separate from each other as well. I have already explained to you how this happened.

Human beings knew—they intuitively understood; they had a cellular memory of the fact—that they were one with all of life. One with the Earth, and one with the creatures of the Earth. One with the sky, and one with everything in the sky. One with the divine, and part of that which *is* divine.

Then the stories of separation began. As I earlier explained, these stories arose out of humans' early experience. Religions codified that experience, transforming myth into dogma. The illusion of your separation was complete. Separation from God, and separation from all of life.

Modern religion has had a chance to break that illusion, to lead you to the truth. But modern religion has chosen to stick with the teachings of pre-modern times, to retain the dogma of hundreds and thousands of years ago. And so, modern religion has failed modern man.

If you are courageous, if you are very brave, you will allow a New Spirituality to enhance your religious experience. This spirituality will not reject outright your traditional religious teachings, but enlarge upon them and alter some of the teachings that you agree no longer apply or no longer function.

You have made that statement repeatedly now. You keep saying that over and over again.

I want it to be something that you will carry from this book firmly in your awareness, for it is, in fact, your only hope for a truly different tomorrow. A tomorrow filled not with fear, struggle, rancor, conflict, outright war, and violent death, but with peace, joy, and love.

What I am doing here is capturing all that I have been telling you over these several years and bringing it all together in one place, saying it over and over again, restating and reiterating comments and observations that I have made earlier here and elsewhere before, and then adding new and very important information having to do with the crisis at hand.

And the human race is facing a major crisis, make no mistake about that. It is a crisis of conflict between ideologies. It is a crisis of beliefs.

As I've said, you have equated your disconnection from God (which itself is a false belief) with a disconnection from Life. It is quite natural for you to have done so, since at some very deep level you knew and understood that God IS all of Life. While you may not have articulated it that way, *you knew at a cellular level that this was true.*

Everything and everyone in Life, therefore, was experienced as Separate From You in the moment you accepted that you were Separate From God.

(Conversely, everything and everyone in Life is experienced as being One With You in the moment you accept that you are One With God. This is something that all masters teach and that all mystics have reported.)

You have accepted that you are Separate From God not because you have *experienced* that you are separate, but because you have been *told that you are*—by organized religion.

One's religion is a product of one's birthplace and early teaching. It is a product not of eternal truth, but of cultural environment. People believe what they have been taught to believe. They do not question it, because they do not wish to question its source.

I invite you to make this inquiry:

Who would you be making wrong if you changed some of your most basic beliefs?

Therein lies the tale.

So long as you believe that there is such a thing as Right and Wrong, you will be willing to risk everything to be "right." You will not change your beliefs if you think that doing so will make you, or someone you love, wrong. Yet as soon as you change the Right–Wrong axis to a What Works–What Doesn't Work paradigm, the difficulty of critically analyzing—to say nothing of changing—basic beliefs is eased.

Today the world lives in a Right–Wrong paradigm, and thus supports the Third Fallacy About God and the First Fallacy about Life—the illusion that Disunity Exists.

Should you dare to say that you have experienced just the *opposite*, that you have known the joyful bliss of complete *union* with others and with the Divine, you will quite likely be told to be wary of such experiences—and certainly to be wary of *talking* about them.

I've experienced that.

I'm sure you have.

And it is this fallacy of separation that allows us to do to each other things that we would never do to ourselves.

Yes.

It also creates the illusion that there is "not enough" of what you need to be happy.

The Second Fallacy About Life.

Yes.

If you thought that there was only One of you— that is, if you thought of yourselves as One Body, which is what you are—

—or one community—

—or one community…you would know that you
always had enough, because you would *create the experience of it.* With such a belief you would share and
share alike; you would ensure each other's well-being.

This is the highest tradition of the Islamic faith, which sees
all Muslims as members of One Community. Islamic teaching
calls upon Muslims to give to the poor, and always to support the
community. Members of the Church of Jesus Christ of Latter-
day Saints — Mormons — also have formed a worldwide community, supported by one of the largest internal systems of organized,
non-governmental assistance to the poor and the needy among
its members of any religious organization in the world. Organizations of Catholic Charities and groups appealing to other
Christian sects, as well as similar Jewish charities, likewise seek
to share the world's abundance with the less fortunate and those
in need.

These are all worthy expressions of a beginning
understanding. The difficulty is that many religious organizations form a closed circle around their own members, thereby demonstrating the limitations of their
understanding. States and nations do the same. As do
cultural, ethnic, racial, and social groups of every kind,
each consciously or unconsciously creating a *cordon
sanitaire.*

Such quarantine living does nothing to promote an
experience of humanity's oneness, and, indeed, produces
a sense of the need for a protective shield, segregating
people according to their most narrow views.

With such a narrow outlook, not everything can be seen as it really is. Because perspective is limited, so, then, is awareness.

What you experience as the safety of your womb becomes the birthplace of your righteousness.

Yet raising your consciousness will lift you out of your womblike segregation. Then you will discover that the quarantine was unnecessary, that the cordon separated you from nothing but your Self.

This will be the biggest surprise. This will be the largest astonishment. You have merely been segregating yourself from *yourself.*

When you break through the circle of your containment, you will discover that everyone else is just like you.

Not only everyONE else, but everyTHING else. Close examination will reveal that you and the rocks and the trees and the planets and the sun and the moon *are all made of the same stuff.* Like beautiful snowflakes, you all *look* different, but you all have identical substance.

When you discover your Oneness, you will marvel at how you could ever have imagined yourself to be separate from anyone or anything else. You will see that when you have treated anyone or anything as though it was *not you,* you hurt no one but yourself.

How did this all happen? How did we become so separated from our Selves?

It occurred when you decided that you were not perfect. Somewhere along the way in your passing on of myths and stories, you landed on the idea that you were less than the world and the life around you.

As I have explained before, you saw the effect that the winds and the rains and the storms and Life Itself had on you, and you determined that the "gods" were more powerful than you. You could never be this powerful, no matter how hard you tried. Thus, you imagined your own imperfection. You were "less than" the gods. In your frustration and your anger, you turned against yourself, judging yourself and condemning yourself for being "not enough."

The first human experience of insufficiency was not in your exterior world, where there was clearly plenty, but within yourself, which measured up as very puny compared to the outward bounty and magnificence of the world around you. One look at the night sky was enough to convince you of the awesomeness of that which you thought of as Not You, and the puniness of that which you thought of as You.

It is from this idea of your puniness that you have never recovered. Yet now can be the time of your healing. This can be the moment of your remembering. For I come to tell you a great secret:

You and the stars are one.

Not figuratively, as in a poem or a song, but *literally.* Your chemical makeup is the same. You will find the same trace elements within you that you will find in all celestial bodies—and, indeed, in *everything else that Is*.

Does this surprise you? Are you amazed to learn that nothing is composed of anything except differing combinations and concentrations of the *Only Substance There Is?* It should not. I have been telling you this for a long time.

Yes, you have, but I think most humans thought that this was meant figuratively, not literally.

It is a literal truth, my child.

YOU ARE ALL ONE.

In the beginning stages of its development, your species could not comprehend this. Now, in the earliest years of its adolescence, it can.

Our species is in its adolescence?

In the *earliest years* of its adolescence. Yet it may never reach maturity the way things are going. You are quarreling with each other like children unwilling to share your toys.

18

Do you think we will ever learn? Do you think we will ever find a way to get along, to do something as simple as live together in peace and harmony and happiness?

You will if you will give up your false beliefs and the human constructions you have built up around them.

I have come here to help you. I have always been here. I have never left. That Which You Are cannot leave you, but remains with you always. And so, even before you ask, I will have answered.

Yet you do not know this, because you do not know Me. You imagine Me to have separated myself from you. You imagine yourselves to be separated from each other. Neither imagining is true. Neither serves you.

The first three of the Five Fallacies About Life... "Human beings are separate from each other"... "There is not enough of what human beings need to be happy". . . and, "To get the stuff of which there is not enough, human beings must compete with each other". . . are sufficient to create crisis, violence, killing, and war in and of themselves.

How did we ever get to that Third Fallacy About Life, the one about competition?

As soon as you accepted that there was "not enough" of the stuff of life, you concluded that you had to do whatever it takes to make sure that *you and yours* had enough. In the beginning, you just reached out and took it. In this scenario, the hand with the most muscles won.

Later, as you began to move into the adolescence of your species, you evolved to the point where it did not seem fair to you that the biggest and the strongest always won. Yet you had not evolved to the point where you chose to see *everybody* win. (You still have not.) So, you began to devise other "reasons" for one person or one group, rather than another, having the lion's share of whatever it was that you thought you needed to be happy.

You developed *competitions,* where brute force was not the only factor in determining life's winners and losers, the haves and the have-nots.

All of this would have been disadvantageous enough (enlightened beings do not compete with each other for the right to grab and hoard that which belongs to everyone), but you did not even construct the competitions fairly. You chose to create competitions in which *the winners were declared ahead of time.*

What do you mean?

I mean that, in your particular culture, you decided that if you were rich, white, Christian, American, and male, you were among the winners *going in.*

Each culture, each sub-group of the whole of humanity, has its own list, its own idea of who the "winners" are in life's competition for the Stuff of Which There is Not Enough, and had I been referring to other cultures, I could just as easily have said that being black, Russian, or Muslim placed you on the winner's list.

But being "female" does not place you on the list in hardly any of humanity's cultures.

That is true, and it is because, in order to create competitions in which you declare the winners ahead of time, you had to revert *back* to the use of force to quiet the losers. And so, brute force, primitive muscle, was the ultimate determiner.

Because you continue to allow primitive physical force or brute economic force to decide most of the issues and all of the major conflicts within the human experience, in virtually every present-day human culture, "rich" and "male" are the primary elevating categories. If you are both of these, you are in a dominant position because you have the strength and the power, and you are declared the "winner" ahead of time in your human competitions for the stuff of life.

In the earliest days, male predominance was demonstrated with a club. Today it is demonstrated with money,
influence, and power—which you make sure is controlled and retained mostly by males. So males continue
to get their way by using force. And since you've imagined a God who uses force to get God's way as well,
you've decided that God must be male.

Well, of course God is male. *Isn't He? Aren't You?*

No.

But I was *taught* that God was a "He."

By whom?

My religion.

Most of your religions are male-dominated, and were
created by male-dominated societies. Some of these
religions even *teach*—that is, they hold as a matter of
doctrine—that women are to be subservient to men.

Yes, we've talked a number of times now about this unfortunate tendency of Muslims to treat women as if they were second-
class citizens.

As in this mandate?
"Every man praying or prophesying, having his head
covered, dishonors his head. But every *woman* who prays
or prophesies with her head *uncovered* dishonors her
head, for that is one and the same as if her head were
shaved.

"For if a woman is not covered, let her also be shorn.

But if it is shameful for a woman to be shorn or shaved,
let her be covered.

"For a man indeed ought not to cover *his* head, since
he is the image and glory of God; but woman is the
glory of man.

"For man is not from woman, but woman from man.

"Nor was man created for the woman, but woman for
the man."

Yes. You can see how such Islamic edicts really put women
down.

Except that is not an Islamic edict. That is from the
New Testament of the Bible.

No, no, wait, no. It's *Islam* that has repeatedly placed women in
such positions of inferiority, not *Christianity!*

I think you'd better read I Corinthians, 11:4–9. Or
try Ephesians 5:22–24, which makes things very clear:

"Wives, submit to your own husbands, as to the
Lord. For the husband is head of the wife, as also Christ
is head of the church....

"Therefore, just as the church is subject to Christ,
so let the wives be to their own husbands *in everything.*"

Whoa. Hold it. Wait a minute. Okay, so maybe I had it wrong.
It's not just Muslims who reduce the standing of women in their
society. It's Christians, too.

Actually, it's virtually every ancient religious culture.

You're right. Now that I page back through the introduction to *Bhagavad-Gita As It Is*, written by His Divine Grace A.C. Bhaktivedanta Swami, I see these words:

"What is material nature? It is explained in Gita as inferior prakrti, inferior nature. Prakrti is always under control... Prakrti is female, and she is controlled by the Lord, just as the activities of a wife are controlled by the husband."

Brother, it's really been soaked into *every culture on this planet*, this woman-is-inferior thing, hasn't it?

> **Yes, it has.**
> **Under Islamic law the testimony at court of a woman is worth half that of a man.**

You're kidding!

> **I wish I were.**

Well, maybe, what with this kind of thing showing up in so *many* religions, God really *meant* that women are subordinate to men.

> **They are not.**

Are you sure?

> **I am sure.**

But they've got to be *protected,* kept in their homes, not allowed to work, not allowed to be educated. They must have their sexual organs mutilated, so that they cannot enjoy sensual pleasure.

And while they are not to *have* sexual pleasure, they are to *provide it* to men, usually upon demand, often as an unspoken expectation and condition of their contract of marriage.

They also can be bought and sold, again for the purpose of providing sexual pleasure for men.

Women cannot walk in public except in the company of a male blood relative, and then must have their bodies completely covered so as not to be seen. They cannot vote, or hold positions of authority.

They cannot be present in corporate boardrooms or places of political power. They may not be ministers or priests, bishops or popes, rabbis or *ulamas,* or even sit in the same section of the temple with men. If they do hold jobs, they are not to be paid the same as men, even if they do the same work. But it would be very difficult for them to hold jobs in any event, because they have specifically assigned duties, besides providing sexual pleasure, that make men happy. They must cook, clean, stock the pantry, handle the laundry, raise the children, and get everyone to piano lessons, soccer practice, and wherever else they need to go.

Let me see . . . have I omitted anything?

Not much.

I've been trying to think of some of the ways we've treated women in our world's various societies, and how we've justified that.

It really *is* our various organized religions that tell us many of these things, and create the breeding ground for the others, isn't it?

I'm afraid so.

And many people have believed them. Many people believe them still. Basically, the idea is that women are simply not equal to men. But how could our well-meaning religions come to such a conclusion if this is not a Direct Teaching from God?

My friend, it is not simply discrimination against women that your holy writings have said is a direct teaching from God. Your organized religions have also taught, at one time or another, that God's Laws forbid people of differing races to marry, that people of the same gender may not physically demonstrate their love for each other, and even that blacks may not be priests.

Yes. The Church of Jesus Christ of Latter-day Saints — the Mormon Church — has always taught that all men within the faith were considered priests. But for a long time the Mormon Church said that this did not apply to men who happened to be black. Blacks were felt to be inferior to whites and were, therefore, not qualified. It was only a relatively short time ago that the church fathers relented and allowed as to how blacks were *not* inferior to whites and could become priests after all.

Now if only they could decide the same thing about women....

Don't hold your breath. But how is this sort of thing possible? How can *religions,* supposedly the very model of love and acceptance, actually sponsor such discrimination?

Their justification stems from the Fourth Fallacy About Life, which states that some human beings are better than other human beings. It is this fallacy that allows your societies to follow in the footsteps of organized religions and practice discrimination of all kinds.

You even use discrimination in your everyday language. You may have noticed that in this conversation I have used the terms "he" and "she" interchangeably when referring to God. This is something that you do not do.

I have noticed that, and I've wondered about it.

I do it because I know that language is a very powerful part of the creation of the cultural story of humans.

Because your race has used the word "he" exclusively to refer to God in most recent millennia, it hasn't taken long for the young among you—the young of both sexes—to get the picture: God is a male, and so, by inference, males are superior to females.

Now when the New Spirituality encompasses the planet, such inferences will be a thing of the past.

A big part of the New Spirituality will have to do with creating true equality for females, ending at last the disenfranchising and the outright abuse of one half the human race.

This is one of many reasons why you can expect the New Spirituality to be opposed by people in power. Most of the people in power are now men.

And men believe in this fallacy that they call their superiority, although many men have by now convinced themselves that it is not really their superiority they are declaring with their actions and decisions regarding women, it is their *concern* for women, and their sensitivity to the fact that men and women have different roles to play in society.

What we will label the Concerned Group says that all it is doing by proclaiming and supporting laws and customs that restrict women is *protecting* them from being exploited and mistreated. Yet its own protection produces massive and pervasive exploitation and mistreatment.

The Different Roles Group says it is merely seeking to keep clear the important and separate roles men and women have been given to play in human affairs. It, too, massively exploits and mistreats women under this pretension. It claims that God has *assigned* men and women their roles, and it proclaims that the very reason the human race is struggling for its survival is that these roles have been subverted. Women are going around doing "men's jobs" and wearing "men's clothes" and wanting "men's authority," and, according to this group, that's what is creating upheaval in our society.

> Well, it *is* creating upheaval, but it is upheaval that is necessary if you are to produce a society of New Humans who understand that neither race nor gender nor nationality nor religious persuasion nor sexual orientation nor any other aspect of a person's individuality should disqualify that person from participating fully in the human experience at the highest level and in whatever way he or she chooses, so long as that choice does not impinge upon the rights or safety of others.

Now *that* statement could be a preamble to an Earth Constitution for New Humans.

"*Nothing in a person's race, gender, nationality, religious persuasion, sexual orientation, or any other aspect of individuality, shall disqualify that person from participating fully and equally in the human experience at the highest level.*"

Whoa.

> Yes, that would be a revolutionary idea. "Revolution" means to "revolve," or to turn around, and such an idea would turn around much of your reality. It would correct the Fourth Fallacy About Life.

19

I'm fascinated by this Fourth Fallacy About Life..."Some human beings are better than other human beings." It seems to me that when we add this to the first three life fallacies, we've quadrupled the odds in favor of disaster.

> Your assessment is correct.
>
> The human idea of "better" is the most harmful concept ever devised by the mind of any sentient being anywhere. It is what has allowed you to rationalize and justify all of your most primitive behaviors.
>
> Some of you have the idea that Christians are "better" than Jews, or that Jews are "better" than Christians. That whites are "better" than blacks, or that blacks are "better" than whites. That Americans are "better" than Arabs, or that Arabs are "better" than Americans.

And that the French are better than anybody!
(That was a joke.)

(I know.)

You think that Catholics are "better" than Protestants, that Protestants are "better" than Catholics; that Republicans are "better" than Democrats, that Democrats are "better" than Republicans; that Lutherans of the Missouri Synod are "better" than Lutherans of the Evangelical Lutheran Church, and that Lutherans of the Evangelical Lutheran Church are "better" than Lutherans of the Missouri Synod.

You think that straights are "better" than gays, that Capitalists are "better" than Communists, that ecologists are "better" than industrialists, and finally, that believers in God—*any* kind of God—are "better" than atheists.

I think I'm right in saying that Muslim religious teachers divide sin into two categories, great sins and little sins, just as Catholics talk of mortal sins and venial sins. But for Muslims, *unbelief* is the greatest of the seventeen great sins. It is considered a greater sin than theft, a greater sin than adultery, even a greater sin than murder. So much "better" are believers than nonbelievers that unbelief can be punishable by death, and ending your own life in the process of "killing the infidels" gets you straight to heaven!

In human society, this idea of "betterness" goes on
ad infinitum.

Yet surely you're not saying that it is not okay to prefer one thing over the other. If everything were "just the same," we would be bored to tears. Differences are good. Variety is the spice of life.

Agreed. Yet differences do not have to mean divisions, and in your world they often do. You have allowed your differences to weaken you rather than strengthen you.

Some of you have claimed that you are more than merely "different." You have claimed that you are "*better.*" Improved. Superior. Advanced. Enhanced. Greater. Finer. Preferred. Chosen. Selected. Uplifted.

You think that because you are "this" rather than "that," that you are *more*. More appropriate, more desirable, more fitting, more suitable, more useful, more valuable, more attractive, more competent, more preferable.

In some cases, you have added the phrase "in the eyes of God" to these descriptions, so that you think you are "more preferable" *in the eyes of God,* or more fitting, or more suitable *in the eyes of God,* to be a priest, or to be called a saint, or to "go to heaven."

Some organized religions say that only if you have a penis can you be a priest or a religious cleric. If you do not, you cannot. Some religions say that only if you believe in Jesus can you go to heaven. If you do not, you cannot. Some religions say that only if you follow the teachings of Muhammad can you know God. If you do not, you cannot.

These and other of your notions have created a caste system in your religious experience—the last place where such a system has any place at all.

What can we do about all this? This idea of our being "better" than the next person is pretty deeply ingrained. I don't know how we can get rid of it.

> Actually, the illusion of superiority is an easy one from which to step aside. A simple look at your behaviors when you think you are superior will reveal you to be acting inferiorly. The bigger you think you are, the smaller you become. The better you think you are, the worse you act. The evidence of your own eyes will lead you to this truth.

> Yet you must open your eyes. You cannot walk around in a daze, as if sleepwalking. And that is what most humans are doing. Sleepwalking. Living in a dream, and watching it turn into a nightmare.

> That nightmare logically leads to, and produces, the Fifth Fallacy About Life: It is appropriate for human beings to resolve severe differences created by the first four fallacies by killing each other.

And as you have pointed out here again and again, many organized religions only help to promote and perpetuate this idea.

> Oh, yes. Very obviously and very definitely so.

> It is your organized religions that have made it clear through their most sacred scriptures that cruelty and killing is an acceptable response to human frailty and human differences.

> This goes against every human instinct, but organized religion has reorganized human thoughts.

Some humans have even been turned against their own instinct for survival. And so people go around maiming and killing each other, because they've been told quite directly that this is what *God* does to *them*— and what God wants them to do to each other.

That seems to be going a bit far. No religion teaches that.

Are you sure? Have you read the Qur'an lately? Or the Bhagavad-Gita? Or the Book of Mormon? Or the Bible?

Do you remember what happened to the Israelites who worshiped the golden calf? Were not 3,000 of them slaughtered by the Levites at my command? Did I not instruct you thus in Exodus 32:27 to "take every man his sword by his side, and go in and out from gate to gate throughout the camp, and slay every man his brother, and every man his companion, and every man his neighbor"?

And what about the 24,000 Israelites who worshiped Baal? Did I not say unto Moses, as recorded in Numbers 25:4–9: "Take all the heads of the people, and hang them up before the Lord..."?

You know, I would say that you are picking out a few isolated examples and are not being fair, but there have been many books written about the history of massacre and slaughter in God's Holy Name as extensively recorded in many places in the Bible. In these books, we are told how the Bible relates that 12,000 men, women, and children of Ai were killed in an ambush that God Himself inspired and supervised (Joshua 8:1–30), and that the armies of the Amorites were destroyed when "...the Lord...slew them with a great slaughter" (Joshua 10:10–11).

These Bible critiques tell us that a reading of the books of Exodus, Leviticus, Deuteronomy, Joshua, Judges, Samuel, Numbers, Amos, Kings, Chronicles, Esther, and Job, to name a few, will produce a toll of no less than *one million people* in Old Testament history alone who were smote by God's hand, including all of those who died during a seven-year famine in Samaria sent by the Lord (II Kings 8:1), or the 185,000 Assyrians slain overnight by one angel (II Kings 19:35)—or by people working at God's behest—such as the 100,000 Syrian footmen, killed on a single day by the children of Israel (I Kings 20:28,29,30), or the prophets of Baal, numbering 450, murdered by Elijah (I Kings 18:40,46), or the *half million* men of Israel slaughtered by the army of King Abijah of Judah, whom, we are told, "God smote" (II Chronicles 13:16,17, 20).

> You may also find it interesting to read the Book of Mormon. It gives humans some very interesting pictures of God. For instance, it says:
>
> "Howl ye, for the day of the Lord is at hand; it shall come as a destruction from the Almighty.... Behold, the day of the Lord cometh, cruel both with wrath and fierce anger, to lay the land desolate; and he shall destroy the sinners thereof out of it...and I will punish the world for evil, and the wicked for their iniquity...every one that is proud shall be thrust through; yea, and every one that is joined to the wicked shall fall by the sword..."

Wow. That sure tells us how vicious you get when you are offended.

> Wait, there's more. Not satisfied with punishing evil men, the Lord God Almighty, Creator of Heaven and Earth, goes after innocent offspring and spouses as well.
>
> "And their children shall also be dashed to pieces before their eyes; their houses shall be spoiled and their wives ravished."

The Book of Mormon says this?

> Look in 2 Nephi 23:6–16.

Man, that's unbelievable.

> Indeed. What you must now admit and acknowledge is that you have told yourselves in many of your holy scriptures that God, Himself, kills people who offend Him, and that God wants you to go out and kill for Him, too.

Perhaps now it is time — while we still *have* time — for all of us to ask ourselves some very important questions.

Is it possible that the Word of God as put down by humans in their holy books *has some errors in it?* Is it possible that there is something we don't know about God and about Life, *the knowing of which could change everything?*

If only there could be a New Gospel.

> There can be. It was proposed before, in the book *Friendship with God.* Fifteen words that could change the

world. A two-sentence gospel that would turn your
planet on its ear.

Yes, I remember now. Two sentences that would alter everything.

They are sentences that could not be uttered from
many pulpits or lecterns, by many religious or political
leaders. You can dare them to say it, but they will not.
You can beg them to repeat it, but they must not. You
can cry out for them to declare it, but they cannot.

Why? Why can't they say it?

Because to utter this New Gospel would be to inval-
idate everything they have taught you, everything of
which they have sought to convince you, everything on
which they base their actions.

You're right. It's a New Gospel that could save the world, but
the world cannot preach these two sentences. The world cannot
proclaim them. They are too powerful. They are too disruptive.

Still, maybe I'm wrong. Maybe there are some brave religious
and political leaders who might take up this proposed New
Gospel and repeat it. Let's proclaim it here!

"We Are All One."

"Ours is not a better way, ours is merely another
way."

What a message that would be coming from the pulpits of the
world! What a declaration that would be from the podiums of
all nations!

How powerful those words would be, uttered by the Pope or the Archbishop of Canterbury or the leading cleric in the Baptist Church or the world's Islamic voices or the president of the Mormon Church or the head of the Lutheran Church – Missouri Synod!

I invite them now – right here, right now – to say them, to declare this their truth, to include it in their next public sermon.

Imagine the Pope saying, "God loves all God's children, and we are all one. There are many paths to God, and God denies no one who takes a path with humility and sincerity. Ours is not a better way, ours is merely another way."

The world would shake. The foundations of all the world's major religions – Separation and Betterness – would crumble!

I challenge every political party spokesman, every international chief of state, to place this in their party platforms and to announce this in their speeches.

Imagine the candidates in the next U.S. presidential election saying, "This is a complex time, and there are many approaches to the challenges we face. I have my thoughts and my opponent has hers. My opponent is not a villain. She is not a bad person. She simply has ideas that are different from mine. Listen to our ideas carefully, and then see which one of us it is with whom you agree. But in the end, I want you all to know this: These are the *United* States, and we are all one. Ours is not a better way, ours is merely another way."

The political process would never be the same. Gone would be the demonizing. Gone would be the character assassinations and the impugning of motives and the "make-wrongs" and the belittling. Standing in every election would be two candidates presumed to be good people whose aspirations are to serve the public interest, who admittedly are seeking power because there are things they would like to get done, and who simply disagree on how to do them.

> That is a wonderful picture you paint. That is the picture of a transformed world.

But no major political party leader could ever say that. No major religious leader could ever declare it. Their whole message, their very *credibility,* is based upon just the opposite premise. *The whole structure of humanity is built upon the idea of separation and betterness.*

> That is the situation in your world, precisely. That is the point being made in this conversation.

> There are many humans who cannot abide the thought of living with such new ideas, and so they die instead, clinging to the Fifth Fallacy About Life as their truth. They declare:

> *It is appropriate for human beings to resolve severe differences created by all their other fallacies by killing each other.*

20

My God, *why are we so stubborn?* What will it take for us to alter our beliefs, to mend our ways, to change our minds? How much more death and destruction do we have to bear before we say *"enough"?*

> You've said "enough" a long time ago; you simply don't know how to stop what you are doing even after you've all had enough.

Is there any way that we *can?* There does not seem to be a way.

> Oh, there is a way. There most definitely is a way. And I've already given it to you.

Give it to me again.

> You can stop the death and destruction *if you will give up your false beliefs* and the mental constructions that you have built up around them.

Okay, we've taken a very close look at our false beliefs—these are what you call the Five Fallacies About God and the Five Fallacies About Life, yes?

Yes. These are the major false beliefs of humans.

Okay, we've taken a very close look at those. Now what do you mean by "mental constructions" that we have "built up around them"?

You have stitched together in your world a complex interweaving of spiritual, philosophical, political, and economic concepts that pretty much govern your collective experience. These concepts arise from certain mental constructions that you have formed on the basis of your false beliefs, and those mental constructions—ideas about "how things are" that you have literally built up in your mind—produce, in your outer experience, certain human social conventions. These conventions are ways of doing things, collections of behaviors, that create a framework into which you pour your lives.

Many of you consider the mental constructions that have produced these social conventions to be the most important and worthy in your entire human value system—when, actually, they can be among the most detrimental.

They are often what *stop* you from doing something as simple as living together in peace and harmony and happiness.

What *are* these mental constructions? Can you name them?

There are many of them, and they are all temporary. They evaporate as soon as you alter your beliefs,
because they are *based* on your beliefs.

Still, you must keep in mind that in cosmic terms,
"temporary" means anything from five minutes to
hundreds or thousands of years. If something lasts "only"
2,000 years, it is barely a blip on the radar screen of
Eternal Life. Yet in human terms, this can *be* an eternity.

However long it takes—and for some human beliefs
it takes a *very* long time—as soon as your beliefs
change, so do the mental constructions that support
your life.

Once, you believed that the world was flat. Then you
came to understand that it is round, and all of the mental constructions that supported your life changed
around that.

Once, you believed that the sun and the entire solar
system revolved around the earth. You said that your
planet was the center of the universe. Entire theologies
were created around this belief.

When Copernicus offered proof that this assertion
was false, he was denounced as a blasphemer by the
creators and teachers of those theologies. And when
Galileo later confirmed Copernicus's findings, he, too,
was labeled by the church as a heretic, and was forced
to recant, renouncing his own findings.

It was not until late in the 20th Century—*300 years
later*—that the Most Holy Roman Catholic Church

reversed its position and granted Galileo an official pardon.

And so we see how the changing of your most basic beliefs remains your most difficult challenge—for humans hang onto their beliefs even in the face of clear and incontrovertible evidence that those beliefs are mistaken.

Thus has it been said, "All great truth begins as blasphemy."

The "blasphemy" spoken here, in this dialogue, is multifold. This conversation is a Multifold Blasphemy.

The first blasphemy is that God would speak to humans at all in this day and age.

The second blasphemy is that God demands nothing of humans.

The third blasphemy is that God and humans are One.

The fourth and greatest blasphemy—the statement that will be the hardest for humans to accept—is that many of the most sacred beliefs of human beings are fallacies. They are simply false.

False beliefs create mental constructions that do not serve you.

Such as?

Such as this human convention we talked of earlier, called "morality."

This is one of your more prominent mental constructions. It is an idea created in the mind. You cannot

feel it, taste it, touch it, smell it, or hear it. It is a concept, nothing more. And it is a concept built up around
beliefs that are false.

What are you saying, that there should be no morals?

I am not saying what there "should" or "should not"
be. That is for you to decide. I am saying that this and
other mental constructions are based on false beliefs
about Life and how it is, and that, because of this, you
have produced certain social conventions that have
made it virtually impossible for you to be able to live
together in peace and harmony and joy.

The philosopher and social commentator Bertrand Russell once
said, "It is not only intellectually but also morally that religion is
pernicious. I mean by this that it teaches ethical codes which are
not conducive to human happiness."

Yet, the "mental construction" that we call "morality" is the
underpinning of our entire way of life.

That's right. That's my entire point. And that's why
I've brought it up again here. That's why I chose it as an
example.

But if our "mental constructions" are based on "false beliefs,"
and if "morality" is one of those "constructions," what are you
saying — *that our entire way of life is wrong?*

I am saying that much of your way of life *is not working.* If what you say you want is to live together in
peace and harmony and happiness, it is not working.

Many say that it *would* be working if people would just *adhere to* this "mental construction" called "morality"! They say that what *stops* us from living together peacefully is that people and nations do not *honor* this construction. They say that it's not the philosophical *construction* that is at fault, it's people's *behavior.*

> And yet, many of their most damaging behaviors are based on this construction.
>
> By human measurements and human standards, you would say that many people act their worst when they think they are acting their best.

Ouch. That's tough to hear.

> I have no judgment about these behaviors (or anything else that humans do), but if humans say that what they seek and desire is to live in peace and harmony, they may notice that they often do things when they say they are acting their best that do not lead to peace and harmony.

Can you give me an example?

> I can give you hundreds of them.
>
> How about a father kicking out his unwed pregnant daughter? Or rebuking his son because he married outside the faith or outside the race? Or a family disowning a child for being gay?
>
> How about a 23-year-old woman strapping a bomb to her body and walking into a crowd in Jerusalem to set it off?

How about a nation occupying the land of another people for decades and keeping those people economically, politically, and militarily subjugated, refusing to grant them even the most basic human rights, and then becoming angry when they become angry, doing desperate things when they do desperate things, and being utterly and totally blind to the role that it is, itself, playing in creating an ongoing human tragedy?

People do things like this because they are making moral judgments.

Yes, I see that now.

This twisting of everything that to you seems "right" occurs because your construction of "morality" itself is based on the fallacies we've discussed earlier.

People think they are doing "right," based on what they believe that "God wants" or that "Life requires"— yet their information on that is inaccurate.

And that is why, often, it is not when people *ignore* morality that difficulties arise, but when people *pay too much attention to it.*

Boy, this is really something. We've got God here, telling us that we get into trouble when we *pay attention to morals.*

If you pay *too much* attention to them, yes. If you put too much credence in them, yes.

And that can happen.

In fact, it often does.

Your "morals" are merely mental constructions—

your current "ideas" about things. If these ideas change
from time to time...

That's the problem. That's the problem *right there.* It's the problem
that our social commentators call *shifting morals.*

Wouldn't it be interesting if those social commentators had the problem all backward?

Look at the world today. The problems you've experienced in the past several years have not been created
because of morals shifting, but because of morals *not*
shifting—sometimes for thousands of years.

Let me say again that morals are nothing more than
ideas about *how things are* and *how they should be* based
on what you believe about God and about Life. They
are *ideas*—nothing more and nothing less. And they
are *your* ideas, not God's ideas.

Human beings tied Matthew Shepard to a cow fence
in Wyoming and beat him to a pulp, leaving him there
to die, not because of God's ideas, but because of the
ideas of human beings. Because of morals that have *not*
been shifting.

Human beings have ruthlessly discriminated against
women, blacks, and other people who are minorities
in their midst not because of God's ideas, but because
of the ideas of human beings. Because of morals that
have *not* been shifting.

Human beings have strapped people into electrically
wired chairs and turned on the current, killing them in
the most inhumane way, in order to teach others that

killing is bad, not because of God's ideas, but because
of the ideas of human beings. Because of morals that
have *not* been shifting.

And human beings have created an environment on
their planet in which all of this is even *possible* not
because of God's ideas, but because of the ideas of
human beings. Because of morals that have *not* been
shifting.

Your mental constructions, based on false and *ancient*
beliefs about God and about Life, have produced wildly
dysfunctional social conventions—behaviors that you
call "conventional," based on "conventional wisdom."

Of course, human beings have not developed these
kinds of mental constructions to be "mean." All of your
mental constructions are sincere attempts of the mind
to articulate and express underlying principles that
support life. Yet, when you pay more attention to your
mental constructions than to the underlying principles
they seek to express, you can indeed "get into trouble."

What do you mean by "underlying principles"? This is a new
concept being introduced here. What are we talking about?

There is a set of Basic Life Principles that lies behind
All Of Existence, and you *know it,* you *remember it* at a
cellular level, you recall it from some Time Before Time,
when you were not experiencing yourself as who you
imagine yourself to be right now.

Still, you have not been able to get close to the core,
to pull out the essence, of these principles, no matter

how hard you've tried. The false beliefs that you hold about God and Life are clouding them over, covering them up, hiding them from your view, and stopping you from knowing them. This is the cloud of unknowing. It conceals the truth from you.

It is not that humans do not want to live according to life's truest principles, it is simply that it is impossible for humans to do so when these basic principles are so clouded over by their beliefs that humans cannot even know what the principles are.

In short, human beings are trying to live the truth through beliefs that are false. In this, they have set themselves an impossible task. And that is why so much of life on your planet is not working.

Now please let me acknowledge here that some of your life on Earth *is* working. You have grown and evolved and become a grander version of humanity. You have learned from some of your mistakes, you have progressed in some ways, and you have become in some ways a magnificent species. And, as I said earlier, you have done this against all odds.

That is why it seems such a shame to see you making collective choices at this point in your development that could so drastically and negatively impact the life of your species as you know it—if not completely end it.

Those humans who understand deeply what is now going on see that the saddest part of all this is that so much could improve so quickly with a few simple changes in the things you choose to believe.

Well, then, let's make that happen right now! Let's turn the tide right here!

> That's exactly the purpose of this dialogue. That's why we're here, having this discussion. That's the purpose of these New Revelations.

Okay, so reveal more. You talked about "life principles" that you said human beings are seeking to articulate through our mental constructions. What are these principles?

> The Basic Principles of Life are:
> Functionality.
> Adaptability.
> Sustainability.
> All of Life exhibits these principles. All of life demonstrates them.
> One of these eternal principles stands behind each of your temporary mental constructions, waiting to be revealed. Yet they are covered and hidden by these mental constructions, for they, in turn, are based on false thoughts about life.
> Because your mental constructions are distorted attempts to express underlying Life Principles, they produce distorted results.
> For instance, here are three of your species' most popular mental constructions—the first one I've already mentioned. These are simple ideas you hold in your head that you have translated into social conventions, customs, and practices:
> Morality.

Justice.

Ownership.

These are among your most cherished philosophical, political, and economic concepts.

What are the Life Principles they seek to express?

In the case of "morality," the underlying principle is
Functionality.

In the case of "justice," the underlying principle is
Adaptability.

In the case of "ownership," it is Sustainability.

Well, I certainly don't understand this. Functionality, adaptability, sustainability... whatever. "Morality," "justice," and "ownership" make more sense to me. We've built our whole lives
around them. How could we live without them?

The idea is not to live without them, but to *elevate*
them, to lift them up to the next level of articulation
and expression, to move from *concept* to *principle* in
the living of your lives.

This is about raising consciousness, or becoming more
fully aware of all that is involved in the process of life
expressing.

For many people, this may not be easy, given the
human penchant for keeping beliefs as they are, no matter how unworkable they have become (or always were).

There is, however, a fast track that you may take, a
way to do this more quickly.

What's that?

The Five Steps to Peace. This produces not just peace in the world, but peace in your inner world.

That is the peace we are talking about here. Inner peace, as well as outer peace.

Most human beings have not had much inner *or* outer peace lately. Neither the state of your world nor your state of mind has allowed it.

Yet now you can take the Five Steps to Peace and raise your consciousness, moving from concept to principle in considering, exploring, and deeply understanding life.

Should you wish to take this fast track, here, again, is what you must do. Here, again, are the Five Steps to Peace:

1. Acknowledge that some of your old beliefs about God and about Life are no longer working.
2. Acknowledge that there is something you do not understand about God and about Life, the understanding of which could change everything.
3. Be willing for a new understanding of God and Life to now be brought forth, an understanding that could produce a new way of life on your planet.
4. Be courageous enough to explore and examine this new understanding, and, if it aligns with your inner truth and knowing, to enlarge your belief system to include it.
5. Live your lives as demonstrations of your beliefs, rather than as denials of them.

You keep saying some things over and over again.

Repetition can be very useful.

It can also be annoying, and cause people to grow impatient.

The serious student never becomes impatient at the repetitions of the master.

Those who live fully never become impatient at the repetitions of life.

Life itself is a repetition. It is impossible for anything new to occur. It is only possible to have new experiences of that which has occurred many times before.

God is a Repetition. Life is God, repeating Itself.

Acquire a taste for repetition. When you do, you acquire a love of God, and of life.

You will know this this Spring, when you once again see the flowers bloom. This Summer, when you once again bask in the sun. This Fall, when you once again smell the freshness in the air. This Winter, when you once again stand in wonder of new-fallen snow.

You will know it when you smile at the sound of a favorite melody that you have heard over and over again, yet of which you never tire. Or when you next move into love's fond embrace, of which you cannot get enough.

These things you have done over and over again, and you love the repetition.

That is not exactly the same thing.

No. These experiences, wonderful as they are, are trivial compared to the repetitions involved in explorations of eternal truth.

Tire not of seeking the truth, nor of finding it.

You have asked for my help at a time of great challenge for the human race. The things being said here have been said over and over, in many ways, across the span of human history. That form of repetition has not produced a change in basic human behavior. You are invited, here, to try a new form of repetition. Perhaps the hearing of the same thing over and over again in a very short span of time will impact human behavior.

It is all up to you.

Do you truly wish your world to change?

Yes.

Then I am going to make some points very clear here—through repetition. Circular logic gains its power from the circle it creates. To travel a circle is to journey over the same ground time and time again. To travel a circle wisely is to journey over the same ground for the first time. In this way, the ordinary becomes extraordinary, and the circle, a path to where you wish to be. And when you notice at last that the path has circled back into itself, you realize that where you wish to be is where you have already been...and always were.

21

I have never—and now *I'm* repeating *myself*—*never* heard so many of life's common experiences explained with such uncommon insight. My God, you make everything so clear, so simple, and so obvious. *Thank you.* And go ahead, repeat yourself all you want. I get, now, that this is perfect.

> You *can* change your world, and the fastest way to do that will be to step away from your fallacies and embrace a new revelation and a new spirituality. This would be the most courageous thing that human beings have done for centuries. It could change human history.

I'm for that! So, let's get back to our discussion of mental constructions that produce social conventions that distort basic life principles. You said that "morality" is one of those mental constructions, and that we can actually be led astray by it.

> Not only *can* you, you *have* been.

Fair enough. So how do we live a life without morals? And how does the "mental construction" called "justice" relate to the life principle called "adapability," or our concept of "ownership" relate to the life principle called "sustainability"?

Help me to see the relationship between a humanly re-created mental construction, a social convention, and a life principle. And what makes the last better than the first?

The last is not "better" than the first in terms of being morally superior. It is simply more functional. Basic Life Principles *work*. Many of humanity's mental constructions and its social conventions *do not*. It is as simple as that.

Many of humanity's ideas and behaviors are not functional. They are dysfunctional.

Have you not noticed, for instance, that most human relationships are dysfunctional? They do not work the way they were intended to work. They break down. They fall apart.

This is because humans have abandoned Basic Life Principles in favor of their own personal mental constructions and the social conventions that emerge from them.

Now if the beliefs upon which your mental concepts are based were accurate, your social conventions— that is, your collective behaviors—would be as workable as the Basic Life Principles are. Yet your beliefs are not accurate, but are full of fallacies.

We've already looked at your most damaging false

beliefs. Now let's see how they produce social conventions that play their effect in your life in a negative
way.

Great! I've been waiting to get to this. I really want to understand this more deeply.

We can't look at all of your social conventions,
because this dialogue would never end, but we can
take one very good example, giving you a chance to
see how...
False Beliefs create Social Conventions producing
Societal Dysfunctions threatening Species Survival.
Species survival is what we have been talking about
here, of course. That is what we have been discussing
from the beginning.

I know. I'm aware of that. We've got to get our act together
here; we've got to come to some new levels of awareness, if our
species is going to survive.

Because of the way humans are behaving, yes.
Because of how far you've advanced in your ability to
destroy each other, but failed to advance in your ability to get along with each other, yes. That is what is
creating the crisis.
So let's go back to the first word on our list of examples of humanly created conventions: Morality. That's a
good one because it's cross-cultural. It touches just
about every society on earth.

Our "morality" has almost destroyed every society on earth as well.

That is an accurate observation.

So what is the false belief that created the mental concept that we call morality, and the social conventions that emerge from it?

Your belief that God needs something—namely, that you behave in a certain way—is the fallacy from which your "morality" has emerged.

Okay, good, I get that. But even if God does *not* have ways in which He wants us to behave, what's wrong with having "morals"? They help us to live our lives.

The problem with "morals" is that they have to be based on some Supreme or Final Value. Morals without moral authority, like currencies without a gold standard or any other thing of value behind them, are worthless.

Agreed. Morals have to have some authority behind them.

And in the earliest days, as societies were beginning to form themselves, as differing human cultures were emerging, what was the authority behind their morals?

Well, I suppose, their idea of what is "right."

And from where do you suppose they ultimately got those ideas?

From God?

Exactly. At least, that's where they *said* they got them. Please let me clarify again how this occurred.

Most early civilizations mixed what today would be called religion and politics thoroughly, citing godly codes to support earthly rules.

Primitive cultures turned to "the gods" for all that they wished to call forth—not just rain or a good harvest, but also the authority to lay down behavioral rules, or what you would today call "morals."

Later cultures did the same. Most civil laws began as religious codes, given to the people through one "revelation" or another. Whether the humans who grouped around them believed in a plurality of gods or in a single, omnipotent God, their earliest ideas of "right" and "wrong" came from their understanding of what their Deity wanted and needed.

And, oh, what a difference it would have made had they decided *that their Deity needed nothing.*

Alas, this is not what they decided. And so, many sets of rules governing day-to-day life were said to have been "handed down" directly to Man by God. One collection of these was actually described as God's *commandments.*

Your conception of the needs and desires of some power greater than your own, with wisdom deeper than your own, and with an authority far surpassing your own, is what lies behind virtually every set of moral imperatives or behavioral standards that earthly society has devised.

That includes societies that do not now profess a belief in God at all, declaring that such a belief is erroneous or superstitious and nothing more than "the opiate of the people."

Even these societies have merely usurped the earlier teachings of their own ancestors with regard to "right" and "wrong"—which earlier teachings were rooted absolutely in some form of idol worship and attachment to "the will of the gods."

Ever it has been so, for it is natural for humans to experience themselves as part of a larger whole, and to know deeply that that is a thing called God. Atheism is a learned reaction; Deism is a natural response, an intuitive "knowing," a deep-seated awareness at the cellular level.

Yet what humans "know" about God in their cells and what they "believe" about God in their minds are often two entirely different things.

Today there are millions of people (not a few, but *millions*) who continue to believe that God has set down a whole system of laws for human beings to follow, and these people declare that God's Law should govern, guide, and control all behavior of civil society. There are entire countries in which people accept God's Law as Civil Law, ruling every aspect of their daily lives.

Well, we could do worse, I suppose. I mean, what's so bad about that?

Nothing, so long as what you imagine to be "God's Law" is fair.

If it's God's Law, how can it *not* be fair?

If that law said that no individual has the right to think or decide for himself, but has to accept God's Law as interpreted by learned teachers, would that be fair?

Uh . . . it doesn't sound fair, but I guess it would depend upon what those teachers said that God's Law was. It would depend on how they interpreted that.

If the learned teachers said that, according to God's Law, a woman's testimony at court is worth half that of a man's, would that be fair?

Oh, yes, you mentioned that earlier. And no, of course that would not be fair.

What if the learned teachers said that, according to God's Law, a woman is not free to marry whom she wishes, and her rights of divorce are not equal to that of a man, would that be fair?

No.

If the learned teachers said that, according to God's Law, a person of the "wrong faith" cannot testify at all in a case brought against a person of the "right" faith, would that be fair?

Of course not. Don't be silly.

> If the learned teachers said that, according to God's
> Law, a male child's inheritance shall be equal to that of
> two female children, would that be fair?
> What if the teachers said that blasphemy toward
> God or God's prophet is punishable by death—and
> made matters worse by not making it clear exactly what
> "blasphemy" was? Would that be fair?

No. No, it would not. And I get the point. The point is that
millions of people are governed by such "civil" laws in Muslim
countries where the *Sharia* is used in place of legislation, or where
the civil laws that do exist are based on it.

As I understand it, the *Sharia* is a combination of the words of
the Qur'an, the teachings in the *Hadith* (a collection of oral
reports, ultimately placed in writing, about Muhammad and how
he lived), and what is known as *ijma* (the consensus of Islamic
teachers, doctors of law, and scholars as to how to interpret the
first two). Is this correct?

> Your understanding is basic, but not inaccurate.

And those religious "laws" that you just mentioned here—they
are all part of the *Sharia?*

> Yes.

I have a hard time believing that God would be so unfair, so
patently unfair. Are you certain that the people who have quoted
you have gotten all this right? That stuff about male superiority,
for instance. That is Divine Law?

> Could you ever doubt it?

Is this just the opinion of Islamic scholars, or is there actual Scripture that backs up this teaching?

> Oh, the Qur'an is very clear on this.

Give me one example.

> Sūrah 4:11:
> "Allah thus directs you as regards your children's inheritance: to the male a portion equal to that of two females. Of two females, if only daughters, two or more, their share is two-thirds of the inheritance; if only one, her share is a half."

Wow. Right there in Holy Scripture.

But really, you don't expect me to accept this, do you, or to believe that this is Your Holy Word? Most people in this day and age would reject a God who said stuff like this.

> Then they will be punished with everlasting damnation.

Naw. Not for simply dividing your inheritance among your children equally, and rejecting a God who says not to do so.

> Read Sūrah 35:36:
> "But those who reject (Allah)—for them will be the Fire of Hell...thus do We reward every ungrateful one!
> "And the fire will neither consume them wholly, that they should die, nor will its torment be lessened for them. And they will cry for help, 'Oh, Lord, let us

out, that we may do what is right!' But I will not do so! Never! I will say to them, 'Did you not live long enough to think on these things? And did I not send one to warn you? So now, taste the punishment!' The iniquitous will have none to help them."

This is what you would say? This is what the God of mercy would say if the soul realizes its mistake and begs for another chance?

The God of mercy shows no mercy to those who do not believe. So your Scriptures say.

And when you have cultures and entire societies basing their laws on such scriptures, they, *too*, like God, are *allowed to show no mercy, and to act in horrible ways with impunity.*

Human societies create "morals" out of such "instructions from God."

Well, perhaps in some cultures, but not in the United States. We pride ourselves on separation of church and state. We don't claim, as some other countries and cultures do, that God is the authority behind our morality and our laws.

Really?

The Pledge of Allegiance to your flag does not describe your country as "one nation, under God..."?

You have not read "in God we trust" on your coins?

The artwork on the back of your dollar bill has nothing to do with God?

You do not swear an oath by placing your hand on a Bible and saying "So help me, God"?

You do not open sessions of your Congress with a prayer—after which you pass laws safeguarding prayer in schools? Read the words of the third stanza of your national anthem.

I see what you mean.

Whether governments want to admit it or not (and more and more governments are now coming right out and saying it), it is the religious views of the majority of the people in a society that consciously or unconsciously form the foundation of all laws and all local moral codes.

In order to give your system of morals any authority, millions of you have relied on what you assume to be God's Law.

Many people would say, "It's not what we *assume* to be God's Law, it's what we *know* to be God's Law. That law is very clear, and it has been laid down for us."

What if one doesn't believe there *is* a God?

That person must still obey civil laws. Yet I really see what you mean. Most of our civil laws are, in fact, based on the moral authority that we derive from the "best idea" we have of what God wants. And, as you point out, in some countries there isn't even any attempt to dance around this. They come right out and *say* that the civil laws *are* the laws of God, as contained in Scripture.

And if your laws and morals are ultimately based on
some interpretation of God's Will, then God's Law as
contained in whatever the locally accepted Scripture is
becomes the "gold standard."

That's right.

So your *source* for God's Law had better be accurate.

That's not a problem, because God gave the Torah directly to
Moses. The New Testament is also correct down to the last word.
The Qur'an is likewise perfect. The Bhagavad-Gita is magnificent.
The guiding principles of the Book of Mormon were delivered
directly by God to Joseph Smith through the Angel Moroni. The
Pali Canon contains breathtaking wisdom. And so on, and so on.

These *are* the "gold standards of morality" in the cultures in which
they are prominent, and they are considered by many of their
adherents to be completely and literally accurate.

So let's look at some of God's Laws.

Not again.

Wait. There are many that we haven't even touched
on yet.

Is this necessary? All you're going to do is quote again, from
one of humanity's scriptures, some text that is no longer applicable to modern society.

Are you willing to concede that many of the words
of many of your holy books were *never* applicable in
any civilized society?

Yes, I'm willing to concede that. Some of God's Laws as contained in various Holy Scriptures probably never made sense.

> Like the "Word of God" that says that if a man has a stubborn son who refuses to obey and is a drunkard, his parents shall take him to the gate and all the men of the town shall stone him until he dies?
> Like that one?

Yes, yes, like that one.

> Like the one that says you shall not cut the hair on your head, neither shall you trim the corners of your beard?

Yes, yes, that one, too.

> And many others?

And many others, yes.

> Like the Law of God that says that anyone who touches a dead body is unclean for seven days, or that if you are a priest you may buy a slave, or that no work of any kind may be done on the Sabbath, or that your impoverished brother may be bought and forced to become your hired servant, or that after engaging in sex, both partners are unclean? Or that witches and wizards are to be put to death?
> Now it may seem to you as though these are just a few scriptures that do not make sense by human standards today, but the truth is, the list of God's rules that

most of you would say makes no sense to any reasonable person is so long that it could make up an entire
book.

In fact, it does.

I have brought these many examples into this conversation—and I will bring in still others later as well—
so that you might understand a larger point:

*You have based your moral authority on Sacred Laws that
you apply on a take-it-or-leave-it basis, depending upon how
you feel about them at a particular moment, in a particular culture, under particular circumstances.*

If you are saying that we disregard the words in our Holy Books
when we clearly see they no longer apply to our lives, I concede
the point.

In other words...

Your morality has *no standard at all* except *what works
and what doesn't work.*

That is the truth, and everything else is a fiction.

Even you agree, as demonstrated not by what you
say, but by your *behaviors,* that the Word of God as
recorded in your many Holy Scriptures is not to be
followed to the letter because it is not infallible.

Clearly it is not, because in all of those books, it has been put
down by humans. Yet if the "gold standard" on which we base
our morality in our various cultures is not infallible, then what?

Then you are basing your morality on spiritual laws
that, when taken as a whole, make no sense. They con-

tradict themselves *within* a particular Scripture, and they contradict themselves from one Scripture to the next. Thus, the human race has been given laws from which you must pick and choose in order to render them sane.

You do not want to admit that you are doing this, of course, because then you would fall prey to the charge of *relativism,* a very dirty word in your vocabulary. You want to be an *absolutist.* You want to believe and to assert that there is *absolutely* a "Right" and a "Wrong." Yet, in the end, YOU have to decide what that is. You cannot rely on your laws, and you cannot even rely on your God.

You *have* to decide for yourself, because the words of both your laws and of your God have been shown to be foolish when swallowed whole, when applied indiscriminately, when adhered to absolutely, literally, and without flexibility in every case and circumstance. They can't function in that way. Nothing can function that way.

Many of your religious laws, by your own admission, should simply be ignored. They could hardly be the source of your entire society's true moral underpinnings.

Therefore, by your own actions, you have proven that: "morals" = "functionality."

The underlying Basic Life Principle is revealed. That is the point that you have been trying to make.

Yes, and your species has already determined this, by the way. You have already decided on your planet that what is "right" is *what works,* depending upon what it is you are trying to be, do, or have. *You simply are not willing to admit this.*

To make matters more complicated, you have not been able to come to an agreement on what it is that you are trying to be, do, and have as the collective called humanity.

And these are the impediments—the second chief among them—to peace and harmony on Earth.

22

So in this New Spirituality that you keep talking about, we're to forget all about morals, is that it?

"Morals" are a dangerous thing, precisely because they change from time to time across history, and from culture to culture across the planet.

The reason that they change is that they are based on beliefs that are fallacious, and what many people do when they discover that certain moral instructions don't work in real life is *change their morals without changing the beliefs from which they emerged.*

People adamantly refuse to change their most basic beliefs, but they change their morals (that is, how they *apply* their beliefs) at the drop of a hat, to suit the situation.

For example, most people hold a basic belief that

God wants them to be honest. They then cheat on their taxes—*and say it's okay.*

"Everybody does it. It's expected."

They've refused to change their basic belief, but they've changed their morals (that is, how they *apply* their belief) at the drop of a hat, to suit the situation.

Yet if they change their *morals,* they *have* changed their beliefs, for morals are simply beliefs expressed. Therefore, they are hypocrites. They do not have beliefs at all. They simply *want to believe that they have beliefs.*

This makes them feel good, but it also makes the world crazy.

I think I see the same thing that you do, all over the place.

Of course you do. You'd have to be blind not to see it.

So you *are* saying that we should just throw out all morals.

You keep wanting to generalize, to come up with a thirty-second "sound bite," but that is not what I am saying.

What I am saying is that humans have created a social construction called "morals." I am explaining how your morals shift, even though you say they don't. I am observing that you won't acknowledge this, and so you become righteous.

It is your righteousness that is killing you.

You insist on labeling all errors of functionality matters of moral decay. This creates judgment, and judgment creates justification. By your judgments about whether a person or nation has behaved morally, you justify your response.

You call this response your "moral obligation." You claim that you are morally compelled to act in a certain way.

Your death penalty is a perfect example. You claim the moral code (or God's Law) of an eye for an eye and a tooth for a tooth is justification for this punishment. It is not even about rendering society safe, because life imprisonment would accomplish that. No, it is a simple matter of evening the score, plain and clear.

Yes. We try to soften this edge by calling it justice, but there is a saying, "If it looks like a duck, walks like a duck, and quacks like a duck, it's probably a duck." In this case it's a duck named Revenge.

But what if morals—which are moveable feasts in any event—were not part of the equation? What if the only question was *functionality*—whether a particular action or reaction worked or did not work, based on what it is you were trying to be, do, or have?

Now you have an entirely different context within which to consider your response. Now you're looking at things in an entirely different way. Now you are "outside the box"—the box in which you have trapped yourselves as a species in a never-ending cycle of violence, destruction, and death.

So, to use the example above, does the death penalty do what you want it to do? Does it have *functionality*?

If the purpose of the penalty is to even the score, it does. Yet if the purpose of the penalty is to deter other crimes, it does not. Statistics clearly show that the states and nations using the death penalty the most have no lower crime rates than those using it the least.

What is that about? If the death penalty deters violent crime, why don't the rates go down and stay down?

> Could it be that a society that practices violence in order to end violence has something a bit backward?
>
> That is the problem with many "moral" justifications. They can breed insane behaviors. Your planet saw evidence of that on September 11, 2001.
>
> Again.

Yet, if we don't rely on "morals" to tell us what is right and wrong — what to do and what not to do — on what do we rely?

> Functionality.

There's that word again. I was wondering if we were going to get back to a deeper exploration of those Basic Principles of Life.

> Yes, we will, starting with this one. So let's bring the discussion down to a level at which "functionality," the principle, can be more easily understood as it relates to "morality," the mental construct.
>
> Supposing you are driving westward in the United States, heading toward the Pacific Ocean, and you wish to go to Seattle. It would do you no good to turn south to San Jose. If you did so, you would be said to be going the "wrong" direction. Yet that label would be

misleading if you equated the label "wrong" with the word "immoral."

There is nothing immoral about going to San Jose. It simply is not where you intend to go. It is not what you wish to do. It is not what you chose as your destination.

Trying to get to Seattle by driving south to San Jose is a lapse of *functionality*, not a lapse of *morality*.

A thought, word, or deed either works or does not work, given what it is that you are trying to be, do, or have. If it works, it is called "correct," or "right." If it does not work, it is called "incorrect," or "wrong."

When it is called "wrong" it has nothing to do with a breakdown in morality, nor with the thwarting of "God's will." It is *your* will that has been thwarted. You didn't get to be, do, or have what you wanted to be, do, or have.

Your society might do well not to place moral judgments on alternative choices or actions. In highly evolved societies, it is simply noticed whether choices and actions "work" or "do not work" in producing the result or outcome that is collectively desired.

In your own life, by taking the "moral value" out of your choices, you remove the "moral authority" from them. (They never had moral authority anyway. You have been making this all up.)

Your earthly societies would then no longer find it possible to invoke the Word of God, or Divine Law, or *Sharia,* or any other version of what is purported to be

a spiritual mandate, in order to justify enforcing codes
of behavior or personal restrictions on everything from
diet to dress to decorum.

But that would lead to anarchy! Everybody doing whatever they
wanted, based on their "desire"—in other words, a "what works"
and "what does not work" world—would produce nothing but
chaos.

Much would depend on what it was you all agreed,
as a world society, that you were trying to be, do, or
have. What are you seeking to experience?

If you are seeking to experience a world of peace
and harmony and cooperation, then "what works" and
"what does not work" would be measured against that.
Currently, you are not using this measurement, or you
would never do the things you are doing in your world.

I think it is worse than that. I think that we *are* seeking to create a world of peace and harmony and cooperation, but that we
are unwilling to look at, unwilling to notice, and *unwilling to give
up,* all the things that are not working. They allow us to experience too much *other* stuff that we enjoy—such as power, self-
indulgence, etc.

Which means that you are *not* seeking to experience
peace, harmony, and cooperation. You are seeking to
experience power and self-indulgence. You are saying
one thing and doing another.

When what you *really* want is peace, harmony, and
cooperation, you will witness what you are now doing,

> assess very clearly that it is not working to bring you
> the experience you seek, then choose behaviors that
> *do* work.

I still wonder whether a world of "what works" and "what does not work" could produce anything but chaos.

> As opposed to the peace and tranquility produced
> by your current "right" and "wrong" world?

Okay, but at least we *know* when somebody has done something wrong, and we can do something about it.

> Such as punishing them and demonstrating that two
> "wrongs" make a "right"?

It is not "wrong" to punish someone!

> That is accurate. It is not "wrong" to punish some-
> one. "Right" and "wrong" do not exist. There are no
> such rigid standards in the Universe. A thing is only
> "right" or "wrong" depending upon *whether it works* or
> *does not work* in producing an outcome you wish to
> produce.
> So we get to ask again, what is it you wish to produce
> by punishing someone? An experience of "payback"?
> Of revenge? Of safety, by removing a threat?

Probably all of those things. If we were to be honest, we'd probably have to say it's a little bit of all of those things. But most of all it's something that you haven't mentioned.

> What's that?

Justice.

I would say we are seeking to experience Justice. Punishment is part of our justice system.

> Hmmm...another one of your interesting human constructions. And what, exactly, is "justice," as you understand it?

It's a system by which society makes sure that what is "just" is what occurs. Our dictionary defines justice as "the impartial adjustment of conflicting claims or the merited assignment of rewards or punishments."

> Wait a minute, did you say "adjustment"?

Yes. That's what the dictionary says.

> Fascinating. That's very close to the Basic Life Principle that I said your mental construction called "justice" was related to.

Oh, yeah. Looking back at the list, I see that now. You said that justice was our distorted attempt to express the Basic Life Principle called Adaptability.

> Yes, and adaptability is just another word for adjustment.
>
> Life always expresses the principle of Adaptability. Life is, first of all, functional. That is a basic quality of life. It *functions*. And it functions in a particular way that allows it to keep *on* functioning.
>
> When functionality is threatened in any way, life

finds a way to adapt, or adjust, in order to *keep on functioning.*

This principle of adaptability is what is called, in evolutionary theory, selectivity. Life selects, through the process of life itself, the aspects or functions of all living things that allow that living thing to continue living. By this means, a species evolves. And when it does, a third Basic Principle of Life is expressed: Sustainability. Life becomes sustainable by adapting its functionality.

All life everywhere expresses these three principles, and the principles are circular, allowing life itself to continue eternally. Life, and everything in life, is functional, or, if it can no longer function in a particular way or mode, it adapts, adjusting whatever it needs to adjust in order to become sustainable. Sustainability creates a circling back to its being functional again, and on through the cycle, over and over again and again, forever and even forever more.

Using what you call your "justice system," your society seeks to express the principle of adaptability, fairly adjusting conflicting claims, and appropriately assigning rewards and punishments.

Well, it tries to.

What does that mean? Does it do it or not?

Most of the time. We like to think that it does this most of the time.

Most of the time?

The truth is, your "justice system" has so many flaws in it—not the least of which is its vulnerability to influence by the rich and powerful and its complete inaccessibility to the poor, the weak, and the downtrodden—that any resemblance between what occurs in your societies and what you dream of as "justice" is far too often purely coincidental.

And, I ask you, where is the "justice" in that?

As true as that may be, it is not an argument for not even *seeking* justice. Listen, we can't just ignore wrongdoing. We have to "set to right" that which is "wrong."

Why not seek to make "work" that which "does not work"?

When you seek to "right a wrong," you imagine that punishment is required as part of the process. That is because you see the "wrong" that was done as a moral failure rather than a functional nonviability.

When, on the other hand, you seek not to punish, but simply to make something work that does not work, you merely put in a correction. You change course. You find a new way. You alter your thoughts, words, or deeds. You *make an adjustment.*

This is "a justment."

So we see that "justice" is really "a justment." It is the system called life adapting itself in order to go on in a way that works.

In highly evolved societies, all of this is understood perfectly. The behavior adjustment is put in, and while consequences are part of that process (it is through the consequences that are experienced that behavior adaptation becomes desirable), punishment is not.

You are amazing, you know that? That is not something that I would ever have come to. My own reasoning would never have taken me there.

I am happy that you are open to getting there, by whatever means. Clarity is the place to which you are going. You are moving to a state called Clear. Once you are clear about these things, you can never live in confusion again.

It is from this state of confusion that you have wished to remove yourself. That is the purpose of this dialogue, and of your having come here. That is true for everyone who is reading this. For the moment is at hand when all the world calls upon all the people to look at all things in a new way.

Yet *how do we do that?*

See the truth. Admit the truth. Do not be self-righteous. Notice that what you are doing is evolving, *adapting,* and of course you are "changing the rules" as you go along. Not to do so would be silly. You can't live today's life by yesterday's rules. You couldn't even live *yesterday's* life by yesterday's rules.

If what you choose is to live in peace and harmony, then *what the world needs now is a new set of rules.*

That is the point I am making here. It is the point of this entire dialogue.

Functionality has all but disappeared from the human life experience. Your species cannot go on as it has been going much longer. You are going to have to express the Basic Life Principle of Adaptability very soon now if you want Life to sustain itself in its present form.

Can we talk about that third life principle for just a bit? How does Sustainability have anything to do with "ownership"? You said that "ownership" was a human mental construction, and that it was a distorted attempt to express the life principle of Sustainability. I don't understand that, exactly.

Life seeks always to sustain itself. That is a Basic Life Principle. You, as an expression of life, will seek to do the same thing. You have built a mental construct around how to do this that plays itself out as a social convention that you call ownership.

You claim ownership over all those things that you wish to see sustained. Seeking to express the Life Principle of Sustainability, you claim ownership of your own body, then of the body of your mate, then of your children. You say that your children are "yours," and you say the same thing about your spouse, and you treat these people as if you "own" them.

So, too, with land, and other articles and property. You have it that the very planet on which you live, this sphere that revolves around the Sun and spins in its majesty one complete cycle every 24 hours, is something that you actually "own," at least in parcels.

You have decided that this heavenly body, this celestial element, does not belong to Life Itself, but rather, to *individual human beings.* Or, in some cases, to their representatives—that is, their governments. And so, you have divvied up the very Earth itself, placing imaginary boundaries on that which has no boundaries, and claiming personal ownership not only of the land itself, but of the ground as far down as it goes and the minerals and resources within it, and of the sky as far up as it goes—which is, of course, forever... leading to intriguing international political questions about fly-over rights and "how high is up"?

You take these "ownership rights" so seriously that you start wars over them and kill and die over them—when the truth is, you cannot ever "own" any part of a planet in the solar system, even if it is a planet on which your species evolved.

You are all merely stewards, seeking to take good care of that over which you have been given stewardship—including your bodies, the bodies of your mates and children, the land on which you live, and all else that you have in your care.

These things are not your possessions, but simply articles that have been *placed in your care.* They are yours temporarily, only for safekeeping. You are asked by Life Itself to sustain them, to express the Life Principle of Sustainability, but not to declare that you "own" them and that they belong to you and no one else. Such a thought is not in any lasting sense functional.

Nothing that is possessed by anyone is possessed by them forever. Nothing. Things may be *in your possession,* but they are not your *possessions.*

Ownership is a temporary fiction. It is an invention of the mind and, like all mental constructions, it is temporary, having nothing to do with ultimate reality.

As with all of your social conventions, the idea of ownership arises from the fallacies that you hold as firm beliefs—in this case, the Second Fallacy About Life, which is that there is "not enough" of whatever it is you think you need to be happy.

There *is* enough of everything you really need to be happy, but you do not believe it, and so you seek to "own" whatever it is that you most desire, imagining that if you own it, you can keep it forever, that no one can take it away from you, that you can do what you want with it—and that from this experience of ownership will come your security, your sustainability, and your happiness.

Nothing could be further from the truth, as anyone who "owns" many things can tell you. Still, the idea persists.

This idea that you can own things has caused more harm to your psyche and more damage to your species than you could ever know.

This is because you think that "ownership" gives you "rights" that you do not intrinsically have.

Oh, man, there is so much here. So much to understand, to absorb. I've never had a conversation like this before. I sometimes feel as if I have to go over everything that's being revealed to me four or five times in order to really understand it, to really get it.

That is why I have repeated several times much of what has been said here. Now you understand.

So what can I take from this conversation that I can use as a tool to help life go on?

Do not worry about Life Itself. It will go on. I promise you. You could not put an end to life if you wanted to. Life will simply adapt to whatever conditions have been created, and continue. Yet if you want life to continue *in its present form,* if you want life to go on as it has been on the Earth, you are going to have to *create* the adaptation that life now needs to make, rather than simply stand by and watch it occur.

That is what this dialogue invites you to do. That is what this conversation is about. It is an invitation to you to create the world of your grandest dreams, to end the nightmare of your present reality, and to discover the tools with which to do that.

Do you think the world is ready to do this? Can we play an active, conscious role in our own evolutionary process?

The world is more ready for this now than it has ever been. The world is hungry, the world is starving, for a new spiritual truth—a truth that works in sustaining life, not a truth that brings an end to life. The world is searching for a new spiritual path, begging for a new set of understandings. Most of its people simply do not dare to say so publicly. Saying so would mean having to acknowledge that the world's present spiritual path is not getting humans where they say they want to go.

It is very difficult, it can be very fearful, for people to go against the prevailing notion of things—even when the prevailing notion of things is killing them.

Then what's to be done?

Encourage people to *become* the spiritual leaders for which they hunger, to *provide* the leadership for which they are starving.

But what about their fear?

Ask them what they are afraid of. An end to their way of life? The loss of their personal safety and security? *What they are afraid of has already occurred.*

Look at your world. The last vestiges of your way of life disappeared on September 11, 2001. Nobody can be safe and secure anymore, if you are using human standards of what that is.

The challenge now is not to keep from losing your safety and security, but to get it back.

You can seek to accomplish this at the physical level by using bombs and tanks and soldiers and economic or political might, or you can choose to accomplish this at the spiritual level, by changing beliefs.

The first belief you can change is the belief that you can somehow *not* be safe and secure.

Loss of safety and security is an illusion, given who and what you are. If you are using human standards, you

have lost these things. If you are using spiritual measures, you can never lose them.

Inner peace is not achieved by outward means. Inner
peace is achieved by understanding who you are. When
inner peace is attained, outer peace becomes possible
at last. In the absence of inner peace, outer peace is
impossible—as your species has discovered over and
over again. And as it is discovering once more, right
now.

The outer peace of your worldwide society is so very
fragile because the inner peace of your worldwide
society is virtually nonexistent. Your world keeps falling
apart, and you keep trying to put it back together using
the wrong tools. You keep trying to get the world to
change its behaviors, rather than its beliefs.

Humpty-Dumpty sat on a wall.
Humpty-Dumpty had a great fall.
All the king's horses and all the king's men
Could not put Humpty-Dumpty back together again.

But God can.
And God will.
As soon as you allow God to.
For God is the essence of inner peace.
But not the God about whom you have been taught.
Not the God of anger and of war, not the God of death
and destruction, and not the God of guilt and retribution.
Not the make-believe God in whom you have had to

make yourself believe, but the God of unconditional love, in whom you have your very being.

If the world were taught of *this* God, the world would change. Yet, where are the courageous spiritual leaders who will give up the God of fear to teach about the God of unconditional love?

Could you be one of them? Spiritual leaders do not have to be members of the clergy. Regular, ordinary, everyday people can be spiritual leaders. Plumbers, doctors, salespeople can be spiritual leaders. Corporate executives, members of the police force, and members of the military can be spiritual leaders. Hardware store owners, mechanics, nurses, and flight attendants can be spiritual leaders. Television news anchors, print media reporters, and politicians can be spiritual leaders. Teachers and baseball players and grocery store managers and movie stars and postal workers and research scientists and exotic dancers who take off their clothes in public can be spiritual leaders.

Do you understand this? *Do you hear what I am saying?*

This is the opportunity, this is the challenge, this is the invitation.

And so, the idea now is not to hide out, but to *come* out, so that others will find the courage to do the same, and all the world may know that it is not alone.

What can people do? Give us some concrete steps.

Now I'm going to call *you* on being repetitious. We've discussed this all before.

Please go over it again. Lay it out for me once more, all in one place. Summarize it. I need to hear it again — one last time.

> The first thing they can do is take the Five Steps to Peace. They can acknowledge that what they've been doing up until now no longer works—if it ever worked. The bravest among them can do so publicly. They can say, "Hey, wait a minute. Has anyone noticed that what we're doing here is not working?"

Yes, I was saying earlier that we could publish the Five Steps to Peace in newspapers and magazines and get high-profile people to sign onto them. We could put them on billboards and handouts, hold meetings around them, begin dialogues, discuss where humanity can go from here.

Then, we could put the building blocks in place for a New Spirituality. A spirituality that will not be a complete rejection of the old, but that will bring to people a new and larger understanding of ancient truths, and some new truths to go with them. We could use the New Revelations found here as a starting point for explorations that lead to the deepest revelations within each human heart. We would make it clear that these New Revelations are not "the answer," but only AN answer — one inspiration that can lead to many others.

> Yes. Do not seek to make the New Revelations a new religion, but rather, allow the New Revelations to reveal the simple and awesome truth that *new revelation is possible*. In so doing, you empower humanity to reveal true humanity to humanity itself.

Did you hear that? I said...

Empower humanity to reveal true humanity to humanity itself.

For when true humanity is revealed, it will be found to be Godly.

23

That is an extraordinary statement.

And it is true. All the grandest qualities of God—love, compassion, caring, patience, acceptance, and understanding, the capacity to create and to inspire—are what true humanity is all about.

Yet humans don't always act with such humanity. What is it that stops us?

The fallacies you hold in your mind about God and about Life, plus the fear those fallacies create, and your mental constructions, which create dysfunctional social conventions—such as the convention of using violence to solve human problems, and of proclaiming that God actually commands, condones, and *rewards* such killing.

All human action and reaction originates in one of

two places: love or fear. At its basis there is no other place from which life may emerge, no other source from which thought, word, and action may arise. And of these two, fear is the predominant leader as the sponsor of human behavior.

Most of your mental constructions and social conventions are fear-based. You have put them into place to protect you from something.

Your "morals" protect you from doing "wrong" and being punished (by God or man). Your "justice" protects you from being "treated unjustly." Even the construction called "ownership" is a protection. You imagine that it protects you from having something taken away from you.

None of these protections work in the long run, as the living of your life has proven. And so once again your battles begin.

It never stops, does it?

It does not, and it will not, until you let go of your fears and the fallacies that produce them. Then your social conventions—the ways you interact with each other that rule your life—will change, and more closely reflect the Basic Life Principles that they now seek, unsuccessfully, to express.

Why have we not been told these things before? Why have I had to wait until this conversation with God to be given the truths about life that are so clearly articulated here?

Largely, because of another one of your mental constructions: "What you don't know won't hurt you."

The things that are being said here are things that your religious leaders and your politicians will not tell you. Even if they believed them, they would not tell you.

More than one religious mystery has been withheld from the people on the theory that "it is too much for them to handle." More than one social truth has been left unspoken with the same justification.

Indeed, keeping secrets from each other has become a way of life for human beings.

Today you live in an essentially secret society, where more is unsaid than is said, more is concealed than is revealed, more is covered than is discovered.

Humans have created this environment quite intentionally, fearing that if everybody knew everything about everyone, no one would be able to be, do, and have what they want.

Your idea is that the only way to get what you want is by not telling anyone else what you're after, much less what you are doing to try to get it.

The strange thing is, you don't really want to be less than totally transparent. You don't enjoy it. It does not make you feel good. Yet you are convinced that everyone else has their "cloaking device" on, and so you keep yours on, too.

I certainly get that we have built a social convention called "secrecy" for sure. We even have categories for this now. We use the terms "social lie," "industrial secret," "government security," and

even "religious mystery" to categorize the ways that we lie to each
other, either by omission or by commission.

> Yes, and humans have created other, equally damag-
> ing social conventions as well. And so on it goes, each
> of your constructions built on your mistaken beliefs
> about God and about Life, each of them created out of
> a sincere seeking to enhance life and to bring a higher
> truth into your experience, yet each of them distorting
> that truth in ways that produce dysfunctional behav-
> ior—and an extraordinarily dysfunctional and danger-
> ous world.

When I hear this, I begin to think that our entire human value
system is more destructive than constructive. Is this what you are
up to in this dialogue, trying to get us to abandon our entire set
of values?

> I am showing you that *you are already doing that.*
> You do it whenever you wish, depending upon what
> it is that you seek and desire in any given moment.
> I am suggesting that maybe the reason you so often
> abandon your values is that the *beliefs upon which they
> are based are mistaken,* and that somewhere deep inside
> of you, you know this.
> Among the beliefs that you have secretly identified
> as mistaken is the notion that *nothing of any real moral
> value ever changes.*
> Your religions and your traditions and your cultures
> seek to tell you that moral values never change, but your
> heart knows this is not true.

With this conversation I am confirming for you what you already know. I am causing you to notice that you *know* that morality does, indeed, change, that ideas that had high moral value in one time and place may not have high value in another, that beliefs held in one millennium are not necessarily—and, in fact, *rarely*—applicable to the next.

I am inviting you here to adopt a new set of core beliefs from which you can create basic values that you do not have to abandon. (They are functional.) Core beliefs that can change as conditions and awareness and experiences change. (They are adaptable.) Core beliefs that will always serve the human agenda because they serve the *soul's agenda.* (They are sustainable.)

Currently, the beliefs that undergird human society are beliefs that serve the *body's* agenda, and so, they lead you into massive dysfunction.

What do you mean, "the body's agenda"?

The body's agenda is to survive, to be fed, to be kept safe, and to feel pleasure.

The soul's agenda is quite different. The soul knows that survival is not an issue, nor is keeping safe or feeling pleasure. The soul understands that the soul is Life itself, locally manifested. Safety and pleasure are its inherent qualities. The soul does not seek these things, because the soul *is* these things.

What is the difference between soul and spirit? Is there a difference?

Your soul is the individuation of the Divine Spirit, which is All There Is. The soul is the universal life energy, focused and localized and vibrating at a particular frequency in one specific time and space. Energy vibrating in such a highly specific way is a Singular Outflow of Universal Life. You may abbreviate that in English as S.O.U.L.

The soul uses the rest of Itself—that is, it draws upon the Energy of Universal Life, of which it is a part— as one of three tools with which to fashion a particular experience. The Energy of Universal Life is sometimes called the spirit. The other tools are the body and the mind.

Your soul is who you are. Your body and your mind are what you *use* to *experience* who you are in the Realm of the Relative.

The home of your soul is in the Realm of the Absolute, where Divine Spirit dwells. Your soul is now living in the Realm of the Relative, and is on a journey home. When it returns home, it joins once again with the Rest of Itself. That is, it reunites with Divine Spirit, fusing with It to become One Spirit once again.

This fusing into One is called, in some Eastern mystical traditions, *samadhi*. It can be achieved even when the soul is in the Realm of the Relative, with a body and a mind, although the experience is generally very brief. The soul can also leave the body and the mind in order to refresh and reenergize. This is done during the period that you call sleep. Finally, the soul can fuse with its Universal Energy, becoming One with Divine Spirit, for very long, extended periods. This is what occurs at the moment that you call death.

Of course, there is no such thing as death. Death is simply the name you have given to the experience of your soul transmuting the energy of your body and your mind as it reunites with the All In All.

This, the soul does as part of an endless cycle. Then, having reexperienced the bliss of *samadhi* and the ultimate Knowing of Oneness, the soul emerges once more from the All, controlling and regulating its vibration and transmuting its energy at a localized point on what you would refer to as the Space-Time Continuum.

Its most recent journey through this never-ending cycle of Divinity Experiencing Itself produced the Being that you call "you."

But please, explain this: I have always heard that the soul yearns to know itself as One with All That Is.

That is true.

Yet if this is what the soul yearns for, how come, once it finally reunites with the All In All — once it finally goes home to God — it doesn't stay there? Why does the soul reemerge from The All to become "individuated" again?

Because That Which Is Divine also yearns to experience all of the individual aspects of its Divinity. It wishes to know Itself completely, *experientially,* and to expand and re-create itself anew—to become a larger and larger version of Itself—and the way that it does this is by entering the Realm of the Relative in Individuated Form.

Divine Spirit emerges *from* The All as individual projections *of* The All, in order to have a total experience of All That Is through an endless multitude of distinctive expressions, which you rightly call the breathtaking Miracle of Life.

It *is* a miracle! And it *is* breathtaking. But as beautiful as it is in so many, many ways, life on this planet is being threatened now. We are destroying it, little by little, and *we don't seem to know how to stop ourselves.*

That's why I have come to you here. I am *telling you* how to stop yourselves, in this conversation. That is what the New Revelations are about.

When you study these revelations, when you put them all together to form one new cosmology, your understanding will increase, your awareness will expand, and you will *automatically* stop yourselves.

And now, receive this, the EIGHTH NEW REVELATION:

You are not your body. Who you are is limitless and without end.

24

I know what is meant by that. I know that, as beings in the Universe, we are more than a body...

> No, you are not "more" than a body. You are not your body *at all*. Your body is something that you have, it is not something that you are. Who you are is limitless and without end.

I understand. You are saying that I am what I call my soul. This is the essence of who I am. Yet even if I accept that as a spiritual truth, what does it have to do with the problems of the world?

> A great deal, which I will demonstrate to you presently. In order for me to do so, we shall have to take a short but intense journey into the esoteric, and it may seem, while we are on this journey, that this conversation has gotten very much out of touch with reality. In truth, it will be touching reality in a very deep way.

So you may have to have a little patience here, and trust that as "far out" as we may get in just a bit with this next part of the new revelation, I am going to circle around and bring this all back to the matter that this conversation was designed to address. Namely, what is wrong with your world, and what can you do about it?

Are you ready for a little diversion?

Yes, I can deal with that. But first, tell me how the statement "you are not your body" can be called a "new revelation"? Practically every religion in the world has taught some version of that.

You are right, it has been taught in some form or another by virtually every organized religion that speaks of an afterlife. The problem is that it has been taught incompletely. What is new in the present revelation is that it goes further than traditional teachings.

Remember that I said that the New Spirituality will not be a complete rejection of the old, but rather, it will *expand upon* the old. It will eliminate from the old what clearly no longer serves you, and bring new and deeper understanding to that which does serve you. It will retain the best of your ancient wisdoms. And so, some of what you find here you will have heard before. Yet, now we are going one step further. Now we are moving one level deeper.

Most religions have taught that you are "more than a body." The message here is that you are not your body at all. You are the essence of that which breathed life *into* your body.

This is the key.

This is the core.

This is the central truth around which every other truth that humans live must now revolve if you do not wish to experience perpetually the cycle of violence, destruction, and killing that has plagued your planet for thousands of years.

You are not your body. Who you are is limitless and without end.

This is the key.

This is the core.

All of the other New Revelations gather meaning and increase in force when this revelation is understood.

This is the Base Truth. The Prime Number. The First Cause. Everything else has new meaning when this meaning becomes clear.

The building of your newer world starts here. The foundation of the New Spirituality rests here:

You are not your body. Who you are is limitless and without end.

May I ask again, what does this have to do with the world's present predicament?

Everything, because the fact that you think you are your body is what has caused and allowed the human race to do all that it has done to itself.

So now, let us seek to understand the meaning and the implication of the thirteen words of the Eighth New Revelation.

The words themselves mean exactly what they say. You are not the conglomeration of bones and muscle and tissue and internal systems that you call your body. That is not Who You Are.

Your body is yours, but it is not you.

It is something that you are using. It is a tool. A device. A mechanism that responds and reacts in particular ways under particular influences and when subjected to particular stimuli.

This mechanism can be hurt or damaged or destroyed, but "you" cannot. This tool can be rendered completely inoperable, but you cannot. This device can cease to function, but you cannot.

The Basic Life Principle of functionality expresses itself eternally, in, as, and through you.

There are those who believe that the body is that which holds you, which houses the essence of you. That is the thought—that the body houses the Life Essence that is called the soul. That is not correct. It is the soul that houses the Body.

Your soul does not live within your body. It is the other way around. Your body lives within the force field that you call your soul. It is housed within the energy configuration, within the localized expression of Universal Spirit, that is the Essence of Who You Are.

This force field, this radiating, pulsating energy package that surrounds your body, is sometimes thought of by you as the aura. It is more than that, much more than what you imagine the aura to be, but that is nevertheless

good imagery for your earliest venture into understanding, because it presents you with a picture that
you can hold in your mind.

The part of you that some of you think of as your
soul is the energy of Life Itself, localized and concen-
trated at a particular point on what you would call the
Space-Time Continuum. This Life Energy vibrates and
shimmers and pulsates and glows around every physical object in the Universe. Depending upon the frequency of its vibration, this energy may sometimes be
seen. It can also produce other effects, such as heat.

Some people call this glow the Light, the Eternal
Flame, the Source, the Soul, or by other names that suit
their particular poetry. It is, in fact, the Prime Essence,
the Base Substance, the Core Material of all things.
This Light is Who You Are.

In your misunderstanding, you have thought that
this Light radiates from all physical objects. In fact, the
process is exactly the reverse. This Light radiates *into*
all physical objects, and thus creates them.

The energy field that you call this Light, or the soul,
envelopes the physical object it has created and extends
outward from that object into eternity. That is, the
energy never ends. There is No Place where your energy
field stops and another energy field begins. This means
that there is no place where your *soul* ends and
another's begins.

It is like the air in your house. In your home, there
are separate rooms, yet there is only "one air." The air

in one room is not separate from the air in another—
which you discover quickly when you are in your living
room and you smell that bread baking in the kitchen.
There is no place where the "living room air" ends and
the "kitchen air" begins.

What is true is that the farther you move away from
your kitchen, the less you can sense the portion of All
The Air Everywhere that is there in the kitchen. Yet
your dog can smell that bread from *outside the house.*
That is because the air that surrounds the house, that
envelops the house, is not in any way separate from the
air within it.

This is my analogy, to help you understand. And have
I not said, in my Kingdom there are many mansions?

The force field that is your soul becomes thin and
expanded the farther it extends from its localized
source, but it never disappears completely, nor ceases
to be. Instead, it mixes and merges with other force
fields, forming other localized concentrations and creating a complex, interweaving pattern extending infinitely.

We are talking here about a force field without
borders. We are describing a soul that never ends.

This is, in fact, what you are.

You are an energy that never ends, in time or space.

I've never heard the soul described quite like that before. I
keep having the experience here of hearing life explained in a
way that makes it seem as if I'm really hearing about it for the
first time.

That is why these are called the New Revelations. Not because the *information* is new, but because the presentation is. For many people, this information will be "hearable" for the first time—which *makes* it new.

But now let me ask, if my soul goes on forever, and my neighbor's soul goes on forever, and every soul on earth —

—and in the Universe—

—and in the Universe, goes on forever, and if there is no place where one soul ends and another begins, and they all mix and meld and blend ... then ... then ...

You're right, you're right ... *go ahead.* You're right on top of it, you're right at the truth. Just *say it.*

Then there is no individual soul, and every soul is just One Soul, locally and individually expressed!

That is exactly right.

Then that One Soul must be the Soul of God, manifesting Itself as All That Is.

That is exactly what is true. *And that is what traditional, exclusivist religions do not teach.*

If organized religions taught this truth, they could never also teach that any one person is better than another, or that any one soul is more pleasing to God than another, or that any one path is the only path to Divinity.

They could never teach that some souls go to "heaven," while others are condemned to "hell."

It is the teaching of their separatist philosophies and their exclusivist theologies that make some organized religions not merely inaccurate, but dangerous.

Yet the New Spirituality can change all that.

Yes. It can present a new point of view, one that is not exclusivist, not elitist or separatist. It can invite people to seriously consider, for the first time in centuries, some new theological ideas. It can offer, for exploration and discussion, some New Revelations.

The New Spirituality will open minds to larger concepts than present theologies embrace, to grander ideas than present theologies consider, and to greater opportunities for individual experience and expression than present theologies allow.

Such as the idea that there is, in fact, only one force field. That there is only one energy. That this is the energy of Life Itself, and that it is this energy that some people call God.

Yes. Now you have it.

This energy has what you would call, in your terms, intelligence. It is at once the repository and the source of all knowledge, of all awareness, of all data and information and understanding and experience.

It is the All In All, the Alpha and the Omega, the great Am/Not Am, which you have heard described in much of your sacred literature.

You *are* this energy, and this energy is *you,* and there is no separation between you. You are one with everything, and everything is one with you, for everything is comprised of this energy. This means that you are one with everyone else in the world, not in a theoretical sense, but in a very literal and specific sense.

There is no one, no human being anywhere, of whom you are not a part—an *intrinsic and intimate part.*

What this means in practical terms is that what is good for another is good for you, and that what is not good for another is not good for you. It means that what you do for another, you do for you, and what you fail to do for another, you fail to do for you.

This is the truth, and if human beings lived this way it would have a remarkable impact on the life that human beings are collectively creating. Earlier you asked whether this spiritual exploration could have "practical implications for the world today," and I tell you this: Living this way would change the world.

The simple awareness that you are all One—One with God and One with each other—and the creation of behavioral codes and international agreements reflecting that awareness, would shift the political, economic, and spiritual reality on Earth in ways that the teachings of your present day exclusivist religions can never do.

This is why, if you wish to change your world as you say that you do, you are invited to now create a New Spirituality, based on New Revelations. For your old exclusivist religions and your elitist, separatist theologies no longer serve you.

Not only do your biggest, most powerful organized religions teach you that you are separate from each other, they also teach you that you are not worthy of God. They teach you that you are shameful, guilty creatures; that you were born in sin and do not deserve to be the dust under God's feet. They rob you of your self-esteem.

They teach you not to be too proud of yourself and of your talents and accomplishments. The glory of you is not to be contemplated or announced, but only your sinful nature. You are not to go to God smiling with wonderment at your own magnificence, but begging for mercy for your countless transgressions.

Yet people who are robbed of self-esteem rob others of theirs. People who do not love themselves cannot love others. People who see themselves as unworthy see others as unworthy.

The core message of most organized religions is not joy, innocence, and self-celebration, but fear, guilt, and self-denial.

Rev. Robert H. Schuller, the American Christian minister who founded the famous Crystal Cathedral in Garden Grove, California, said twenty years ago in his book *Self-Esteem: The New Reformation* that what is needed is a second reformation within the Church, to move it away from its message of fear and guilt, retribution, and damnation, and toward a theology of self-esteem.

"The church," he flatly declared, "is failing at the deepest level to generate within human beings that quality of personality that can result in the kinds of persons that would make our world a safe and sane society."

Dr. Schuller went on to suggest that "sincere Christians and church-persons can find a theological launching point of universal agreement if they can agree on the universal right and uncompromising need of every person to be treated with great respect simply because he or she is a human being!"

This extraordinary minister also declared, "As a Christian, a theologian, and a churchman within the Reformed tradition, I must believe that it is possible for the church to exist even though it may be in serious error in substance, strategy, style or spirit." But, he said, ultimately "theologians must have their international, universal, transcreedal, transcultural, transracial standard."

> Rev. Schuller was profoundly astute in his observations and incredibly courageous in making them public. *I hope he is proud of himself!*
>
> I suggest that such an international, universal, transcreedal, transcultural, transracial standard for theology is the statement: "We Are All One. Ours is not a better way, ours is merely another way."
>
> This can be the gospel of a New Spirituality. It can be a kind of spirituality that gives people back to themselves.
>
> That is the work I am inviting you to do in the world. I am inviting you to give people back to themselves. People are returned to themselves when they are allowed to think their own highest thought about

themselves, and to announce it. You give people back to themselves when *you announce it for them.*

Do not let a moment go by in which you have an opportunity to tell someone how magnificent they are. Do not let an opportunity pass in which you may offer praise. Give people the gift of self-esteem, and you will have given them a gift that many cannot find a way to give themselves. Yet when they find themselves through you, and return to their own most glorious vision and their own grandest idea of who they really are, they are lost no more, for you have returned them to themselves. Once they were lost, but now they are found.

To change people's behavior, change people's ideas about themselves. To change people's ideas about themselves, change their beliefs about Life and about God.

If you think that you were born in sin, are a sinner now, and will be a sinner always, how are you most likely to act? Yet if you believe that you are One with God, that you walk in step with the Divine, how, then, will you behave?

I tell you this: You are an angel.

You are the angel for whom someone is waiting today.

That is one of the most wonderful things that has ever been said to me. I only wish it could be true.

It *is* true. Yet if you cannot believe it is true, that may be because you have been told you are an unworthy sinner.

I agree with you. And I'm not the only human being who does.

"As one who believes in a loving, cleansing, forgiving God," says Rabbi Harold S. Kushner, "and as one who advocates religion as a cure for the afflictions of the soul, I am embarrassed by the use of religion to induce guilt rather than to cure it, and by the number of people I meet, of all faiths, who tell me that they are constantly burdened by feelings of guilt and inadequacy because they 'made the mistake of taking religion seriously' when they were children."

In his book *How Good Do We Have to Be?*, Rabbi Kushner also says, "It is so sad to meet people who think of themselves as deeply religious and to discover that what they think of as religion is, in fact, a childish fear of losing God's love if they ever do anything against His will."

> Rabbi Kushner has spoken with a voice that is courageous, clear, and true.
>
> Now you have a choice between beliefs. I say you are my angel. You say you are but a lowly, groveling sinner.
>
> Which belief do you think better serves you? Which do you think better serves humankind?

25

You are making this all so... irresistible. I don't know what to say.

> Say the truth, and then be it. Say but the word and your soul shall be healed.

"I am an angel. I am one with God, and God is one with me."

> Good. Very good.

Can this be true? Really true? I am not separate from you? All my life I've been told...

> Your elitist, exclusivist religions have not served you *or* humankind, but created in both a huge misunderstanding. That is because the core message of those religions is a message of separation from God, when the reality is that you are eternally unified with me.

You are saying that, at its basis, all of *life* is unified.

Yes.

Yet humans have always had a question in their minds about this. Science has been trying to resolve this question for centuries, has it not? Is this not what the search for a Unified Field Theory has been all about?

That is exactly what it has been all about.

And now we're hearing terms like the Super String Theory and other such descriptions from our physicists as they try to explain to us scientifically what you've just explained to us spiritually.

Yes, science and spirituality are coming closer and closer together on your planet, and soon it will be discovered that the two were always one. It is the same discipline, approached from different angles. It is the study of life, and what life really is, examined and explored from different perspectives.

Very soon now, science will confirm a great many things that spirituality has been telling you all along.

When it does, the human race will be faced with ethical and philosophical decisions, the likes of which it has never been faced with before.

What does that mean? I don't understand.

Spirituality has been saying to you that life is eternal, that you are immortal, and death is only a horizon. Science is now about to show that to you—and to show you ways that you may push back that horizon into the very distant future.

You mean, extend our lives.

Yes. Beyond anything you might ever have imagined.

Spirituality has been telling you that you create your own reality, that you have all the secrets and power of life within you. Science is now about to show you that—and to show you ways that you may use that power and those secrets.

Spirituality has been telling you that you are God. Not only that you are a *part of God,* but that you *are gods, in human form.* ("Have I not said, ye are gods?") Science is now about to show you that—and to show you ways that you may impact life with the power of the gods.

When you begin to be able to do this—and this is coming now not in a matter of decades, but years, and even months—you will be faced with many, many decisions. "Are we to play God?" you will be asking yourself.

This will be the central question of the 21st Century.

To what extent are you to "interfere" in matters that you used to think were supposed to be "left up to God," and to what extent is God calling upon you to use the tools you have been given *by God* with which to perform miracles?

These are the kinds of ethical decisions that religions are hoping to prepare you to make in the future, just as they have been trying to help you in the past to make social, political, and economic decisions. Yet unless they expand their own belief systems, religions—well-meaning as they are—will be no more successful tomorrow than they were yesterday.

Organized religion is going to have to vastly expand and deepen its understandings of Life and God before it can tackle *today's* problems, much less tomorrow's.

Will the problems of tomorrow be even worse?

Not worse, more complex. You could hardly have any worse problems to face than the threat of your own self-extinction, which you face today. Yet, the challenges of tomorrow will be far more complicated than the simple question of whether you want to live or wish to die.

More complicated than the question of whether we want to live?

Yes. In the future, should you get past this decision, the question will not be *whether* you want to live, but *how?* And how long?

Okay, wait a minute. You've opened a whole new area of discussion here. First of all, you categorize today's problems as a "simple question" of whether we want to live or die. Is that really how you see it?

Certainly, because that's really how it is. That's all that the human race is deciding now.

As with most beginning cultures, your species is making a very early developmental decision: Does it wish itself to continue, or does it choose extinction? Does it wish to survive, or does it choose to self-destruct?

With every choice you make in your life at this early developmental stage, you are making that larger decision.

I'm sure we don't see it that way.

No, you do not, and that is what marks you as a culture in the early stages of development. Like children, you do not see the long-term implications of your in-the-moment decisions. Like children, you are largely interested only in short-term outcomes. You want what you want, and you want it now.

Yet, as you move from the childhood of your culture into its adolescence, you will begin to identify long-term goals that cannot be met with short-term thinking. Instant gratification will have to be replaced by long-range satisfactions if you choose to prolong your existence and to experience it peacefully and joyfully.

This is by no means a closed matter. This is by no means a decision already made. Had you already decided to do this, you would not be behaving in many of the ways that you are now behaving, individually and collectively.

In a very real sense, you are making this decision every day, in every moment. Every moment is a Choice Point. It is in each moment that you decide whether you want to "live long and prosper," as your popular television science-fiction character Spock would say, or to die young.

We are deciding this in every moment?

Oh, yes—for yourself and for your species. In some
ways that are obvious, and in some ways that are sub-
tle. Your decision to breathe is a decision to live. Your
decision to eat is a decision to live.

Oh, well, of *course* at *that* level we are deciding between life and
death, but who decides not to breathe? Who decides not to eat?

All sorts of people. People make these decisions all
the time. You've never heard of a person who decided
to stop eating? Or who asked for a respirator to be
turned off?

No fair. Those are people who are dying already, and are being
kept alive with extraordinary measures. They're simply asking
for "no extraordinary measures."

And they are dying now because of *other* decisions
they have made *throughout their lives*. Collective decisions and individual decisions.

Decisions to pollute their environment and then to
live within the pollution. Decisions to poison their soil,
and then to eat the foods grown in the poison. Decisions to inhale and ingest into the body things that
should never be put there, have no use there, and do
not belong there. All *sorts* of decisions, large and small,
made all day, every day.

You do not think of these decisions as "life and
death decisions" because you are an awakening culture,
not yet fully aware of the consequences of your own
actions—and, when you *are* aware, ignoring what you

know because you cannot say no to short-term gratification.

As you mature, both individually and as a species,
you will give up short-term gratification in favor of long-
term goals, and many of your day-to-day and moment-
to-moment choices and behaviors will change.

Then, ultimately, you will make the decision that
you want to live long and prosper, and that you want
the same for your entire species. That is when the more
complex questions will arise.

I've thought about it, and I think I know the kinds of questions you're talking about.

Yes? Good. What kinds of questions do you think
that I am referring to?

Well, I read an article on March 8, 2002, in the *Arizona Republic* from the Associated Press, which said that "for the first time
scientists say they have used the ethically sensitive technology of
therapeutic cloning to repair an inherited disease in a lab animal."

The article goes on to report, "Experts say this demonstrates
the potential of the approach to correct many common ills that
affect humans."

That is exactly the kind of thing I am talking about.
And that is only the beginning.

I know, I know. I also just read about a new and very expen-
sive item that's going to be appearing soon on the menus of the
finest restaurants: Cloned Cow Steak.

I beg your pardon?

Cloned Cow Steak. *USA Today* reported in the spring of 2002 that "in the quest for the perfect steak, scientists have created the first cloned cow from a two-day-old side of beef. The feat means cattle producers could choose beef cells from a slaughtered cow after its meat has been graded, then create a herd of grade-A clones. The first such clone was born at the University of Georgia, and is part of a research collaboration between the school's College of Agricultural and Environmental Sciences and a private company."

> Yes, well, that is a good example of where your society is heading with its new technologies, and humans are going to have to make decisions very soon that you never could have imagined you were going to have to make.
>
> Stem cell research is going to open vistas that you once thought of as the stuff of science-fiction movies, including the possibility of greatly extended life, of repairing bodily damage and curing major diseases with a simple injection, and of preventing many major diseases from ever occurring, through genetic manipulation before birth.

Wow. This will raise questions like, "Is it appropriate to let a child be born with a genetic predisposition for, say, muscular dystrophy, if pre-birth genetic transplantation therapy can prevent it?" Or, "What makes it okay to treat a child for MS *after* birth, but not *before* birth?"

Exactly.

But isn't it for *God* to decide which child gets to live a normal life and which child gets to be crippled? We are not supposed to *prevent it,* are we? If you didn't want a child to be crippled, you wouldn't have made it happen.

Is that what you believe?

Some of us. Things happen because you want them to happen. It is the "will of God."

I see. And who "made it happen" that medical researchers found a way to prevent such tragedies through pre-birth gene therapy?

The devil! *The devil made them do it!* This is science run amok! This is taking things too far! That's what many people will say. That's what many *are* saying right now.

Yes. It is the current belief of many people on Earth that God is the one who decides which humans suffer and which do not. It will come as a great shock to humanity to learn that *you are the ones making this decision.* You are making it every day, and you are pretending that you are not.

You will shrink from "playing God" until the evidence that you were always *meant to* act as gods mounts so high that you can no longer ignore it.

Like Hermann Kümmell in Hamburg in the late 1800s, your researchers of today will have a terrible time convincing others that it is a good idea to use advanced medical techniques in the prevention of debilitating disease until it becomes painfully obvious—and I mean those words literally... until it become *painfully* obvious—that not to do so would be inhumane.

Mind you, if it were a matter of pure science, there would be no question about any of this. But you have not allowed it to be a matter of science alone. You have made it a matter of theology.

The issue becomes clouded when you get into what you think that "God" wants, when you begin claiming that the area of genetics is "God's domain" and not the proper domain of medical science.

Now it becomes a "moral" issue—a matter of "right" and "wrong," not a matter of "what works" and "what doesn't work."

Even if it can be shown that it "works" to prevent crippling diseases in children by genetic transplantation therapy before birth, that will make no difference. Humans will still insist that it is "wrong" if they contend that it is "immoral."

These are the kinds of complex issues you will face and difficult decisions you will have to make in the very near future and throughout the 21st Century— assuming that you answer yes to the first question, "Do we as a species wish to survive?"

Yet you cannot even effectively explore that question, much less answer it, so long as you see yourself as separate from everyone else, and that is the core message of your present belief systems.

But I don't understand why that thought—even if it is inaccurate—has been such a destructive force in the human experience. Even if we do think that we are not "all one," can't beings who think of themselves as individuals still find a way to get along?

> The problem is this: The chief instinct of your species is survival. Remember what I told you. The Basic Principles of Life are Functionality, Adaptability, and Sustainability.
>
> At this stage of your collective development you are still not clear that your Sustainability is not in question.

You mean it isn't?

> No. It is not possible for you to not survive. This will be explained to you further when we explore the Ninth New Revelation, very shortly. For now, I'm going to ask you to accept it.

Okay.

> That Which You Are (and remember, you are *not* your body) will always "survive." It cannot *not* survive, because it is the essence of Life Itself—and Life expresses the Principle of Sustainability in, as, and through you, eternally.
>
> So it is not a question of whether you will survive, but in what form.

Supposing we wish to survive in our present form, in *human form?*

> Well, of course, that *is* the form in which you wish

to survive, largely because you do not know about any other forms. You have forgotten. You do not remember.

Many of you are not even certain that you survive the death of your body at all, in *any* other form. So you are understandably deeply attached to survival in the physical body. Deeply attached.

What's wrong with that? That's healthy, I would say.

There's nothing wrong with it. You might even say that "it works"—so long as you know that this "body" you imagine yourself to be is much larger than it appears. That is, if you realize that ALL bodies are part of One Single Body. In that case, your fight for survival will be a *collective one,* and an expression of a Basic Life Principle itself—the principle of Sustainability.

If you thought that all bodies are part of One Single Body, you would do nothing that would reduce the chances of survival for all of humanity, and do everything that would increase those chances.

This is exactly the opposite of what you are doing now.

With your mistreatment of the environment and your ecology, with your misuse of politics and your economies, with your incomplete understanding of spiritual truth as expressed in so many of your religions, with the mistakes of your mental constructions and your social conventions, and with all the behaviors that emerge from all of this, you are doing a great many things that reduce the chances of survival for the collective called humanity. *So* many things, in fact, that those chances are growing slimmer and slimmer by the day.

Humans are doing these things precisely because most humans do not think of themselves as part of a collective. They think of themselves as *separate beings living separate lives* on a planet where *other separate beings are living other separate lives.*

And while they know and fully understand at some level that separate beings may do better when they cooperate with each other than when they don't, they very quickly revert to a "survival of the fittest" mentality whenever they or theirs feel threatened.

It is this "my-survival-first-and-yours-if-I-agree-with-it-and-can-manage-it" mentality—not exhibited by every human being, but exhibited by most—that works against the collective good, and, in fact, creates a world in which the collective good is repeatedly threatened, and may soon be destroyed.

Because you imagine yourself to be a separated body, you believe that the experiences you create for yourself are experienced only by you. You also believe that the things you think, do, and say with regard to others have no direct effect on you. It is this idea that allows human beings to commit unthinkable and merciless acts of violence.

But not all human actions and not all human beings are violent. There is goodness and courage and charity and kindness and compassion that resides within people.

That is profoundly true, and this frequently emerges through human behaviors. Acts of heroism and kindness, compassion and goodness abound in the annals of human history, and they are in evidence everywhere today.

And so it's a question of which side of human nature will win out.

No!
No, no, and a thousand times no.
It is not "human nature" to be violent.

I hate to say it, but from what I observe, it somehow looks very normal to me.

"Normal" is not "natural."
Saying that a thing is *normal* simply means that it is often and usually done. Saying that a thing is *natural* means that it is intrinsically a part of something.
Violence is not an intrinsic part of human beings. Yet the illusion that it is effective in solving human problems has become so pervasive that it is *assumed to be natural* to the human condition. Yet human beings are not *by nature* violent.

But what of those who say that it is the nature of *life* to be violent? They argue that life itself is violent. They point to violence in the animal kingdom and violence in nature and violence in the Universe, with stars exploding and imploding and asteroids colliding and whole galaxies disappearing, to support their claim that of *course* humans are violent by nature. *Violence is the nature of things.*

There is a huge difference between outcomes of natural occurrences—such as the process of star systems that you describe—and outcomes of conscious creation, such as a decision to violently respond to a human circumstance.

There is also a difference between the Instinctual Response of some living species and the Conscious Response of others.

Life expresses itself at many different levels of consciousness, or self-awareness. The higher the level of consciousness, the greater the degree of self-determination, the greater the ability to choose and decide, announce and declare, express and fulfill, the grandest notion one has of who and what one is.

Every act is an act of self-definition.

I'm confused. I thought you said that the idea of being "better" is what gets human beings into trouble. Now you're saying that some living beings operate at a higher level of consciousness than others. How does all this square with your earlier statements that superiority is an illusion?

A higher level of consciousness is not "better" than a lower level of consciousness, it is merely higher.

Being in the sixth grade is not "better" than being in the third. It is simply being in the sixth grade. By the actions they take, by their way of being, animals announce what grade they are in. So, too, do humans.

Animals demonstrate not how life intrinsically is, but *their level of consciousness* about how life really is. And so, by their actions, do humans.

Human beings once declared themselves to be God's greatest achievement, beings of the highest level of development, having dominion over the creatures that creep and the birds that soar and the fishes in the sea. Such was the level of their arrogance.

Gosh, this is a view *still* held and taught by some of the world's religions.

Yes. Yet it cannot continue to be seriously subscribed to by even a casual observer of human behavior.

Then, if violence is *not* natural, why is it so normal? Why is anger such a constant aspect of human behavior?

Just a minute. You have equated violence and anger there. You've made them seem as one. Anger and violence are not the same thing, and should not be confused.

Anger is a natural emotion. It is very natural to be angry at times. It is also very okay. That is, it works, if what you wish is to live a life that is harmonious.

What? I don't understand. I've always experienced anger as discombobulating.

That is because you have not known a peaceful and loving way to express it.

Expressed with love, anger is the *discharge* of disharmony, not the *creator* of it.

I've never heard that before. I've never thought of it that way.

That is all that anger was ever meant to be. It is built into the system. It is part of being human. It is a pressure valve, releasing negative energy.

It is not the release of negative energy, but the failure to release it, that will get you into trouble. It is not the expression of anger, but how it is expressed, that causes your concern.

There are many ways in which anger may be released that do involve no violence whatsoever, neither physical nor verbal. Learning to release anger in these ways is the mark of maturity.

How can I do that?

There are many ways in which you can do it, and many people who can assist you in learning about those ways. Some people attend anger management classes. Some people learn to meditate. Some simply begin making new choices about how they are going to express their anger, based on new decisions about who they are. If one is serious about learning how to express anger with love, one can find helping resources quite easily.

For now, understand that anger is not a negative emotion, it is a healer. Anger releases negative energy. That makes it a positive emotion, because it helps you get rid of something you don't want, and live a harmonious life.

Anger and harmony go hand in hand. Anger that is *fully* expressed, with *wonder* at its healing qualities, is anger that is wonder-fully expressed, and that can make rich any moment between human beings, for it is the stuff of authenticity and truth, and there is no greater healer than that, nor any shorter path to harmony.

Anger that is not wonderfully expressed, but expressed through verbal or physical violence, does not heal, but inflicts injury.

Injury cannot heal injury, no matter how hard it tries.

Then why do we continue to use violence as our chief means of attempting to resolve conflict?

Because violence has been deeply injected into your modern culture.

There are a hundred ways in which humans have allowed this to occur—each one of which humans vehemently deny.

Some humans vehemently deny that images of violence—that movies and television shows of violence, that comic books and video games and the constant barrage of depictions of violence in every conceivable form—have any effect on human behavior. At the same time they pay *millions of dollars* to present *sixty seconds* of images in a Super Bowl commercial, precisely because they *do know how images affect human behavior.*

Based on your own clear sociological evidence, it would seem impossible to conclude that the violent images constantly placed before humans have nothing to do with their conceiving of violence as an acceptable means of resolving human conflict.

And I tell you this: *What you conceive, you receive.*

The process of human creation is very simple. It is a process that you might call Ceiving.

Ceiving? Is that a word?

It is a part of an English word, and it perfectly describes the process by which human beings put creations into place. It is how you build the life you are living.

First, an idea is con-Ceived. That is, it is given birth within your culture. Second, that idea is per-Ceived. That is, you form a point of view about it. Finally, the idea is re-Ceived. That is, it is experienced again, this time in physical form. It has changed from an inner thought to an outer physical reality.

To understand this more clearly, let's look at how this process has worked in creating the experience of increasing violence on your planet.

First, notice that the idea that violence can be effectively used as a solution to human problems is being given widespread birth in your culture. In earlier days and times, it would have been difficult for many people to even conceive of such a thing. Now, such ideas are being shared with even the very young, in a variety of ways.

With this message receiving widespread dissemination, the people of your species, and particularly the young (who have no memory of a time when violence was *not* shown as the way to solve problems), form a personal point of view about the idea. What has been

con-Ceived is now per-Ceived, and the perception is
that violence is effective, and, therefore, acceptable.

This idea then comes back to those who think it. It
returns in physically manifested form. What is con-
Ceived and per-Ceived is thus re-Ceived.

The results of this process is what you are receiving
every day.

But human beings were violent long before the technologies
of mass media spread the idea of violence as a means of conflict
resolution.

Indeed, that is true. Your mass media and your technologies, your ability to now instantaneously and graphically share your most violent communications, has only
raised the problem to planet-threatening propor-
tions. But the problem has, as you point out, existed
for centuries.

It first emerged out of man's earliest misunder-
standings about Life, and about God. Review again the
earlier portion of this dialogue describing this. You will
recall that, in short, humans assumed that the forces of
nature that seemed to from time to time work against
them were the outcome of conscious decisions made
by something outside of themselves that was stronger
than they. This evolved into the thought that they were
the choices of an Angry Deity. The natives thereafter
sought to not "anger the gods." Indeed, they developed
rituals to appease and mollify them.

Later, these primitive ideas gave way to a larger

understanding of Nature, but superstition was not so easily disposed of. Belief systems had already been built up, and when hard physical evidence of how the world worked belied those beliefs, the beliefs were simply adjusted to accommodate the new knowledge.

Ultimately, organized religions emerged, and many of these institutions—particularly those that promulgated doctrines of superiority and exclusivity—encouraged the *perception* of an angry God who wanted things one way, *His way,* and who had to be mollified and appeased.

Thus, retribution and violence became a Godly trait, spoken of specifically in many Holy Scriptures, as we have shown graphically and repeatedly in this dialogue.

And whether the religions of those Scriptures actually encourage violence or not, many of their followers have been willing to *believe* that they do, for in such belief lies their justification to do unjustifiable things... and to call it justice.

I still don't understand this. As human beings developed and grew more and more sophisticated in their understanding of nature and life and how everything worked, surely they would have given up their idea that violence was "natural," and therefore okay. How could we continue to believe that?

Because this belief is supported by other beliefs, *underlying* beliefs, which have never been seriously challenged.

These are your most fundamental beliefs, inculcated

in society just as surely as massive violence is inculcated in your culture today.

The Creation Myth of virtually every human culture
tells, in one form or another, the story of an angry Deity
who separated Himself from humans in a tirade over
humans' inability to do as He asked.

To reinforce the message, scriptures of nearly every
major religion contain passages vividly describing an irate
God's further acts of anger and violence.

The illusion of disunity and unworthiness—the idea
that all of life is separate, rather than intrinsically unified, and that humans are inherently evil—is the cause
of dysfunctional and violent behaviors.

Humans act violently because they believe they are
alone—that, ultimately, they are isolated—and that they
must do whatever it takes to preserve, protect, and
defend themselves in a world filled with evil.

And what is this "self" that they must defend? Why,
it is the body, of course. This is what they think. And
so, survival of the body becomes human beings' prime
motivator, and whenever they feel the safety, security,
or survival of their bodies threatened, they *attack others in defense of the selves they think they are—and call
this Self-Defense.*

Because you have seen other bodies like yours do
the thing that you call "die," you think that you, too,
can die, and so you do everything in your power to
keep from doing that—because you believe that death
is the end of you.

Your observation that your body can "die" (that is, cease its functionality) is correct, but your thought that *you are your body* is not.

This is where your confusion lies, this is where your fear originates, and this is the source of all the horror that you have collectively created and jointly experienced in your life on Earth.

Yet now it is time for your confusion to end. Now it is time for you to stop creating hell on your Earth. For either you will stop creating it, or you will create the ultimate horror, which will be the end of *life* on Earth.

So here is my invitation today:

Do not end your life, end your confusion.

26

That really *is* the choice that we have, isn't it?

> That really is.
>
> I have put it in such stark terms so that you could quickly grasp the seriousness of your present situation.
>
> Make no mistake about this. You have placed your-selves in the direst circumstance. The hearts of millions of humans have been filled with despair, with anger, with hatred, and with desperate intent. And now, thanks to the forward race of your modern technologies, you have placed in the hands of those angry humans the ability to vent their negativity with tools of destruc-tion beyond anything of which you could have dreamed in your worst nightmares.

You keep making this point! Are you trying to discourage us beyond all hope?

No, *I am trying to wake you up.*

Okay, okay, *I'm awake already.* But now that I'm awake and aware, it all looks *worse,* not *better.* Is there any hope?

There is *enormous* hope! There is *extraordinary* opportunity! There is a *breathtaking* possibility! But you must be willing now, *right now,* to seize the moment, to seize the day.

You must decide—here and now, in these days and times, not in some far-off, distant future—whether the world is to be fashioned with tools of devastation or tools of re-creation, with words of hate or words of hope, with acts of war or acts of peace, with thoughts of fear or thoughts of love.

You must decide whether you are going to be DEstructive or CONstructive.

You can now destroy yourselves utterly, or you can re-create yourselves anew in the next grandest version of the greatest vision you ever held about who you are—as individuals, and as a species called The Human Race.

How can we re-create ourselves anew? How can we create a New Human? A New Society? A New Spirituality? A New Politics? A New Economy? A New World? *How do we do this?*

You have asked again, so I will answer again. Begin at the level of belief.

I am telling you that the root cause of humanity's problems is what you believe. Yet many people will not believe this. They would rather believe the beliefs that have produced the unbelievable.

Your current belief systems have produced unbelievable horror, unbelievable devastation, unbelievable destruction, unbelievable cruelty, unbelievable sadness and suffering, unbelievable oppression and anger and hatred and conflict and warring and killing.

The ways in which human beings behave, the things human beings do to each other, are unbelievable. Yet many humans would rather accept what they cannot believe than change the things that they do.

So, then, it *is* hopeless . . .

No, it is not, because for the first time in a very long time, the number of those people is dropping.

The number of people who see that *their old beliefs no longer work* is growing. The number of people willing to say, "There must be another way" is increasing.

That number is rapidly reaching critical mass—and what you can do is help it get there.

Now here is something you should know. "Critical mass" is not that difficult to achieve. It is not nearly as high a number as most people think. It takes a very small percentage of the whole to form sufficient mass to affect the whole.

Critical mass is not one more than half, it is not 25 or 30 percent, it is not even 10 percent. *Critical mass can be achieved with less than 5 percent of the whole moving in any one direction.*

Put another way, it takes only one domino to make the rest of the dominoes fall.

And so, it is as I have said twice before. What is needed now is a small number of people, a tiny percentage, who are willing to become—in their nations, in their cities, in their towns, in their villages and neighborhoods and churches and synagogues and temples and mosques and community halls and political party meetings, and even in their homes—The First Domino.

What does that look like? How can people do that?

It looks like people standing up for what they believe—but first, being willing to look at what they believe, to test what they believe against the results that are being produced, and to change what they believe, should the need for a change be clearly indicated.

In other words, it looks like taking the Five Steps to Peace.

Yes. Each person, individually, must do that.

Then it looks like having the openness and the courage to explore and to examine, in a serious way, whatever new revelations are given to the human soul when the human heart opens to create an open mind.

You may wish, as a starting point, to consider the New Revelations I have given to you here. Neither dismiss them out of hand, nor praise them to the sky, but, rather, look into them deeply. See if there could be any truth in them for you; determine if there could be any value in them for the human race.

You owe yourself that. That much, you owe yourself. There has not been a serious new theological construct presented to the human race in millennia. There has not been an expansion of your theologies in a hundred generations. *You have not challenged your God in a very long time.*

The time has come for you to have more courage than any war has ever called upon you for, than any hardship has ever demanded, than any suffering has ever required. The time has come for you to confront yourself at the level of belief. The reason this will require so much courage is that your beliefs form the basis of who you think you are.

You must challenge yourself.

You must challenge your society.

You must challenge your world.

You must collectively ask:

Is this who we are? Is this who we choose to be? Is this the only way we can live? Is this the only way we know how to behave? Is it possible that there might be another way?

Might this other way bring us closer to what we say, as a species, that we really want? *Are we missing something here?* Do we have the courage to seriously look at what that might be? Do we have the courage to accept the answer that our searching uncovers?

How can we do this searching, this asking, in a way that makes a difference? People have been asking themselves these questions forever. I don't see that the asking, the searching, or even the finding of new answers, ever changes very much of how the world works or how life is. Things go on pretty much as they have before.

Group action is what is required now. You cannot do this alone, nor can one charismatic leader or one spiritual teacher produce a miracle. The time for individual gurus who come along and change the world is over. The time for collective consciousness and collective action to change the collective reality is at hand.

This is as it should be, for your present reality has been collectively created. It is now time for you to collectively re-create it anew.

Work, then, in a collective. Do not follow individual masters, but master collective consciousness individually. Then work collectively to awaken the collective called Humanity.

The world is now ready and able to take such action, for group communication is now possible as it was never possible before. The whole world is now linked. The entire planet is now connected. You have tools that you never had before.

You mean the Internet?

All of your modern technologies. All of them. The Internet. Cell phones. Faxes. E-mail. Easily made, home-made videos. CDs that you can burn right on your home computer, and send anywhere.

You name it. You have moved into the era of instant and easy worldwide communication.

It has been said that your rapidly advancing technolo-

gies are threatening to destroy humanity. They are also
that which can save it.

Use them to create the New Reality that you wish
to experience. Use them to create the New Human
that you wish to become. Use them to build the New
Spirituality that you wish to express.

But remember to use them *collectively*. It is *collective
action* that is destroying the world. It is only collective
action that can save it.

Yes. That is why it has been suggested here that people form
groups that will collectively commit to taking the Five Steps to
Peace. Have petitions signed. Sponsor discussions and dialogues.
Print booklets and flyers.

Publish the Five Steps in the newspaper, something like this:

AS WE SEEK TO CREATE HARMONY IN OUR WORLD,
WE, THE UNDERSIGNED, HEREBY PUBLICLY COMMIT
TO TAKING THE FIVE STEPS TO PEACE:

1. We acknowledge that certain old beliefs about Life and
   about God are no longer working.
2. We acknowledge that there is something we do not understand about God and about Life, the understanding of which
   could change everything.
3. We are willing for new understandings of God and Life to
   now be brought forth, understandings that could produce
   a new way of life on this planet.
4. We are willing to explore and examine these new under-

standings, and, if they align with our inner truth and knowing, to enlarge our belief system to include them.
5. We are willing to live our lives as a demonstration of our
beliefs.

Ask prominent figures in the community — including political
and business leaders — to sign on to it before it is published, and
have their signatures included at the bottom. Create a ground-
swell. Get groups involved. Citizens' groups, civic and service groups,
church and religious groups, cultural and educational groups, senior
and youth groups, government and legislative groups. Create
coalitions of presently existing groups. Form new groups. *Don't let
this idea go away.*
Yet what can be done to motivate people to step to the line
like that?

> The excitement of new possibilities. And the assur-
> ance that they do have the power to change the world.
> If people think they are impotent, they will do nothing.
> If people really believe there is something they can do,
> they will do it.
> You must convince people that there is something
> they can do. Then, show them how it can be done more
> easily than they could ever have imagined, if they will
> first create a state of being, then allow what they do
> to flow naturally from what they are being, rather than
> try to find something to do just to "do something,"
> without changing what they are being at all.
> Just doing something is not the answer. The whole

world community has been trying to "do something" about its problems for a very long time. Nothing has made a lasting change. The human race is still acting as it has been acting for centuries.

Being something is the answer. The whole world community has not tried to "be something" in response to its problems for a very long time. Yet this is what would produce lasting change. The human race could then stop acting as it has been acting for centuries.

When what you are doing is a reflection of what you are being, rather than an attempt to create what you wish you were being, you will know that you have produced lasting change in *yourself.* This is what produces lasting change in the world.

Remember what was said earlier. You cannot "do" peaceful, you can only "be" peaceful. You cannot "do" loving, you can only "be" loving. You cannot "do" unified, you can only "be" unified.

Seek, then, to shift your state of being. Do not seek first to change the world, seek first to change the self.

When you achieve that, your actions will *automatically* change.

Hold it. Do not seek to change the world? This *entire conversation* has been about changing the world!

I said, do not seek *first* to change the world. You will not change the world by trying first to change the world. You will change the world by first changing yourself. You must first decide some important things about yourself, come to some new conclusions within yourself about who you are, about God, and about Life, *and then begin to live those decisions.*

This inner process can, in fact, produce changes in the world around you, for the world that you touch is affected by how you touch it.

Who you are, and *how* you are, affects the world to a much larger degree than you might imagine. Yet remember this. You cannot achieve inner peace by being agitated if you do not achieve outer peace.

Therefore, do not tie your efforts at personal transformation to a result called planetary transformation, or you may achieve neither.

Share with the people of the world, if you wish, but share with them not what you think their experience should be, but what you know your experience has been. Teach others if they ask, but teach them not that *you* have their answers, but that they have their own.

And drop any expectation that any decision you are making, or any information you are sharing, about who you are and what you choose to be will have any impact on anything or anyone else at all.

Do not require those results.

Why? I just don't understand this. Don't results bring us a sense of satisfaction that allows us to go on?

If it is results that bring you a sense of satisfaction that allows you to go on, then *lack* of results will bring you a sense of frustration that will cause you *not* to go on. And in this you will defeat yourself.

I see that, but how do we get around it?

By being clear *why* you are engaged in whatever you are being and doing to begin with.

Which is?

Self-realization. To realize the Self at the next highest level. To know who you really are, and to experience that.

This is called evolution.

This is the work of the whole humanity. And this is its joy. For your joy is in becoming greater than you are, and in knowing yourself as that. Entire species evolve in this way, and in no other.

Do not change your beliefs because you want other people to change theirs. Change your beliefs because your new beliefs announce more accurately who *you* are.

Yet even as you change, do not be surprised if other people change, and if the world around you changes. For the change in you will act as a catalyst in producing change in others. Not because you have *sought* to produce change in others, but, more probably, because you have not.

People do not change because they are told to change. People may temporarily alter their behavior because they have been told to do so by those who have power over them, but that is not real change. That is merely a surface shift of outward demeanor. Inner truth has not shifted. As soon as the power over them has been lifted, or can no longer be exerted, people's behavior returns to that which is motivated by their inner truth.

The parent of every teenager knows this.

The tyrant who would rule any country finds it out.

Change is an act of freedom, not an act of compliance.

Obedience is not creation, and creation is the only act of evolution.

Seek not, therefore, to change the world. Seek to BE the change you wish to SEE in the world.

Didn't Gandhi say that?

Yes. And he demonstrated it.

First, he attained a state of being. This is work that he did from within. Then, and only then, did his outward "doing" become the kind of "doing" that changed the world.

He did not achieve a state of being as a result of what he was doing. *What he was doing reflected the state of being he had achieved.*

Do you understand this now?

I understand it—you've explained it quite well—but I don't understand how to make it *work.* I mean, I don't understand how to get it going, how to make it happen. How do you change your inner state of being? And can't what you are doing affect what you are being? Doesn't listening to soft music sometimes help you to "be" more calm? Doesn't prayer or meditation sometimes help you "be" at peace?

Yes. You can achieve a state of being by what you are doing. You are quite correct in this. You have noticed it, and it is true. Yet getting to a place of being through something you are doing is a very long way around. And, much more important, it is rarely more than temporary.

Most people do not put on a piece of soft music and remain calm the rest of their lives. Most people do not pray and continue to be at peace in every succeeding moment.

A decision to come *from* peace and love, rather than try to get *to* them, turns everything around. It completely shifts the axis of your experience. It places the source of what you desire within you, rather than outside of you. That makes it accessible to you at all times and in all places.

This is genuine power. The kind of power that changes lives and changes the world.

This level of complete inner peace and total love for all humankind can be reached in a single moment. It can also take a lifetime. Everything depends on you. Everything depends on how deeply you desire it.

You may achieve any inner state of being you wish by simply choosing it and calling it forth.

At present, most of your states of being are "reactions." They do not have to be this. You can make them "creations."

Help me with this. What do you mean? What are you talking about?

Let me give you an example as a means of explanation.

Right now when you move into any moment, you rarely do so with your state of being determined ahead of time. You wait until you see what the moment contains and provides, and then you respond by being something.

Perhaps you wind up being sad. Perhaps you wind up being happy. Perhaps you wind up being disappointed, or elated.

But now, suppose you decided *ahead of time* how you were going to be when you moved into that moment. Suppose you decided that you were going to be peaceful, no matter how that moment showed up. Do you think it would make any difference in the way that you experienced the moment itself?

Of course it would.

Let me tell you something. It is when you decide how *you* are going to show up before the *moment* shows up that you have begun to move to mastery. You have learned to *master the moment,* and that is the beginning of mastery in living.

When you decide ahead of time that your inner state of being is going to be peaceful and loving, understanding and compassionate, sharing and forgiving, no matter what any outer moment brings, then the outer world loses its power over you.

Others cannot convince you to join them in their behaviors if their behaviors do not coincide with your inner state of being. Political or religious leaders will seek to rally you to their cause, but it will be no use—unless you are in harmony at the deepest part of your being with what they are saying or doing.

This sounds so wonderful! But what could make me choose an inner state of being that is different from what the outer world is sending me? I mean, how can I "be" something that the world is not letting me be? Do you understand the question? How can I be "peaceful" if the world is destroying itself? (To use one example.)

You can be peaceful no matter what the outer world is doing—and the wonderful irony of this is that what the outer world is doing will very often be affected by what you are being.

I'm sure you have already heard the advice that if you chance upon a rattlesnake, the best thing to do is to stay calm, back away slowly, and you will come to no harm. The last thing to do is to turn and run.

I'm sure you've heard the advice that when you are getting on a horse, the last thing to do is to let the horse think that you are afraid. If you do not let the horse know that you are in charge, the horse will be in charge of you.

You have heard these things, yes?

Yes.

Good. I am using them here as a metaphor for life.

How do you remain peaceful when the world is demonstrating everything but peace? Loving, when the world is demonstrating everything but love? Forgiving, when the world is demonstrating everything but forgiveness?

You insist on being who you are no matter what the rest of the world is being.

Slowly, the world you touch will change.

Now imagine what would happen if everyone did this.

Yet you cannot insist on being who you are if you do not *know* who you are. Thus, this decision must be made *ahead of time.*

Remember this always: What you are being is who you are.

You are not what you are doing.

You are a human, *being.*

27

God, you make it sound so easy. But it's *not* that easy.

> The most effective of your earthly master teachers
> have demonstrated that it is.

Here we go again. Do you think that we can be like them?

> They have all *promised* you that you can! Wasn't this
> their greatest promise?
> Many spiritual teachers have shared with you the
> secret that deciding who you really are, and being it,
> is the fastest means of affecting and creating your
> inner self and your outer world. This is not a new
> teaching. Yet what may be new is your decision to
> try it.

I *have* tried it. The whole human race has. Do you think this is
the first time we've heard these things? Do you think that we
haven't tried it?

I observe that many humans are scared to death to try. I mean, to *really* try. To claim sovereignty over their own lives, to believe that God has given them that power, much less that authority.

I observe that many humans are afraid to believe that the wisdom of Divinity lies within them.

I observe that many humans would actually feel guilty about creating a New Spirituality based on having real conversations with God, forging a genuine friendship with God, and creating an experience of communion with God.

I observe that fear and guilt are the biggest enemies of humans.

What is it that we are so darn afraid of?

Why, me, of course! You are afraid of death, that's clear, but the reason you are afraid of death is because of what you've been told about Life, and about God.

Most humans are so afraid of dying that they have become afraid of living. And so they *surrender* their living to those who are *not* afraid of dying. Suicide bombers and the nations with the biggest armies and the most bombs.

Yet you cannot go on like this. Your world cannot sustain itself with fear as its guiding principle. Love must become its guiding principle.

Yet how can we believe in love, and not be afraid of dying? We have been taught to believe in a God who loves us in very unloving ways, who then lets us die, and who punishes us after death.

That is why, if you wish to live in peace and harmony, you must change your world at the level of belief. One person at a time. Starting with you.

And now I have given you some new tools. Here, in this conversation, you've been shown some new steps that can move you away from fear and into love. Here are some new revelations that can help you find the path.

These are major philosophical and theological statements. They carry monumental implications for all humankind.

And now I want to bring you the last of these revelations. Consider it carefully. Look deeply into its larger message.

This is the NINTH NEW REVELATION:

You cannot die, and you will never be condemned to eternal damnation.

Oh, my God, if that were true, it would change everything!

It *is* true, and it *will* change everything, the moment you decide to live it as your personal truth.

Most of your world's religions have taught the first three words of this truth, yet what they have said to you after those three words has turned this truth into a nightmare.

They have told you that your soul never dies, but they have also told you that your soul could spend eternity in hell. And their description of what could *cause* you to spend eternity in hell—as well as what could cause you to spend it in heaven—*has created a hell on earth.* For some religions have taught that *killing others* for the "right reasons" will send you straight to heaven, while others have taught that *believing in God,* but doing it in the "wrong way," will send you straight to hell.

Now if that doesn't twist your head around, nothing will.

I declare to you now that these teachings are wholly and completely inaccurate.

They were brought to your world not by God, but by human beings. Human beings who assumed that God must be angry, vindictive, revengeful, and retributive because *humans* are angry, vindictive, revengeful, and retributive.

Human beings who imagined that God must be petty, nitpicking, particular, and exclusive because humans are petty, nitpicking, particular, and exclusive.

Human beings who thought that God designed eternal life based on a system of reward and punishment because humans designed life on Earth based on a system of reward and punishment.

Reward and punishment, as I have pointed out, is a human social convention, having nothing to do with divinity. It is not a divine notion at all, but a human contrivance replacing the divine notion of unconditional love.

Reward and punishment is the human attempt to express the Life Principle of Adaptability. Humans have created "rewards" and "punishments" in order to cause themselves to adapt their behaviors to what they imagine God wants. Yet this social convention is distorted by the fallacies that humans hold about God and Life—and, thus, some humans exhibit behaviors that *no* God could *ever* want.

There are many millions of people who do not do that, of course. People who are beautiful in the depth of their soul, and who spread and share beauty wherever they go.

There are people who teach only love, and people who heal by their very beingness. You all know these kinds of people. It is quite possible that you are one of them. It is absolutely certain that you are seeking to be one of them, or you would hardly be engaging in the sort of personal and spiritual growth work that could lead you to this kind of conversation with God.

And so to you goes humanity's thanks. On you rests humanity's hope. In you resides humanity's highest vision.

It is a vision that soars beyond humanity's limited beliefs in things that are not true.

There are those who see the world as it is and ask, "Why?" And there are those who dream of things that never were and ask, "Why not?"

To those who dream the dreams of angels, I declare that I will help you create that dream, and turn it into reality.

Thus have I come to bring you this Ninth New Revelation, and to now repeat it, so that humanity cannot miss it and cannot ignore it, nor its implications.

You cannot die, and you will never be condemned to eternal damnation.

With this final New Revelation comes your vision. Through it comes your freedom and your movement into your True Self.

When you understand that you are not your body and that Who You Are never can, and never will, die, AND... when you understand that you will never be condemned by a judgmental, angry, and vindictive God... THEN will your lifelong worries about your happy survival be over.

The end of these worries will transform you completely, causing you to interact with the world in an entirely new way. You will become, quite literally, a New Human. You will live, quite naturally, a New Spirituality. And you will create, quite spontaneously, a New Society.

You will be thrilled at the new way in which you look at life, see other people, and treat them. You will be uplifted by the new priorities you will set and the new ideas you will hold about what is important and what is not—to say nothing of what you will think is important enough to kill each other over.

You will be amazed at how you have been walking around in circles all these years, as if in a maze. Your entrapment in this cycle of violence has been an a-maze-ment, and your release from this cycle of violence will be achieved by your at-one-ment—or what you would call atonement.

But if we thought that we were never going to be judged or condemned, there would be no reason to "atone" for anything. *And then what would stop us from acting worse than ever?*

> Do you need the threat of eternal damnation to not hurt others, to do what is in the best interests of all?

We are not convinced that it is in our best interests to act in a way that is in the best interests of all. We think it is in our best interests to act first on behalf of ourselves.

> Of course you do. And that instinct is a basic instinct, built into all of life. It is the Life Principle of Sustainability, expressing itself. Self-interest is the highest interest. And it should be.

Then I don't understand. Now you've got me really confused. If self-interest is the highest interest, and it *should* be, then everything else you've been saying here falls by the wayside.

> Only if you have a very limited definition of the Self. And so, we come full circle. It is your false beliefs that limit your definition of the Self. When you see the Self as including all others, your definition of self-interest expands—and the world changes overnight.
>
> I said to you very early in this conversation that the problem now facing the world is easy to solve. The answer is obvious. Simply enlarge your definition of "Self."
>
> Now you are able to understand this statement more completely.

Expand our definition of "Self"? It's as simple as that?

> It's as simple as that. When you believe your Self to be one with all others, you will abandon your self-destructive behaviors. When you believe your Self to be one with God, you will create new behaviors, new ways of *being*, that will change your life and change your world forever.
>
> The New Revelations that I have given you here can serve as a catalyst in enlarging your awareness, opening you to a consciousness that will allow you to expand your definition of Self.

Yes, I see that now. These New Revelations feel so *redemptive,* because they deliver us from evil, telling us that *ours* is the kingdom, and the power, and the glory, forever. They release us from fear. They allow us to love again. To love God again, and to love each other again. They give us back to ourselves. We can love *ourselves* again. And life. And yes, even death.

> Now you can believe the unbelievable—that God wants nothing but good for you. You can stop being afraid of God now. You never had to be, and you will never have to be again. You *can* have a conversation with God. All of you. Any time. You *can* have a friendship with God. All of you. Every day. You *can* experience communion with God. All of you. In each moment.
>
> You can release, at last, the thought that God *wants* you to suffer... that suffering is *good*... that you are *not supposed to be happy.*

But what about James, Chapter 4, Verse 8 of the New Testament? Does it not say:

"Cleanse your hands, you sinners; and purify your hearts, you double-minded. Lament and mourn and weep! Let your laughter be turned to mourning and your joy to gloom. Humble yourselves in the sight of the Lord and He will lift you up."

> This is what I was talking about earlier. This is the religion of low self-esteem. If you wish to live in peace and harmony, this is a part of your religions that needs to be reformed.
>
> I do not want your laughter to turn to mourning, nor your joy to gloom. Why on earth would I want that? There's been a slight error there. James was more than a little overzealous on this point.

And was Peter also in error? He said, as recorded in I Peter, Chapter 4, Verse 19:

"Therefore let those who suffer according to the will of God commit their souls to Him in doing good, as to a faithful Creator."

> Yes, that is a mistake, too. It is not my will that you suffer.

Yet the *Qur'an* also says that it is *the will of Allah* that some will be led to knowledge and truth and that some will not, and will suffer for it.

> Those books are in error. It is as simple as that. It is time for you to release some of the thoughts that you have been carrying around about what I want and need from you. And one of the most important thoughts

for you to release is the idea that I want you to kill others for my sake.

But it is difficult to believe that God does not command this. Especially when reading passages in all our holy books. Take this passage from the Bhagavad-Gita, for instance. The Gita is also a dialogue book, in which Arjuna—who, in a sense, represents Everyman—has an ongoing conversation with his God, Lord Sri Krishna. In the excerpt which follows, Arjuna turns on the eve of battle to Lord Krishna, asking how killing can be justified. Listen to Lord Krishna's answers . . .

ARJUNA: I do not see how any good can come from killing my own kinsmen in this battle, nor can I, my dear Krishna, desire any subsequent victory, kingdom, or happiness.

Alas, how strange it is that we are preparing to commit greatly sinful acts. Driven by the desire to enjoy royal happiness, we are intent on killing our own kinsmen.

LORD KRISHNA: O son of Prtha, do not yield to this degrading impotence. It does not become you. Give up such petty weakness of heart and arise, O chastiser of the enemy.

Lord Krishna goes on to explain that the soul can never die; therefore, "the self slays not, nor is slain." In other words, you may go ahead and kill the body "without lamentation."

Do you believe that?

I believe the part that says that the soul cannot die. I do not accept as my truth that this gives me permission to slay without lamentation.

Why not?

Because that is not who I am, nor who I choose to be. Because I wish to help create a different kind of world.

I see.

Most of the people of the world want that.

You are right, they do.

But they don't know how to get from where they are to where they want to be.

You can help them. You can all help each other. Build your world anew. Work together to create a new reality. First, a new inner reality, then a new outer one.

Begin where the human race would have benefited from beginning a long time ago. Do not try to change your behaviors; seek to change your beliefs. It is beliefs that sponsor your behaviors, and cause them to be endlessly repeated.

I've got it. I understand that now. And I've seen, thanks to this conversation, which beliefs in particular are causing the most self-destructive behaviors. Those are the beliefs that I'm going to look at very closely. Those are the beliefs that I'm going to change.

Good. Because change them you must, if what you choose is what you say you choose, which is to live long, healthy, and happy lives, at peace and in harmony with each other; if what you choose is the continued survival of humanity.

Your species is choosing now, by its actions, every hour, every day, whether to survive its adolescence and to mature into adulthood, growing in understanding and eventually joining the other highly evolved species in the universe, or whether to render itself extinct.

In each moment you are making a life and death decision. Do you choose more life, or do you choose a quicker death?

When you smoke that cigarette, are you choosing more life, or are you choosing a quicker death?

When you eat that big hunk of red meat at every meal, are you choosing more life, or are you choosing a quicker death?

When you go for days and weeks and months without even the slightest physical exercise, are you choosing more life, or are you choosing a quicker death?

When you work yourself to the bone, pounding away ten and twelve and fourteen hours a day, leaving no time for a bit of silliness, no time for an evening of leisure, no time for a moment of laughter—not even time for a hug and a squeeze and any real intimacy anymore with those who long to be intimate with you—are you choosing more life, or are you choosing a quicker death?

When you squabble and argue with your family and your neighbors over matters that mean nothing—absolutely nothing—in the long run, are you choosing more life, or are you choosing a quicker death?

When you fight and go to war with other nations over matters that could be resolved with just a little

bit of compromise and just a little bit of trust—a willingness to forgive the past, and an awareness that the only
way to create a viable future is to create it together—
are you choosing more life, or are you choosing a
quicker death?

When you insist on continuing to believe, as if they
were true, doctrines and dogmas that are killing you,
are you choosing more life, or are you choosing a
quicker death?

From the smallest day-in-and-day-out decisions to
the largest decisions now facing the human race, are you
choosing more life, or are you choosing a quicker death?

Always the choice is the same. More life, or quicker
death.

Of course, as I have said to you many times, death
does not exist. The word is used here in the context
within which you have understood it. It is used to
mean the end of life as you have known it, individually
and collectively.

Within the context of the human adventure, what
shall the life experience be? Indeed, what shall humans
be? Or shall humans be at all?

Your wonderful writer Shakespeare said it perfectly.

To be, or not to be?

That is the question.

28

Now take this message to the world. Carry it to all people whose lives you touch, through your own life, lived.

I say now to all humanity, move forward in your lives with excitement and joy, for the most extraordinary time in your history lies before you.

Wondrous is the opportunity, and unlimited is your potential. The challenge is great, but your talents, your abilities, and your resources are greater.

Whenever you have trusted your abilities and used your talents at the highest level, have you not always won the day? Indeed, and you can win it now. And by winning the day you can *save* the day, for your loved ones and for all those who will follow your time upon the Earth.

You can do so by calling forth your highest ideals and putting them into practice in your daily experience, by collecting your grandest thoughts and turning them into living realities, by gathering your courage and summoning your greatest strength and making these available to everyone.

You can do so by sharing your love, your compassion, your wisdom, and your abundance.

Freely have you been given. Now, freely give.

Oh, my wonderful ones, how every room lights up when you enter it with your smile, giving of the wonder of who you are! How the lives you touch are healed when you touch them with the glory of your highest self, reflecting onto them the glory of their own highest selves. How the world changes when you move through it in your own most special way, proposing by your very state of being a way that the world itself might be.

In order to create the life that you desire for yourself and for all others, some big things need to be done. Yet, the good news is that it takes but little things to do them.

A smile. A touch. A laugh. A decision to forgive. A willingness to share.

An ability to cry—and to hear the crying of others.

A love of life. A trust in God. An acceptance of each other.

A choice to live as one.

A determination to dare.

These are things of which you are capable. These are things that you have all done before. Do them now, and always, and you are but one short step from Paradise.

Is this not exciting? Is this not inspiring? With these simple tools of life, you can *change* your life. With the wisdom that rests within your soul, you can re-create your world anew.

I have said that this is a crucial time, and it is. I have said that this is a defining moment, and it is. I have said that in the past many humans have been unwilling to change, unwilling to move forward, unwilling to become unstuck. They have stuck to their old ways and to the old beliefs that have sponsored them. But this is the dawn of a new day, and you can help to give it birth.

For all that I have said about the past will become *part* of the past the moment you decide that *you are the future.* That in your mind lies the wisdom, that in your heart lies the love, and that in your soul lies the truth that will set your world free.

For you *are* all the wisdom, love, and truth that any moment will ever need for that moment to be healed.

Your life, and your world, *can* be healed, one moment at a time. By each of you.

In fact, that is the only way it will be.

So go now, and do this joyous work. Be, now, my messenger. Take, now, my New Revelations, and place them firmly into your mind, deeply into your heart, and permanently into your soul.

These words I leave with you, these gifts I give to you. They can change your world forever.

1. God has never stopped communicating directly with human beings. God has been communicating with and through human beings from the beginning of time. God does so today.

2. Every human being is as special as every other human being who has ever lived, lives now, or ever will live. You are all messengers. Every one of you. You are carrying a message to life *about* life every day. Every hour. Every moment.

3. No path to God is more direct than any other path. No religion is the "one true religion," no people are "the chosen people," and no prophet is the "greatest prophet."

4. God needs nothing. God requires nothing in order to be happy. God *is* happiness *itself.* Therefore, God requires nothing of anyone or anything in the universe.

5. God is not a singular Super Being, living somewhere in the Universe or outside of it, having the same emotional needs and subject to the same emotional turmoil as humans. That Which Is God cannot be hurt or damaged in any way, and so, has no need to seek revenge or impose punishment.

6. All things are One Thing. There is only One Thing, and all things are part of the One Thing That Is.

7. There is no such thing as Right and Wrong.

There is only What Works and What Does Not Work, depending upon what it is that you seek to be, do, or have.

8. **You are not your body. Who you are is limitless and without end.**

9. **You cannot die, and you will never be condemned to eternal damnation.**

These statements are true. These revelations are real. They can be used, if you choose, as one basis for a New Spirituality. Yet turn, first and foremost, to the truth and the wisdom and the love within your own being. Test everything against that. Measure everything by it.

Remember that the greatest tool you will ever have with which to create not only a new spirituality, but a whole new world, is your own life, lived.

Use the moments of your life to demonstrate your own highest truth, to offer your own genuine love, and to heal every wound that you and others have inflicted upon yourselves.

Your lives do not have to be the way they are. Human beings are capable of living together in peace and harmony. Yet some people must decide to show the way. Some people must declare with their lives that they *are* the way. Some people must choose to be the first domino.

I'm inviting you to make that choice. I'm inviting you to *make the moments of your own life*...

... The New Revelations.

IN CLOSING . . .

On the pages of this extraordinary book we have been given all the information we need to change our lives and bring healing to our world. The only question remaining is, will we choose to do it?

Right now humanity needs help. God has given us help, and now help must come from you.

Yes, it's up to you now.

You and me.

We've got to join the others — the politicians and the soldiers and the economists, the industrialists and corporate people, the religious leaders and all those we have "put in charge" in the past. We've got to join them and help them see the kind of world we really wish to create, because, so far, they have not produced the outcomes that we all say we desire. Our world is still on the brink of global calamity, and it is moving *closer to,* not further away from, total self-destruction.

We can no longer ignore the fact that what our leaders and our society's institutions have been doing *is not working.* Look around. Corporate giants are crumbling, brought down by their own self-serving accounting lies. Churches have lost their credibility due to their own shameless hypocrisy. Armies in the thousands and military budgets in the billions have become meaningless in the face of a half-dozen people who don't care if they die. And what is supposedly the fairest and most democratic political system on earth cannot get a presidential election right.

So now it's up to the regular folks, the untitled people, to become members of the team. To *lead* the team. We are going to have to get in there with the others, become leaders ourselves, as we rebuild our world one person, one family, one village, one town, one city, one state, one nation — one *idea* and one *moment*— at a time.

We've waited long enough. We must now get about the task, each one of us, of changing the prevailing notion of who we are in relationship to each other, and of what life is really about.

This book gives us the tools with which to do that. All that's needed now is commitment. We have to care. We have to dare. We have to share.

We have to care enough to be our very best.

We have to dare enough to be that now.

We have to share enough to touch the whole world, each in our own way, with the shining light of our love, and the truth of who we really are and who we choose to be.

What we need right now is a new idea within humanity about humanity itself. An idea that could create enormous and lasting change in how we see and experience ourselves, and in how we live our lives.

The challenge we are going to face is that many people don't *want* to change. Some don't believe that change is possible, while others don't believe that humanity is facing any real peril at all. Still others simply don't seem to have the will to do what it takes to make a difference. Yet a golden age of peace is within our reach. All that is needed now is the will to create it.

All things are created with three basic tools: Understanding, Ability, and Will. We have, at last, the Understanding and the Ability. Will is the final element in every choice-making process. It is the ultimate tool of creation. Where there is a Will there is a way. Without the Will, we can do nothing.

Standing before an audience in Zürich in the Spring of 2002, I talked about the human resistance to change even in the face of potentially disastrous results from failing to do so.

"We want in this life to hang on to our ancient beliefs and prejudices and behaviors, and we do not want to change them, or even to have them be seriously challenged, even though we say we are begging for a different kind of world. We could have the solution put right in front of us and most of us would not avail ourselves of it.

"We don't want to change, we don't want to let go. We want everyone else to change. We want the world to change, but we don't want OUR world to change.

"Yet, if we want the world to change, we had better start looking at the striking contradictions in our own behaviors.

"I am not different from you. I have not corrected my most serious self-defeating behaviors any more than you have. So this is not 'the pot calling the kettle black.' I'm right in there with you. But this much I know. If we don't now help each other, support each other, challenge each other, lift each other to a new level of awareness, then, my friends, we're all going down together.

"And I don't want that for us. We can do better than that. We can change our lives and our world, but . . . *we must deeply desire to do so.* And we must commit to starting here, right where we are, not 'over there,' where that other person is.

"So, I challenge you to challenge me. Wherever you see me behaving in a way that is less than you know me to be, or that brings me results you know that I do not even want, you tell me so.

"Not critically. Not angrily. But with love.

"Simply say . . . 'I know that's not who you are. I know that's not what you really choose. And I would like to give you back to yourself.'

"And then, give me permission to do the same for you.

"If we will do that for each other, the sky is the limit."

And now I'll say the same thing to you, who are reading this book.

Let's wake each other up. Let's end our long global nightmare. Let's be the beacon that shows the way when the other becomes lost. Let's be bringers of the light. Let's be The First Domino.

As this book says, we will be most effective when we choose to work at this together, as a collective. There are many ways to do this. One way could be to join with the Conversations with God Foundation, our non-profit education organization, as partners in a joint creation.

The mission of the Foundation is to inspire people everywhere to *be the change they wish to see*. Our desire is to render the CwG message accessible and understandable in the fastest way to the largest number of people.

The Conversations with God Foundation produces books, audiocassettes, videotapes, interactive online and e-mail courses, and other educational materials, and also presents classes, retreats, and seminars.

If you are as excited about the information in this book as we are, and if you believe it would serve the world to have as many people as possible become aware of this material, you may wish to play a personal role in creating that outcome. Our *Inspire the World Campaign* offers you a chance to do so, in a very direct way, by partnering with us in sharing your talents, your time, your energy, and your resources. There is much that you can do.

To learn more, please go to www.inspiretheworld.com, which will take you directly to the campaign page on our main website. If you are not on the Internet, you may contact the Foundation office at:

The Conversations with God Foundation
PMB #1150, 1257 Siskiyou Blvd.
Ashland, Oregon 97520
Telephone: 541-482-8806

Our Foundation also maintains a worldwide directory and resource network of people and organizations seeking to connect with others and gather new energy as they work to uplift and enhance all of life on this planet by being the change they wish to see. To plug into this network, go to www.beingthechange.net.

If you feel personally called to explore actively partnering with us, our main website offers you comprehensive information on who we are and what we are doing, as well as additional learning and study opportunities should you choose to delve more deeply into the extraordinary material in the *With God* series of books. Included in those offerings is an interactive sixteen-week e-mail course and an online self-paced study course on *The New Revelations,* helping you to integrate its powerful messages into your everyday life. You may immediately access all of this, and connect with us directly, at our main Internet address, www.cwg.org.

I am very grateful that you were led to this book, and that you chose to read it all the way through to the end. Even if you and I ultimately disagree on the way to a brighter tomorrow, we can at least know that we seek the same end. This commonality of purpose is the beginning of unity—and unity of intention can heal the world.

Life proceeds out of our intentions for it, and I know that if the world changes, it will be because of you, and others like you who choose to make a difference through their day-to-day lives.

May you experience God's blessings in abundance, and may you share them with all those whose lives you touch.

Neale Donald Walsch
London
April 15, 2002

INDEX

Absolute, Realm of, 269
acceptance, 338
adaptability, 223, 224, 251–52, 253, 254,
    255, 258, 268, 295, 327–28
adultery, adulterers, 104, 111, 204
Afghanistan, 36, 55, 111–12, 113, 179
aggression, 165–66
agnostics, 100, 101
air, 276–77
Allah, 45, 62, 108, 122, 145, 147, 148,
    236–37, 332
All in All, 270, 271, 279
All That Is, 269, 270, 278
Ammerman, Nancy, 75
angels, 239, 283, 284, 285
anger, 300–302, 308, 310, 327
anthem, U.S. national, 238
apostasy, apostates, 35, 74, 88, 91, 111, 171
Arizona Republic, 42, 291
Arjuna, 52, 333
arrogance, 5, 89, 183, 300
assessment, 152, 156
Associated Press, 291
atheism, atheists, 101, 174, 204, 233, 238
atonement, 329–30

aura, 275–76
awareness, 94, 331, 346

Baha'u'llah, 7, 78, 95
Baptists, Baptist Church, 44, 46, 76, 211
beards, 113, 115, 240
behavior(s)
    adaptive, 253–54
    barbaric, 110–12, 149, 302
    beliefs and, 14–23, 38–39, 100, 179,
        305–6, 315
    changing, 179, 265, 283, 291, 318–19, 331
    dysfunctional, 155, 156, 221, 229, 264,
        267, 268, 306
    errant, 76
    fear-based, 264–65
    God and, 103
    morality and, 217, 247
    Oneness and, 280
    positive, 298
    of righteousness, 206
    self-destructive, 335
    being, state of, 40, 319–23, 338
    beliefs. *See also* fallacies; God; life
        attack on, 114, 176

beliefs (cont.)
  behavior and, 14–23, 38–39, 100, 179,
    305–6, 315
  changing, 2, 57–58, 70, 98–99, 175, 178,
    180, 186–87, 192, 213, 215–16, 222,
    244–45, 259, 260, 268, 305, 309–10,
    311, 318, 326, 334
  dialogue about, 100, 160–61
  emotional attachment to, 152
  fighting for, 38, 145
  mental constructions around, 214–21,
    223, 228–29
  of New Spirituality, 177
  old, 339, 345
  as problem, 49
  Super, 101
Benke, David, 43–44, 45
betterness, 203–12, 299
Bhagavad-Gita, 5, 10, 34, 52, 103, 145, 146,
  159, 197, 207, 239, 333
Bhagavad-Gita As It Is (Bhaktivedanta), 103,
  197
Bhaktivedanta, A. C., 103, 197
Bible, 10. See also New Testament; Old
  Testament
  arguments about, 5
  on evil, 159
  fundamentalists on, 110
  gender-neutral, 75–77
  on genitals, 105, 106
  God and, 34, 75, 76
  interpretation of, 74
  on killing, 207–8
  on slavery, 175
  swearing oath on, 238
  on women, 196
blacks, 199, 203, 220
blasphemy, 89, 91, 144, 153, 171, 215, 216,
  235
body, 40, 268, 269, 271, 272, 273–75, 296,
  306, 307
Bolinder, Scott, 75
Book of Mormon, 5, 34, 96, 207, 208, 209,
  239
bribery, 146
Buddha, The, 10, 86, 95, 96
Buddhists, 90

burdens, 86
burqah, 55

carcinogens, 168
Catholics, Catholicism, 46, 52, 188, 204,
  215–16
Cause, First, 138, 274
Ceiving, 303–4
change
  bringing about, 67–68, 70, 157–58
  Conversations with God Foundation
    and, 346–48
  coping with, 176
  judgments and, 165
  lasting, 316–17
  morals and, 173
  resistance to, 345
charity, 63, 188, 297
chemicals, 168, 290
children, 104, 106–7
choice, viii, 14, 152, 156, 248, 289, 299, 301,
  343
chosen people, 98, 113, 340
Christians, Christianity, 35, 44, 68, 74, 96,
  121, 196, 203
church and state, separation of, 174, 237
Church of Jesus Christ of Latter-day
    Saints, 97, 188, 199. See also Mormon
    Church, Mormons
Clinton, Bill, 62
cloning, 291–92
clothing, 104, 112, 113, 171, 172, 195–96,
  198
coins, "in God we trust" on, 237
Commandments, Ten, 97, 102, 232
communication, worldwide, 313
communion, 44
community, 52, 121, 154, 187–88
competition, 37, 193–94
Concerned Group, 201
conduct, codes of, 153, 158, 159, 170
Confucius, 7, 10, 95
Congress, prayer opening sessions of,
  238
consciousness, levels of, 299, 331, 346
consequences, 126
contraceptives, 115

Conversations with God Foundation, 346–48
Copernicus, 215
corporations, 343, 344
courage, 14, 99, 100, 175, 225, 228, 282, 284, 297, 311, 312, 338
cows, cloned, 291–92
Creation Myth, 306
creations, 320–23
crime rate, 247
Crusades, 35, 36, 62, 148
cry, ability to, 338
Crystal Cathedral, 281

damnation, eternal, 326, 329, 330, 341
dancing, 173
death
  for apostasy, 171
  for blasphemy, 171
  choice of, 288–90, 335–36
  confusion about, 296, 306–7
  for cursing father or mother, 170
  from failure to change beliefs, 175–76
  fear of, 325
  as horizon, 286
  impossibility of, 326
  Life Review after, 126
  loving, 331
  over ownership rights, 256
  soul and, 270
death penalty, 246–47
Decalogue, 102
decisions, ethical, 286–87, 292–93, 294
deism, 233
denial, 79
dialogue, open, 74, 77, 99–100, 160, 163
Different Roles Group, 201
discrimination, 69, 114, 195–201, 205, 220
disease, 291, 292
Divine Spirit, Divinity, 85–86, 87, 88, 149, 269–71, 325
divisions, 122, 154, 205
divorce, 234
Dobson, James, 75

doctrines, 129, 134, 195–200, 305, 336
dogmas, 129, 184, 185, 336
doingness, 40, 319, 320
dollar bills, artwork on back of, 237

Earth Constitution for New Humans, 201–2
ecology. See chemicals; pollution
Eden, Garden of, 125
Elijah, 208
Emerson, Ralph Waldo, v
Emerson's Essays (Emerson), v
emulation, 90, 92
Encyclopedia Britannica, 36
End Days, 159
energy, 135, 269–70, 275, 276, 277, 279–80, 301, 347
environment, 296. See also chemicals; pollution
ESP (extrasensory perception), 140
evangelicals, 75, 204
Everything, Unified Field of, 138
evil, 159, 306, 331
evolution, 128, 152, 173, 193, 222, 248, 252, 253, 258, 318, 319
exclusivity, 48, 62, 121–22, 278–79, 280, 285, 305, 327. See also righteousness; separation

faith, 107–8, 171
fallacies, 71–73, 102, 123, 124, 216–17, 219, 228, 229–30, 267, 328, 330
fatwa, 35–36, 88
fear, 56, 264–65, 266, 281, 307, 309, 325, 331
fighting, 145–46, 147, 161–62, 335–36
flag, Pledge of Allegiance to, 237
Focus on the Family, 75
Forces, Four Basic, 137
forgiveness, 336, 338
free will, 54, 172, 174
Friendship with God (Walsch), 209
functionality, 223, 224, 242, 245, 246–49, 250, 251–52, 253, 255, 268, 275, 295, 307
fundamentalism, fundamentalists, 51, 54, 64, 74, 76, 110–12, 147, 176

Galileo Galilei, 215, 216
Gandhi, Mahatma, 319
Gautama, Siddhartha, 7, 90, 95
genetics, 292–93, 294
genitals, 105, 106, 197
Georgetown University, 62
Giuliani, Rudolph, 45
God, ix. *See also* scripture, sacred; *specific sacred scriptures*
    anger of, 327
    appeals to, 44, 46, 122
    bad things and, 30–31, 33
    barbaric behavior in name of, 144–46, 149, 207–9
    beliefs about, 14, 19, 20, 24, 29–33, 50–51, 68, 100, 101–2, 149, 181, 220, 221, 222, 225, 233, 267, 283, 304, 314, 317, 325, 328
    clashes over, 74
    communication from, 80–81, 118, 340
    communion with, 40, 325, 331
    confused, 158
    disconnection from, 185
    energy as, 279
    faith in, 28, 107–8, 327, 338
    fallacies about, xi, 29–30, 72, 73, 102, 123–24, 125, 129, 130, 131, 133, 134, 180, 182, 187, 264
    fatherhood of, 75
    five senses and, 141
    as freedom, 174
    glory of, 82, 91
    Gods created by, 90
    good graces of, 125
    as happiness, 340
    in human form, 132–33, 173, 184, 287
    justice of, 116–17
    knowledge about, 141
    Law of, 112, 133, 158, 174, 199, 233–34, 238–42, 246
    as Life, 27–28, 139–40, 186
    of love, 260–61
    love of, 172, 226, 284
    maleness of, 195, 200
    of mercy, 237
    message of, 62
    messengers of, 84–85

mockery of, 110
offense against, 170
One, 87, 135
on Oneness, 211
open dialogue about, 77
orders from, 115
paths to, 97, 340
presence of, 131
proclamations of, 113
Protection Racket of, 146
punishment by, 107–9, 117, 125, 126, 145, 265, 306, 325, 327
Qur'an on, 53, 159
religion and, 60–61
repressive societies on, 55–56
requirements of, 102, 103, 116, 129, 131, 171, 172, 182, 219, 231–32, 327, 328, 332–33, 340
righteousness and, 205
servants of, 88, 90
soul of, 278
soul with, 270
suffering and, 5
as Supreme Being, 101
tools from, 81, 172
truths of, 12
as unavoidable, 91
understanding of, 14, 44, 47, 50–51, 64, 66, 70–71, 77–80, 83, 95, 99, 153, 225
unification with, 283, 285
will of, 233, 248, 284, 293, 294, 305
on women, 201
Word of, 11–12, 34, 51, 74, 76, 89, 96–97, 158, 209, 240–41, 248
work of, 93
worship of, 132
Wrath of, 34–35
writing name of, 172
within you, 85
governments, 256
gratification, instant, 289, 291
Grossman, Cathy Lynn, 75, 76
guidance system, internal, 94, 114
guilt, 281, 284, 325

Hadith, 5, 55, 89, 149, 235
hair, 240

Happiness, 183
Harding, Susan, 76–77
Hartford Seminary, 75–76
hatred, 308, 309, 310
healers, healing, 161, 162–63, 190, 285,
    301–2, 328, 338, 339, 341, 343, 348
heart, 40
heat, 276
heaven, 131–32, 146, 279, 327
hell, 144, 279, 326–27. *See also* damnation,
    eternal
heresy, 89, 153, 215
Hindus, 44
Holy Terror (Taheri), 148
Holy War, Islamic, 148–49
homage, 86, 88
Homo sapiens, 31
homosexuality, 69, 113, 114, 199, 204, 218
hope, 308–9, 310
How Good Do We Have to Be? (Kushner), 284
hubris, 53
human beings
    God in image of, 132–33
    on holiness, 97
    interests of, 149–50
    nature of, 160
    on orders, 117–18
    self-consciousness of, 120–21
    special, 84, 91–92, 199–200, 305
humanism, 128, 143, 150
humanity, 262–64, 295–97, 309–10,
    334–35, 343
humility, 69, 88
hurt, 161, 162, 163

idea(s), 63–64, 70, 149, 176, 220, 303, 344
ideologies, conflict between, 13, 175, 176,
    185
ijma, 235
images, graven, 112, 173
immorality, 170, 173
imperfection, 190
infallibility, 52–53, 74, 118
infidels, 159, 204, 237
injury, injuries, 105, 302
innovation, necessity of, 178
inspiration, divine, 11

Inspire the World Campaign, 347
intermarriage, 114, 115
International Society for Krishna
    Consciousness, 103
Internet, 313, 347
intolerance, 42, 43–47, 69
intuition, 140
Islam, Islamists
    in Afghanistan, 55, 111–12, 179
    brutality in, 74, 144–47
    civil laws in, 235
    on community, 188
    on infallibility of Qur'an and *ulama,* 52,
        74
    on inheritance, 236
    male dominance in, 236
    on Oneness, 211
    on women, 195–96, 197–98

James, Saint, 332
Jesus Christ, 7
    belief in, 205
    Benke on, 44, 45
    Christians on, 96
    Crusades and, 62
    examples set by, 90
    as head of church, 196
    holiness of, 97
    identity of, 75
    Lutherans and, 155
    non-specialness of, 88, 89
    Siddhartha Gautama and, 95
    Smith and, 96
    on truth, 78
    words of, 95
Jews, Judaism, 44, 46, 62, 96, 97, 171–72,
    188, 203
jihad, 146, 159
jizya, 147
Jones, James Earl, 45
judgment, 245–46, 248, 330
justice, 126, 128, 133, 224, 229, 246, 251,
    252–53, 265, 305
justification, 245–46, 247, 248–49, 305

kharaj, 147
Khomeini, Ayatollah Ruhollah, 35, 148

Kieschnick, Gerald, 43, 45
killing. *See also* murder
  Bhagavad-Gita on, 207, 333
  Book of Mormon on, 207, 208, 209
  fallacies about life and, 181, 193, 206–7,
    212, 310
  in God's name, 183, 240, 264, 327, 333
  morals and, 220–21
  new thoughts on, 329
  over ownership rights, 256
  for self-defense, 165
kings, royalty created by, 90
knowledge, 90, 125, 141
Krishna, 52, 333
Kümmell, Hermann, 12–13, 293
Kushner, Harold S., 284

leaders, spiritual, 68, 70, 73, 90, 261,
  343
life
  basic principles of, 221–24, 228–29,
    242, 247, 251–52, 255, 265, 275, 295
  beliefs about, 50–51, 67, 73, 220, 221,
    222, 223, 225, 267, 283, 304, 314, 317,
    325, 328
  changing, 339
  decisions and, 67
  disconnection from, 185
  Divinity and, 85, 86
  energy of, 276, 279
  everlasting, 329
  experience of, 82
  extended, 286–87, 288, 289, 291, 292,
    335, 336
  fallacies about, 37–38, 72, 73, 181–82,
    187, 192–93, 199, 202–3, 206, 212,
    216–17, 257, 264
  God and, 27–28, 139–40, 226
  as interest of humanity, 150
  love of, 338
  mastery in, 321
  messages about, 92
  Miracle of, 271
  as One Thing, 135
  purpose of, 152
  review of, 126–27
  secular, 100

soul and, 40
truths of, 77, 138
understanding of, 66, 70–71, 77–80,
  83, 95, 99, 153, 225
unification of, 285–86
Light, 276
logic, circular, 227
Los Angeles Times, 42
love
  anger and, 300, 301
  beingness and, 316
  God and, 56, 62, 172, 260–61, 264
  as guiding principle, 93, 160, 325, 326
  human action from, 264–65
  within ourselves, 331, 339, 341, 344
  repetition and, 226
  of self, 281
  sharing, 338, 346
  soul and, 40
  teachers of, 328
  thoughts of, 309
  total, 320, 321, 323
  unconditional, 47, 327
Lutherans, Lutheran Church, 43, 44, 45,
  46, 155, 204, 211

male dominance, 194–201, 234, 235
marriage, 197, 218, 234
masters, mastery, 6–7, 87, 89, 90, 91,
  142
Mathnawi, 5
media, mass, 302–4
meditation, 301, 320
messages, messengers, 84, 92, 93, 108, 109,
  123, 147, 340
Metropolitan Community Church, 48
mind, 28, 41, 151, 269, 270, 311
minorities, discrimination against, 69
Missouri Synod, 43, 44, 45, 204, 211
mistakes, 170, 171, 173
Mohler Jr., R. Albert, 76
monarchs, 117
morality
  based on false beliefs, 170, 171, 216–17,
    218–21, 223, 224, 228–29, 230–32
  based on scripture, 241–42
  change and, 173, 244–46, 267–68

functionality and, 247–49, 250, 253
of gene therapy, 294
God and, 237
organized religion and, 238–39
punishment and, 265
Mormon Church, Mormons, 97, 188, 199, 211
Moroni, 239
Moses, 7, 88, 89, 95, 96, 97, 104, 207, 239
motion, 136–37, 138, 139
Muhammad, 7, 10, 78, 88–89, 95, 96, 97, 205, 235
murder, 62, 111, 144–46, 148, 204. *See also* killing
music, 112, 113, 173, 179
Muslims
    in Ashland, Oregon, 68
    Benke on, 44
    on community, 188
    Crusades and, 62
    on Muhammad, 90
    on Qur'an, 74, 96
    on Rushdie, 35–36
    on sin, 204
    tribute to, 147
    umma and, 52–53
    violence by, 146, 148, 149
    on women, 195–96, 197–98
myths, 32, 306

nationalism, 69, 72
nation "under God," 113–14
New Gospel, 209–10
New Testament, 75, 96, 97, 114, 196, 239, 332

obedience, disobedience, 106–7, 117, 149, 319
Oberdieck, David, 43
obligation, moral, 246
Old Testament, 103–4, 105, 208
One Being, 269, 278
Oneness, 154–55, 187, 189–91, 210, 216, 270, 280, 282, 285, 296, 316, 330, 331, 338, 340, 348
One Thing, 134–35, 140
One Who Brings The Message, The, 93

order, 117
ownership, 169, 224, 229, 255–57, 265

paganism, 32
Pali Canon, 5, 239
Paradise, 125, 149, 339
Patanjali, 7, 95
Path, The, 93
Patterson, Paige, 44
Paul, Saint, 76
peace
    beingness and, 316
    choosing, 93, 309
    five steps to, 14, 49–51, 64, 66, 73, 74, 77, 99, 225, 262, 311, 314–15
    God as, 260
    Golden Age of, 26, 345
    inner, 317, 320, 321, 322–23
    nature of, 39–40
    seeds of, 70
    sixth sense and, 140–41
    Thousand Years of, 25
Pentagon, 43
Peter, Saint, 332
poison, 168
pollution, 168, 290
popes, 35, 52, 148, 198, 211
Possibility, Space of, 78–80, 81, 83
praise, 283
prayer, 320
prejudice, 112, 113
pride, 281
priests, 199, 205, 240
prisoners, 146
prophets, 6–7, 87, 98, 142, 178, 208, 235, 340
Protestants, 44, 204
punishment
    adaptability and, 327–28
    Book of Mormon on, 208, 209
    evolution and, 128
    by God, 117, 125, 126, 133, 325, 340
    God's Law and, 246–47
    justice and, 250–51, 252, 253
    morality and, 265
    in public, 111
    in Qur'an, 107–9, 145, 236–37

questions, asking, 69, 74, 186
Qur'an
  fundamentalists on, 110
  God's Laws in, 103
  infallibility of, 52, 74, 239
  interpretation of, 4
  on male dominance, 236
  Muhammad's words in, 96, 97
  on punishment, 107–9
  Sharia and, 235
  on slavery, 175
  on suffering, 332
  Taliban and, 55
  on violence, 34, 144–46, 147, 159, 207

rabbis, 87, 172, 198
reality, new, 334
re-creation, 309, 339
relationships, dysfunctional, 229
Relative, Realm of, 269, 271
relativism, 176
religion, organized
  angry God promoted by, 305
  beliefs about God and, 101
  brutality justified by, 62, 143–46, 150,
    160, 206–9
  on charity, 63
  dogma of, 184–85
  on ethical decisions, 287–88
  evolution of, 58, 152–53
  exclusivity of, 41–42, 121–22, 130, 134,
    153, 188–89, 278–79, 280–81, 285,
    305, 327
  experiencing God in, 142–43
  Five Fallacies and, 72
  freedom and, 174
  on human rights, 174
  hypocrisy of, 344
  interpretations of, 64
  intolerance and, 60–62
  male domination of, 195–201
  morality and, 238–39
  multiplicity of, 132
  from myths, 32
  on new ideas, 63–64
  non-religious and, 100
  on one's body, 273

  one true, 97, 340
  as problem, 46–48
  questioning in, 69
  on secular humanism, 128
  on separation, 186
  for soul's afflictions, 284, 326
  spirituality and, 128–29, 142
  stifled debate and, 74
  on women, 205
repetition, 226–27, 334
repression, 55
revenge, 246, 250, 327
Review, Life, 126–27
reward, 126, 146, 251, 252, 327–28
right and wrong, 167–70, 176, 186–87,
  231–32, 233, 234, 242, 243, 248, 250,
  253, 265, 294, 340
righteousness, 154, 189, 203–12, 245. *See
  also* exclusivity; separation
rights, human, 174
rituals, 32, 103, 304
Rumi, Jalal al-Din, 7, 95
Rushdie, Salman, 35, 36
Russell, Bertrand, 217

Sabbath, no work on, 240
safety and security, 259–60, 306
samadhi, 269, 270
Satanic Verses, The (Rushdie), 35
Saudi Arabia, 112
schools, prayer in, 238
Schuller, Robert H., 281–82
science, 286, 291–94
scripture, sacred. *See also specific sacred
  scriptures*
  on angry God, 306
  authors of, 75
  God's Law in, 238–42, 279
  interpretation of, 4, 5, 51–52, 53–54,
    174, 176, 234, 235
  on slavery, 175
  on unbelievers, 237
  violence in, 103–4, 110, 145, 206–9,
    305, 333
  on women, 195–96, 199
secrecy, 266–67
secularism, 128, 134

selectivity, 252
self, 67–68, 92–93, 120–21, 128, 316–17, 329, 330–31
self-awareness, 25, 299
self-defense, 105, 163, 165, 166–67, 171, 173, 306
self-definition, 67, 299
self-denial, 281
self-destruction, ix, 14, 288, 309, 331, 334, 335, 343
self-determination, 299
self-esteem, 281, 282–83, 332
Self-Esteem: The New Reformation (Schuller), 281
self-interest, 330
selfishness, 119–20
self-realization, 318
self-renewal, 157
sense, sixth, 140–41
separation, 182, 184, 185, 186, 187, 188–90, 192, 280–81, 294, 297, 306. *See also* exclusivity; righteousness
sex, 113, 197–98, 240
Shakespeare, William, 336
Sharia, 235, 248
sharing, 338, 344, 347
Shepard, Matthew, 22, 220
shortsightedness, 119
sin, sinners, 125, 145, 170, 173, 204, 281, 283, 284, 332
slaves, slavery, 113, 175, 198, 240
Smith, Joseph, 7, 95, 96, 239
Society, New, 329
soul
    afflictions of, 284
    beingness and, 40
    body and, 272, 275
    Emerson on, v
    as energy of life, 276, 277, 278
    everlasting, 333
    healing of, 285
    joy and, 40
    New Revelations in, 339
    new revelations in, 311
    religions on, 326
    spirit and, 268–70
    wisdom within, 339

Southern Baptist Convention (SBC), 44
Southern Baptist Theological Seminary, 76
Space-Time Continuum, 270, 276
spirit, 268, 269, 275
spirituality
    activism in, 74
    arrogance of, 5
    destructive nature of, 2
    new, 64, 134, 142, 143, 177, 178, 180, 185, 200, 228, 244, 258, 259, 262, 273, 274, 279, 280, 282, 309, 314, 325, 329, 341
    old ideas of, 9, 47, 48–49, 70, 176
    in organized religions, 152
    science and, 286
    secular humanism and, 128–29
St. Louis Post-Dispatch, 43
steak, cloned cow, 291–92
stealing, 111, 169, 171, 204
stem cell research, 292
Strand, David, 44, 45
suffering, 127, 168, 170, 293, 310, 331, 332
suicide, 167–68, 204
suicide bombers, 145, 146, 218, 325, 344
superiority. *See* righteousness
sustainability, 223, 224, 229, 252, 255, 256, 257, 258, 268, 295, 296, 330
sword, 148–49
syncretism, 43–44

Taheri, Amir, 148
Taliban, 55, 113, 179
teachers, teaching. *See also specific teachers*
    altered, 185
    changed beliefs, 21
    fallacies, 34
    fear in, 56
    on God, 116, 174
    Highest, 87, 88
    humble, 87–88
    Islamic, 52, 116, 198
    knowledge of others created by, 90
    of love, 328
    male dominance, 195–200
    of organized religions, 47, 129
    others their own answers, 317, 324

teachers, teaching *(cont.)*
  warrior mentality of, 145–46
  as your whole life, 92
technology, 13, 25, 175, 308, 313–14
Temple Mount, 62
Templeton, Sir John, 68–69
That Which You Are, 295
theft, thieves, 111, 169, 171, 204
tolerance, 46, 47. *See also* intolerance
Torah, 10, 96, 97, 103, 104, 106–7, 114,
  239
tradition, comfort of, 178
transcending, 7–8, 9
transformation, planetary, 317
truth, v, 10, 12, 32, 50, 77, 80, 84, 87, 99,
  216, 274, 315

ulamas, 52, 116, 198
unbelievers, murder of, 111, 144–46, 204
Unified Field Theory, 286
United Church of Religious Science, 48
Unity Church, 47–48
University of California, 76
University of Georgia, 292
Urban II, Pope, 35
USA Today, 75, 76, 292

values, changing, 167–69, 267
Victory, Final, 159
violence
  anger and, 300, 302
  Ceiving and, 303–4

cycle of, 329
to end violence, 247
God and, 264, 305
pervasiveness of, 298–99, 300, 302, 306
in scripture, 110, 305
separateness and, 297

war
  fallacies about life and, 181, 193
  injuries, 105
  over ownership rights, 256
  for self-defense, 161, 165, 166, 171, 259
  self-destruction from, 309, 310, 335–36
What Works, What Does Not Work, 164,
  176, 187, 241, 243, 341. *See also*
  functionality
Who You Are, 152, 275, 276, 283, 301, 309,
  312, 317, 318, 323, 324, 329, 338, 341,
  344, 346
witches, wizards, 240
witnessing, 152, 156
women, 55, 69, 112, 113, 171–72, 174,
  194–201, 205, 220, 234
World Trade Center, 43
worship, 117, 132
worthiness, unworthiness, 11, 12, 306

Yogananada, Paramahansa, 7, 95
You, New, 127–28

Zondervan, 75